The Captain Was a Doctor

Jonathon Reid

The Captain Was a Doctor

The Long War and
Uneasy Peace of POW John Reid

DUNDURN
TORONTO

Publisher: Scott Fraser | Acquiring editors: Scott Fraser and Rachel Spence | Editor: Michael Carroll
Cover designer: Sophie Paas-Lang
Cover image: John Reid, Sendai Camp 1B, shortly after the Japanese surrender on August 15, 1945. *Marjolein de Klerk.*
Printer: Marquis Book Printing Inc.

Library and Archives Canada Cataloguing in Publication

Title: The captain was a doctor : the long war and uneasy peace of POW John Reid / Jonathon Reid.
Names: Reid, Jonathon, 1948- author.
Description: Includes bibliographical references and index.
Identifiers: Canadiana (print) 20200278282 | Canadiana (ebook) 20200278444 | ISBN 9781459747210 (softcover) | ISBN 9781459747227 (PDF) | ISBN 9781459747234 (EPUB)
Subjects: LCSH: Reid, John, 1913-1979. | LCSH: Canada. Canadian Army. Royal Canadian Army Medical Corps—Officers—Biography. | LCSH: Canada. Canadian Army—Medical personnel— Prisoners of war—Canada—Biography. | LCSH: Prisoners of war—Japan— Biography. | LCSH: World War, 1939-1945—Prisoners and prisons, Japanese—Biography. | LCSH: Physicians—Canada—Biography. | LCGFT: Biographies.
Classification: LCC D805.J3 R45 2020 | DDC 940.54/7252092—dc23

We acknowledge the support of the Canada Council for the Arts and the Ontario Arts Council for our publishing program. We also acknowledge the financial support of the Government of Ontario, through the Ontario Book Publishing Tax Credit and Ontario Creates, and the Government of Canada.

Printed and bound in Canada.

VISIT US AT

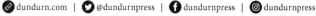 dundurn.com | @dundurnpress | dundurnpress | dundurnpress

Dundurn
3 Church Street, Suite 500
Toronto, Ontario, Canada
M5E 1M2

*To the 1,975 Canadian soldiers and two nursing sisters of
"C" Force and their families*

The captain was a doctor. Not a captain.
— John Reid, "The Captain"

A poignant sense engulfed him of the one-way flow of time,
of the offhand decisions, the slight impulsive mistakes, that
could swell and become a man's fate.
— Herman Wouk, *War and Remembrance*

If I weep for Jack, it is for the bright, gay, sensitive person
who once was a comrade-in-arms, it is for lost dreams, it is
for the inexorable ticking of the clock.
— George Pollak, Letter of Condolence,
Written on Pearl Harbor Day, 1979

Contents

Foreword

Captain John Reid, Royal Canadian Army Medical Corps, was a doctor; a doctor who found himself in a merciless place without medicine or equipment, but a doctor who himself embodied compassion. A doctor who — when he left Canada for war — was expected to return to a stellar career in medicine.

There are two aspects that make his story unique. Firstly, this is a full biography covering his prewar life, wartime experience in Hong Kong and as a POW, and the all-important postwar challenges. And secondly, Reid was the only Canadian officer to travel with the Canadian Other Ranks when they were shipped from Hong Kong to POW Camps in Japan itself. There he fought a war against starvation, cruelty, and rampant disease.

"My endeavour here," he noted at one point, "is to take back as many men as possible to Canada, whether well or ill, and not to concentrate on complete health. I would rather return five hundred men in various stages of beriberi, which perhaps in future can be cured, rather than to return three hundred men in good health and leave two hundred dead behind."

Reid did his best, but whatever decisions he made, those in his care kept dying. For an intelligent and imaginative man, playing at God must have come at a high cost. His men knew how difficult this was for him. "He had to make these decisions, and make'em and make'em and make'em and it was so hard," said Royal Rifles Sergeant "Flash" Clayton. "He didn't have anything to help anybody with, and I can remember when Jimmy Emo died, I can remember [Reid] crying. And when Murray Goodenough died he was eighteen years old. He won the MM [Military Medal] in Hong Kong when he was sixteen. He died in December of 'forty-three [of catarrh pneumonia] and [Reid] just cried and cried and cried. What can you do?"

After almost four long years, the war suddenly ended. And this work's description of the struggle within Japan to accept defeat is as good as I have read anywhere. This is a history to be reckoned with.

Reid survived. But his marriage did not. Every single POW from Hong Kong I ever knew was changed by this war, and their families suffered in turn: wives and children; prewar and post. One might cast blame, but a lifetime of study has led me to the conclusion that there are very few true villains in war. The overwhelmingly vast majority of survivors are simply victims. Without the war, there is every likelihood that Reid would have had a stable family life and that stellar career.

Oh, yes, the captain was a doctor, and one who saved many lives in that war. And he was a brave man and a good one, damaged though he clearly was. But to the Canadian soldiers he escorted to Japan, those same soldiers who he guided through such difficult times for so many years, he was much more: to them, it is clear, the doctor was a captain.

Tony Banham, Ph.D.
Hong Kong, July 2020

Author's Note

This book contains some pejorative and racist language. For the sake of veracity, it has been retained as originally quoted. While acknowledging the Japanese convention of writing family names first, in the case of this book, I have followed the Western practice of given names first, family names second, to which English-speaking readers are accustomed. Imperial measurements, in use at the time of this story, have been retained. However, all place names have been modernized, except in two direct quotes: "Wong Nei Chong Gap" for today's "Wong Nai Chung Gap," page 69; and "Chungking" for today's "Chongqing," page 92.

Finally, it should be noted that prisoner of war (POW) Tokyo No. 5 Branch Camp and Tokyo No. 3 Dispatched Camp (Camp 3D) are one and the same. In Branch Camps, the Japanese Army supplied all housing, food, clothing, and staff. In Dispatched Camps, the Japanese Army only provided staff. Housing, food, and clothing were supplied by the company where the POWs worked. Tokyo No. 5, Reid's first camp in Japan, was renamed 3D on August 1, 1943, when Nippon Kokan (Tsurumi) Shipyard took over "Dispatched Camp" responsibilities.

Preface

I hardly knew my father. After my parents' final separation in 1954, he remained in Vancouver. My mother, brother, and I moved back to Toronto, where Tony and I grew up. Throughout our childhood, we saw him once a year. He would come east in the summer and take the two of us to his father's cottage in Muskoka for a two-week visit. When Tony and I were young, we were enthralled to be with him — our dad, the handsome, charismatic war hero. But as the summers passed and we matured, we became increasingly frustrated that he kept avoiding the discussions we were hoping he would have with us. It was as though the crucial events that had changed his life, and by extension ours — the war and imprisonment, the breakup of our family — had never happened. Our relationship with him, which began in 1955 as a summer regimen of wood-chopping, canoeing, horseshoes, and cribbage, was essentially unchanged when the Muskoka visits came to an end 10 years later, with Tony and I none the wiser about our father's inner life. After the Muskoka visits stopped, I saw him three times before he died in 1979.

His death sowed the seeds of this book. In December 1981, I sat down to write a submission to the Bureau of Pensions Advocates on behalf of my mother, Jean Reid. In question was the veteran widow pension awarded to Cathy Reid, my father's second wife, whom he married in 1951. My point was that Jean, who married him in 1939, was a victim of the war as much as my father. She had a right to a portion of the pension.[1]

I thought the submission would take a weekend to complete. It took six weeks. Investigating the personalities and circumstances from all angles to present a fair and balanced case involved far more than I had first thought. By the time the submission was mailed to the Bureau of Pensions Advocates in January 1982, I had mined deeply into my parents' past.

Yet many questions remained. In the years that followed, I continued to gather information about my father from anyone who knew him. An early and invaluable document was the long letter written to me in 1983 by George Pollak, an American naval officer who was imprisoned with my father and by the end of the war had become his closest friend. Pollak's detailed account of their experiences in Camp 3D, and of the strange, sad ending of their friendship seven years later, made me think that a version of my father's life story could and should be told. By the time I met George MacDonell in 2002, I had amassed an archive of interviews and historical material.

George MacDonell, a sergeant major in the Royal Rifles, was in prison camp with my father in Hong Kong and Japan and knew him well. *One Soldier's Story*, MacDonell's book on his war experience, was published the year we met. Ten years later, when he was planning *They Never Surrendered*, a book of eight stories about Allied prisoners of war who "defied their captors," he asked me to write the chapter on "The Doctor." In two weeks, I wrote 18,000 words. This book had begun.

In the years of writing *The Captain Was a Doctor*, I have tried to plumb the depths of a significant and complicated life. During the war, Captain John Reid was placed in exceptionally difficult circumstances and for 44 months rose to meet them. But he was a casualty of his ordeal. How that was so, for my father and for all the men who were captured at Hong Kong, is best told by one who was there — Lance Corporal Robert Warren of the Royal Rifles:

> In order for a prisoner to survive, he must shut down his feelings. He functions with only those feelings that help him to survive and keep him sane. During my entire internment I did not see one person cry. No one.
>
> The feeling that we could not suppress, however, was uncertainty. Though it was a vague sensibility, it was ever-present. At the beginning, we were easily able to identify it. But as time went on, it became a lot of other things. It became concern, anxiety, nervousness, fear. The moment we were taken prisoner we were being terrorized. Because we did not run around in a panic does not lessen the fact that we were undergoing extreme emotional stress. Any innate feelings of security that we brought with us began to deteriorate the moment the surrender came. We did not stop to ponder it, but it was happening. We did not think about it because we were busy adjusting to a hostile environment. The irony of the situation is that when you have adjusted to a bad environment, you are mentally ill. In striving to survive, we were conditioning ourselves for neuroses and psychoses in our normal world.
>
> We toughened ourselves, individually and in groups. We suppressed compassion and empathy to a point where it became non-existent. God only knows what it did to us spiritually. It certainly left scars, many indiscernible.

When we returned home, one of the most serious problems was our inability to express our feelings. One cannot suppress feelings for such a long time and then, on command, express them with any degree of facility.

So we moved around among our friends and relatives with everything locked up inside. The feelings were there — manifested in nervousness, anxiety, rage, nightmares, and countless other symptoms more subtle. Those of us who did not drink ourselves into an early grave still struggle with them.

I hope this writing will help you resolve some of the feelings you have regarding your father. It will no doubt sadden you. But you will come to rationalize it, gain a better understanding of his behaviour, and realize that it was the war that deprived you of him as you would have wanted him to be. Only the war.[2]

Part I:
1913–1942

I next remember standing in the high office of the D.G.M.S. being told that I had been chosen to represent Canada in a far field, laden with Imperials, who must, by my deportment, be suitably impressed with the Royal Canadian Army Medical Corps.

While this preamble was going on, my mind had been wandering under the influence of sub-tropical stations, from North Africa to Jamaica, finally settling on the latter in view of some late grapevine news I had received a few hours before.

Imagine then, the appearance of my face when the D.G. ended his talk by clapping me on the shoulder and whispering that, while it was a secret that I must impart to NO ONE, yet I was, in fact, going to Hong Kong. The turn of my brain over 12,000 miles was almost vertiginous.

— Captain John Reid, Office of the Director General Medical Services,
Canadian Department of National Defence, Ottawa, October 6, 1941,
Reid Family Papers

– 1 –

There Was a Kindness in Him

John Reid was born in Toronto on October 6, 1913, the only child of Olive Gibson Reid, a 28-year-old tailoress, and Harry Edgar Reid, a typesetter soon to turn 30.

Olive and Harry were the children and grandchildren of immigrants. Harry was born in the town of Innisfil, Ontario, on the west shore of Lake Simcoe, in 1883. His father, Joshua Reid, was an Ontario railway worker whose paternal grandparents were landed gentry in Borrisokane, Ireland, and whose parents, William and Margaret, fled the depression in Great Britain and Ireland following the Napoleonic Wars and were granted land in Weston, Upper Canada, in the 1830s. Harry's mother, Mary Jane Killen, was of French Huguenot descent and the daughter of James Killen, a millwright from Dumdruff, Ireland, whose noteworthy grandfather, also James, fought under Britain's Lord Nelson in the

Battles of the Nile, Copenhagen, and Trafalgar. The Killen family immigrated to Canada in 1873 and settled in Innisfil, where Mary Jane Killen and Joshua Reid met and married in 1876. Harry was the fourth of their seven children.

John Reid's mother, Olive Gibson, was born in 1885, the daughter of Thomas Gibson, a Toronto teamster, and his wife, Mary-Ann Thorogood. Thomas Gibson's parents emigrated from England to Canada West in the late 1840s and opened a shop on Charles Street in Toronto. Mary-Ann Thorogood's English father, Joseph, and her American mother, Theresa, emigrated from the United States to Toronto in the 1850s, where Mary-Ann was born in 1862 and married Thomas Gibson in 1881. Olive was the third of Thomas and Mary-Ann's five children.

How Harry met Olive is unknown, though a possible connection is Joseph Gibson, one of Olive's two older brothers. By 1908, Harry Reid, now 25, had moved from his first job setting type by hand at the *Muskoka Herald*, a small-town newspaper co-founded by his uncle in Bracebridge, Ontario, to the typesetting staff of a large Toronto daily. Joseph Gibson, a year older than Harry, worked as a machinist and may have been employed at the same newspaper, servicing its printing presses and Linotype machines.

Churchgoing was another way of meeting members of the opposite sex, and given their neighbourhood proximity this, too, could have been the case for Harry and Olive. By 1911, the entire Reid family had moved from Innisfil to Toronto and was living at 279 Dupont Street, just west of Spadina Road, a 15-minute walk from the Gibson household at 784 Euclid Avenue. One of the Annex neighbourhood churches was a possible point of contact.

However they met, Harry and Olive were married in Toronto on March 12, 1912, and set up house at 226 Margueretta Street in the city's west end. A year and a half after the wedding, Olive gave birth at the new Toronto General Hospital on College Street, the institution where her son — christened John Anthony Gibson Reid, but almost always known as Jack — would train as a doctor in the 1930s.

Jack Reid, age three.

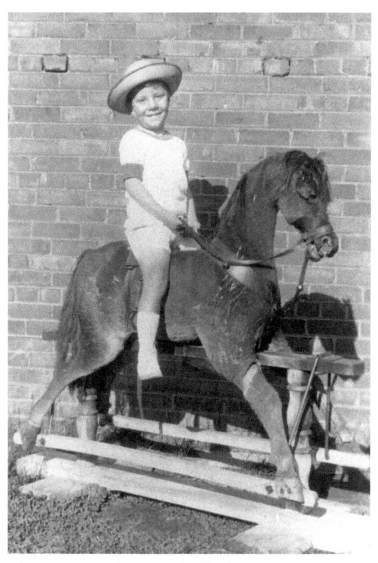

Jack Reid, 226 Margueretta Street, Toronto, circa 1918.

Jack Reid's childhood was happy and secure. By the time he was born, his father had logged five years of experience operating Linotype machines, the ingenious keyboard-controlled typesetting device with an astonishing 5,000 moving parts that was revolutionizing the publishing industry worldwide. In August 1918, the summer before Jack turned five, Harry Reid left the newspaper and landed a job at Canadian Linotype Limited itself, the American company's Toronto office, which sold and serviced Linotype machines across Canada. Here he would rise from novice salesman to sales manager within four years, then to branch manager in 1925 and in the 1930s to vice-president and manager for Canada. Even during the Great Depression, Harry Reid's job was assured.

Shortly after the First World War, the family moved to 396 Durie Street, where Reid attended nearby Runnymede Public School, grades one through eight. From the beginning, he was a great reader. *The Boy's Own* and *CHUMS* annuals were consumed with gusto, as were the many novels of G.A. Henty, featuring historical heroes from Britain and its empire. These yarns and later stories from the Great War likely inspired the battle stratagems the boy employed when he set up his ever-growing collection of lead soldiers — galloping cavalry, kilted Highlanders, Irish Guards in scarlet tunics and bearskin hats — later reinforced by First World War–vintage khaki-coloured infantry crouched behind machine guns or charging the enemy with fixed bayonets.

His literary bent appeared early on. At the opening of the new wing of the Art Gallery of Toronto in February 1926 (today the Art Gallery of Ontario), Reid, age 12, won first prize in Runnymede School's writing competition for the best student essay on the painting entitled *A Canadian Soldier* (the prize itself was a picture — a small, poorly tinted reproduction of fields lined by poplars in a Flanders landscape still untouched by war).

Jack's first salute.

Nourishing her son's interest in cultural matters with her own was Olive, who encouraged Reid's reading, writing, and musical talents, and took him to the public library and to stage shows and movies of the day. Charlie Chaplin, Buster Keaton, Joe E. Brown, and especially Harold Lloyd, the suave, bespectacled, stunningly athletic comedy star of the silent screen, were childhood preferences of young Jack.

Family outings were popular in Toronto in the 1920s, and on these forays, Harry Reid led the way. Toronto's Sunnyside Amusement Park and the Toronto Islands were popular spots, and favourite days for the Reids were communal picnics with family and friends where races, games, and ragtag baseball were part of the fun. A natural organizer of such razzmatazz, Harry Reid was usually at the centre of things, including the softball diamond where, as pitcher, his underhand fastball was renowned. In later years, Harry embellished these exploits and entertained the young with tall tales of his prowess in the father-and-son competitions: chugging to victory in the egg and spoon and potato sack races, little Jack flying in his wake as they crossed the finish line in first place. Harry Reid also had his musical side, a Pied-Piperish pleasure in gathering children for singalongs of such ditties as "Take Me Out to the Ball Game" and "Bicycle Built for Two" — Harry conducting, the children chiming the beat on glass jars with old nails as they raggedly sang the tunes.

In the fall of 1926, Harry and Olive Reid enrolled their son at University of Toronto Schools (UTS), a special "laboratory" high school established on campus in 1910 by the University of Toronto's Faculty of Education for teacher-training and curriculum-testing purposes. Here he excelled as a student and made the close friends — Doug Dadson, Frank Woods, and Leney Gage — he would keep throughout his university years and beyond. In the Class Notes section of the 1927 edition of the *Twig*, the UTS school magazine, Reid's traits of independence and self-direction are wryly noted in the doggerel of a classmate:

> A very fine student is Reid,
> He comes of a ponderous breed,
> He never hurries;
> He never worries;
> This ponderous student Reid.[1]

His extracurricular activities at UTS were basketball, track and field, and tennis, as well as working on and writing for the *Twig*.

Due to preadolescent chubbiness (he weighed 148 pounds by the age of 11), Reid welcomed the growth spurts of teenage years (he would reach six feet in height) and committed himself to a physical regimen that in one form or another, even in prison camp, he kept up until his final illness in the 1970s. In 1930 and 1931, he captained the UTS basketball team, and in his last two years, he competed in singles and doubles tennis (partnered with Doug Dadson), advancing to the quarter- and semifinals, respectively.

His road to tennis mastery revealed Reid's solo approach to new challenges. Taking up the game from scratch in his teens, he borrowed a book of tennis instruction from the library and spent the summer developing his strokes by volleying balls off a brick wall at Runnymede Public School for hours a day. Only after perfecting his shots did he take to the court against live opponents.

University of Toronto Schools (UTS) basketball team, 1930. Reid (front row, centre), Doug Dadson (front row, second from right), Leney Gage (back row, left).

With his strong literary interests, Reid continued his omnivorous reading throughout his high school years and approached this part of his self-education with similar practicality. Some of Charles Dickens's more sentimental novels, for example, he was inclined to leave unopened. But Dickens was part of literature's Western canon, so Reid dutifully read the complete works. When gripped by a story, he found it hard to put down. Preparation for a set of high school exams, he said, was almost sabotaged by John Galsworthy's *The Forsyte Saga*. His taste in poetry was expansive, ranging from the Latin classics and 19th-century romanticism to contemporary works — *Requiem*, for example, a Great War–inspired collection composed by Humbert Wolfe, a now forgotten Italian-born British poet of the interwar period. Something of Reid's quirky sense of humour and his ready appreciation of the lovable and ludicrous can be drawn from his early and enduring affection for Laurence Sterne's *Tristram Shandy*.

As well as reading widely, Reid was writing poetry and stories of his own during high school — clever if derivative juvenilia such as his Gothic-style poem entitled "A Slumbering Legend," which begins:

> Edged by the outflung brightness of the sky,
> A blot, like some dark moon in strange eclipse,
> Vines lingering o'er its skeleton like a sigh,
> Bowed down with age, the ruined castle sits ...[2]

Or his Wordsworthian rhapsody, "May She Return?":

> A fairy path I happ't upon
> That led me drowsily afield,
> A trace that stretched into the dawn,
> As if by wind-borne feet unreeled ...[3]

Noteworthy is "Impulse," a short story written and published in the *Twig* in 1929 when Reid was 16, which strangely foreshadows the nightmare he would experience as a prisoner of war in Hong Kong and Japan more than 10 years later.

"Impulse" tells the story of two newspaper reporters — the narrator and his associate Richard Roberts, whose assignment brings them to the dark, forbidding house of To Fang Chu, a prominent member of New York City's Chinatown and a man reputed to hate white men "like poison." The editor of the *Daily Tribune* wants his reporters to get Chu's reaction to the elopement of Chu's daughter, who has run off with "Renny Basil, idol of New York society." The tone of the story is macabre. As the reporters knock on Chu's door, the narrator thinks he glimpses a ghoulish face leering down from an outcrop of the gable. Once admitted (at their knock, the door swings silently open of its own accord), they make their way down dim corridors into a back room where they are confronted by a smirking To Fang Chu, who seems to be expecting them. Suddenly, the only light in the room crashes to the floor. The narrator hears his partner cry out in the darkness and in panic makes a run for the front door. He takes a wrong turn and by mistake shuts himself inside To Fang Chu's security vault:

> Instantaneously the world was cut off. Every sound ceased.... I felt for the door, its edge. A smooth wall greeted my shaking fingers. Turning, I started on, and stepped into another wall. Of course, the passage branched off. Two steps to the left and I was again halted. Panicky, I turned and ran madly to the right. And then my worst fears were realized. Four full paces and a glassy surface prohibited my further progress. In the next moment all the gruesome tales of Chinese tortures that I had ever heard flashed

into my mind. Insanely I assailed those bare, defiant walls. Kicked and beat them until I was exhausted. It seemed hours since I had slammed that door. And then my frantic, strained nerves impressed upon me that it was becoming increasingly hard to breathe. This realization only urged me to greater efforts. But a few moments later I stopped, panting. Then remembering that warm air rose, I knelt down and breathed a bit easier. But only too soon it again became close, stifling. I was choking. One last assault on those unforgiving walls. Then — oblivion.[4]

Reid won the T.M. Porter Special Scholarship for English and History in 1930 and the Special James Harris Proficiency Scholarship upon graduation from UTS in 1931. That fall, Reid and his school friends, Doug Dadson, Frank Woods, Leney Gage, Alfredo Goggio, and Bruce Charles, entered the honours bachelor of arts program at University College, University of Toronto. For Reid and Charles, who had chosen to become doctors, this four-year undergraduate degree was part one of the University of Toronto's biological and medical sciences courses, a seven-year program.

Thanks to Harry Reid's position at Canadian Linotype, his son not only could afford tuition but drove to school from his home in the west end in a big blue Buick of his own. As far as his friends could tell, Reid always had money, or access to it. For others, the effects of the Great Depression were devastating. By 1931, Doug Dadson's family was in such financial straits that the $100 university tuition fee was beyond their means. Reid, "a very kind man, without show,"[5] said Dadson, gave him the money for first-year university.

Before the stock market crash of 1929, the Reids moved from Durie Street to a corner property at 79 Humber Trail, a spacious house a few minutes walk east of the Humber River and its forested valley. Here at 79 Humber Trail, the last house the Reids would share as a family, Doug Dadson, Frank Woods, and Leney Gage would visit for evenings of bridge, conversation, and cigar smoking. Dadson and Woods remembered the Reids as a close-knit family with little connection to neighbours on the street. Harry struck them as a positive, friendly, uncomplicated man, busy with his work at Canadian Linotype. They found Olive attractive, gentle, and welcoming, with a very close bond to her son. "She was quiet," said Dadson, "but her warmth permeated the home."[6]

As an only child, Reid matured early. He struck his friends, who had siblings, more like a close associate of his parents than a son. He dressed well. Already a skilled bridge player (he didn't sort his hand — one glance and he was ready to bid), Reid excelled at all card games. He was an early devotee of the *New Yorker*, an admirer of its contributors, such as James Thurber and Ogden Nash, for their inventive whimsy, and of Noël Coward, that consummate

On the beach at Foot's Bay, early 1930s. Leney Gage (left) and Jack.

sophisticate, for his stylishness, playwriting, and music (Reid played the piano and apparently wrote tunes of his own). Horse racing was another of Reid's early interests, a visit to the track entertainment of a different sort.

Something of a loner, Reid could also be a receptive and reflective friend. Doug Dadson occasionally stayed at 79 Humber Trail when Olive accompanied Harry on his business trips and describes Reid as someone he could talk with intimately on any subject. Sometime during first-year university their conversation must have turned to summer holidays because it was Dadson who provided the *entrée* for Reid and their other friends to spend a string of summers at Foot's Bay on the Muskoka Lakes — what would become golden interludes in their university lives. It was also where Reid met Jean Hodge in 1933, the woman he would marry just before the Second World War.

Foot's Bay in the 1930s was a sparsely settled tourist community at the southwest corner of Lake Joseph in Ontario's Muskoka region. One of the regular summer residents was Doug's uncle, Dr. Thomas Dadson, a history professor at Acadia University in Wolfville, Nova Scotia, whose Baptist minister father, Ebenezer, had bought an extensive shoreline property before the First World War on which Thomas later built a huge summer home called Cranbrook, named after the market town in Kent, England, where Ebenezer was born.

Down the shore from Cranbrook stood a rambling, pleasantly shabby boarding house-cum-hotel called Staney Brae ("Stoney Hillside"). It was run by a wiry little Scottish spinster named

Georgia MacKenzie with the help of her companion, Miss Ray, and Miss MacKenzie's nephews, Alan and Dunny. In 1931, Doug Dadson, who often stayed at Cranbrook, heard from his uncle that a waterfront shack on Miss MacKenzie's property was vacant and would be available the coming summer for a pittance. At this news, Reid must have pricked up his ears. Inquiries were made, the rental was arranged, and after the university year finished in June 1932, Harry and Olive Reid chauffeured their son and Frank Woods to Foot's Bay. Several hundred yards along the lake from Miss MacKenzie's hotel sat their tiny destination. Although to older eyes, Olive's in particular, it looked disconcertingly primitive, Reid and Woods were delighted by the place and its surroundings.

About 10 feet square, shrouded by trees on three sides and steps from the water on the fourth, the shack was fronted by a narrow, roofless porch and furnished inside with a table, a few chairs, three cots lining the walls, and an old sheet iron stove. Over the ensuing five years, this would be home for Reid during the three-month summer break from university, while Dadson, Woods, Gage, and other friends came and went in changing combinations.

"They were marvellous summers," said Frank Woods many years later. "We had a canoe and a rowboat. We ate well — steaks and chops from MacDonald's Store, and the washing up was easy. We just left the dishes and utensils in the water by the shore and they were clean by the next meal, washed by sand and water motion."[7]

Dark and cramped, the shack was mainly for sleeping. Days were spent on the water and at a splendid sand beach at the nearby entrance to Stills Bay. Photographs show Reid and his friends swimming in halcyon summer weather, sunbathing on the beach with an old log as bench and backrest, reading on the steps of their porch, or gathered around campfires during canoe trips they took to other parts of Muskoka.

For regular supplies, they paddled or rowed to the store at the Foot's Bay public dock, 20 minutes away. Fish were plentiful. Lake trout were especially prized, and a favourite Reid pastime, especially when on his own, was to paddle out to deep water in the evening, drop a line, then stretch out on the floor of his drifting canoe, light a cigar, and watch the fading light and first stars appearing until a fish struck. Cooking the catch — or anything else — on the shack's old sheet metal stove was always an adventure. If bumped, as easily happened in the close quarters, the stove had a tendency to collapse and could only be reassembled after cooling down.

More exotic foodstuffs were imported by the revolving cast of shack dwellers, not always with the intended outcome. One night, after leaving a large jar of pickles on the porch, the sleepers were awakened by strange knocking sounds. They found the jar stuck on the head of a staggering and very unhappy skunk — for whom Reid, Frank Woods remembered, expressed droll sympathy as it lurched away in the dark. Doug Dadson recalled a special burnt offering brought by Leney Gage. Impossible to miss, Leney — a six-foot-five blond Adonis, avid stamp collector, and member of the Gage publishing family, arrived for one visit bearing an enormous cooked ham. Even for this crew of hungry young men, it took days to consume. Hung in mosquito netting from the branch of a tree beside the shack (there was, of course, no refrigeration), the ham slowly darkened from pink to a sort of bluish colour, then from blue to black. "We gave up carving the ham by this time," said Dadson. "It was so rotten we could pick delicious chunks off it till we finally worked our way down to the bone. I'm surprised Jack didn't become nervous [of ptomaine poisoning], but he didn't."[8]

Occasionally, the young men made sorties by canoe down the Little Joe River to Port Carling on Lake Rosseau, nine miles south, to call on girls they knew at the country club or local cottages. Reid was a strong, skilled canoeist, and calm in trying circumstances, as

Frank Woods described one of the Port Carling visits: "We were coming back to Foot's Bay, just the two of us. It must have been three in the morning and we ran into some terrible winds. I wasn't the strongest paddler in the world, but Jack was a very fine paddler. I was scared stiff, but he didn't seem to be worried about it. It was pitch-dark and raining and blowing, but he knew every bend and turn in the river."[9]

Woods had been diagnosed with a cardiac weakness following an illness during his final year at UTS, a condition not considered serious but a factor to keep in mind. During their times at Foot's Bay, Reid always did.

"There was never anything remotely mawkish about Jack," said Woods, "but he was always very kind and understanding of me. Jack, who never had a physical concern at all — I always appreciated the way he'd nudge me out of the way of the heavy lift or the heavy climb. There was a kindness in him that, frankly, not too many people might have seen."[10]

Evenings, the young men often visited their neighbours. Georgia MacKenzie was a warm, welcoming landlady, and the door of Staney Brae was always open for card playing and radio listening. But it was at Cranbrook that they socialized most. Professor Dadson — "Uncle Tom," as everyone called him — was an endearing character of the crusty, old-school variety. A bachelor, a Baptist, an eminent professor of medieval history, he was in person a short, plump, pipe-puffing gnome with huge shaggy eyebrows, dark, sombre eyes, and a dry sense of humour. When the young men learned that his doctorate at the University of Chicago had been on "Persistent Influence of Paganism in the Thirteenth Century," he accepted with amused equanimity their referring to his thesis as "Pernicious Influence of Gasoline on the Lifespan of Sparrows." Both Woods and Dadson roared with laughter as they recalled Uncle Tom's story of visiting Toronto one winter and being conscripted as a human toboggan on the Avenue Road hill, the long, steep slope south of St. Clair Avenue that was once the north shore of prehistoric Lake Iroquois. Uncle Tom was waiting for a streetcar at the top of the hill the morning after a severe ice storm when an unknown woman lost her footing, fell against him, and clutching him for rescue, launched them on their tandem slide to the bottom. As Uncle Tom told it, once gravity brought them to a stop near the corner of Cottingham Street, a third of a mile south, he, winded and bruised from the crushing descent, addressed the weighty woman now perched atop him: "Excuse me, madame, but you have to get off here. This is as far as I go."

In some ways a folly with its two-storey central portion, looming quadrangular tower, and offset wings, Cranbrook was a grand summer house with a veranda and a study full of books, easy chairs inside and out, places to write, and when night fell, ample lamplight. Typical were the evenings when Reid and his friends left the shack and made their way through the woods to Uncle Tom's place for boisterous bouts of bridge and conversation. "It was eight hundred or nine hundred yards away," said Woods, "but we knew the path so well that we could find our way to and fro on the darkest night without a light."[11]

A feature of Cranbrook, usually resorted to on cooler, cloudy days when the bugs weren't so bad, was the crazy, one-of-a-kind croquet course that Uncle Tom had laid out over several hundred yards of rough, hillocky terrain around his cottage. Because of the broken ground, rotting stumps, juniper bushes, protruding rocks, the hazards of scrub and scree at every turn, hooping the ball and pegging out was really a game of wild and woolly bush golf, a far cry from the genteel ball-tapping on manicured lawns the word *croquet* normally conjures up. By now a golfer as well as a tennis player, Reid excelled at hacking his way around the course.

That first summer at Miss MacKenzie's shack established the relationships and pastimes of their Foot's Bay life that Reid and his friends were to pursue and elaborate over their university years. By the time Reid left for the city in August 1932, plans were already laid to come back the following year. As it turned out, Reid did. But the summer of 1933 would be a momentous one: begun in mourning, ending in love.

Olive Reid had been experiencing bouts of fatigue and malaise unnatural for a woman in her midforties. The diagnosis was endocarditis, an infection that damages heart valves and for which medications and surgical procedures of the 1930s were helpless to correct. By the fall of 1932, the condition was taking its toll. One telling photograph shows Olive standing by herself in her garden appearing wan and tired. There are dark circles under her eyes, a look of sadness and resignation on her face, no trace of the beautiful smile that lights up earlier pictures.

She kept her medical condition to herself. A 1932 Christmas letter written to her Montreal sister-in-law, Grace Reid, wife of Clifford Reid, Harry's youngest brother, is newsy and lighthearted. Olive declares Christmas "the children's day" (Grace and Clifford would know — they had five kids to Olive's one). She mentions the flu season as a reason to be careful. Harry's nasty head cold is discussed in order to cluck over the impossibility of getting him to stay in and rest up properly. Olive tells Grace that she has taken up interior decorating: "I enjoy it very much and am acquiring a great deal of useful information." She is about to start an advanced course in January and adds mock-seriously, "so perhaps when you want to do your house over you will require my services." But worry about her health must have been circulating

Olive Reid, 1932, the year before her death.

in the family, for Olive then lightly chides her sister-in-law for spreading rumours:

> Grace, who told you I was taking treatments for my nerves? I have taken osteopath treatments for my intestinal trouble. But have not had any trouble with my nerves — so I guess you have been misinformed! I only take an occasional treatment now — in fact, have not had one since August.
>
> Well, I guess this is about all the news for the present. I hope you are all well now, and will continue so through the winter.
>
> Write me again soon. It is too bad we do not hear from each other more often. Love to you all from we three.
>
> — Olive[12]

Grace Reid preserved the note, pencilling on the corner of its envelope, "Olive's last letter."

A danger of endocarditis is that a small clot can break off from a damaged valve and circulate to the brain, causing a stroke. On March 17, 1933 — St. Patrick's Day — Olive felt unwell. She rested at home. But on Sunday afternoon, two days later, she suddenly lost consciousness while she was lying on the divan in the living room of 79 Humber Trail and died of a cerebral embolism within minutes. That evening, Doug Dadson got a phone call from Reid, who quietly told his friend the news and asked if Doug would come out to the house to keep him company.

Reid's friends found 79 Humber Trail a much-changed place in the months after Olive's death, the two men rattling around the house like lost souls, more brothers in their sorrow than father and son. Adding to the gloom were the effects of the Great Depression that Harry Reid faced daily at work. As economic conditions worsened and business dropped, he was forced to cut jobs at Canadian Linotype. Reid saw the impact on his father, who at the end of the day would come home and curl up on the living room couch too bereaved, glum, and exhausted to talk.

"Jack was always a bit mysterious," said Doug Dadson. "Now he would disappear for a few days. Wouldn't say where. And you didn't ask him. Jack never broke down. He was always very controlled. But his mother's death put him into a strange state for a while. He neglected his studies, drank a bit."[13]

The memories of Jack Reid's early years that Woods and Dadson provided were recorded at Dadson's Toronto home in March 1983, half a century after Olive's death and four years after Reid's own. Dignified gentlemen approaching 70 at the time, Dadson and Woods were by then both retired. Frank Woods,

Frank Woods (left) and Doug Dadson.

who became a chartered accountant and never married, had ended his career as a vice-president of Moore Corporation, the business forms giant. Doug Dadson, a widower and father of two grown children, was an educator who became the first dean of the Faculty of Education at the University of Toronto. During an interview lasting several hours, Dadson and Woods reminisced about their old friend with warmth and humour, the comments of one prompting amendments by the other. After listening to Doug Dadson's description of Reid's rocky, unpredictable behaviour following the death of his mother, Frank Woods quickly added: "But when Jack met Jean and the rest of the Hodge family, he suddenly straightened out again."[14]

2

The Golden Couple and the
Phoney War

I t was a family with five daughters. John Cory Hodge, their father, came from the fishing village of Port Dover, Ontario, the youngest son of Matthew Hodge, the local customs agent, who emigrated with his wife, Jane, from Devonshire, England, in the 1860s, failed at farming northwest of Hamilton Mountain, and ended up in his modest government job on the north shore of Lake Erie.

Leaving school in 1895 to help support his parents, John Hodge (usually known as "Jack") went to Portland, Maine, at the invitation of a Port Dover family friend already working there, and at 16, joined R.G. Dun & Company, the international credit bureau business that later became Dun & Bradstreet. By 1922, Hodge had progressed from office boy, travelling auditor, and district manager for London and Hamilton, Ontario, to become R.G. Dun & Company's manager for the Toronto district, acquiring the three-storey home at 5 Scholfield Avenue in North Rosedale chosen by his wife for its five bedrooms, a den for her musical activities, and Rosedale Park

Jack and Eva Hodge, Jean's parents, bought the 5 Scholfield house in Toronto's Rosedale in 1922. It still stands.

across the street for their girls to play in. By 1933, the year R.G. Dun & Company merged with John M. Bradstreet to form Dun & Bradstreet, Hodge was general manager for Canada.

His wife, Eva Luttrell, was the daughter of Alexander Luttrell, a Bowmanville, Ontario, baker distantly related to the ancient

Luttrell family of Dunster Castle, Somerset, England. One of eight children, Eva grew up to become an accomplished musician, and until her marriage at the age of 30, travelled weekly by train from Bowmanville to Toronto to teach piano and organ at the conservatory and to serve as sole accompanist for the Toronto Male Chorus conducted by J.D.A. Tripp, chorus founder, distinguished Canadian pianist, and composer of such popular ditties as "Woodland Love Song," "The Salt Sea Foam," and "Hail, Britain, Hail! — Song of the Canadian Patriots." Hers must have been a prized role: Eva's memento of those years, always on display over the family piano, was a formal photograph showing her seated in a long white concert dress, like a queen with her courtiers — Tripp and the six chorus members encircling her on three sides in their black tuxedos. Eva Luttrell and Jack Hodge met in 1905 while lodging at the same Toronto boarding house — the widow Mrs. Thom's very respectable residence at 185 College Street — and married in 1909.

Jean, the third of their five girls, was born on August 6, 1914, two days after the First World War began, her name in honour of Jeanne d'Arc, patron saint of France. Throughout childhood, Jean's shy, artistic personality hardly conformed to her historic namesake. But her toughness did. In the winter of 1926, at the age of 12, she suffered a ruptured appendix, often a death sentence before antibiotics, and spent several months at Toronto's Sick Children's Hospital, her life hanging in the balance. Against the odds, she pulled through, fortitude that would stand her in good stead in difficult times ahead.

At Toronto's Central Technical School on Bathurst Street, where she pursued her artistic ambitions after high school, Jean Hodge became friends with Miriam Fox, a fellow art student, Rosedale neighbour, and daughter of Edward Carey Fox, a Canadian business tycoon with mining and meat-packing interests. "Mim," as Miriam was called, had met Frank Woods through another connection, and in the winter of 1933 had been escorted by him to a University College dance. Frank Woods and Mim Fox stayed in touch, and when the Fox family rented a cottage at Foot's Bay in the summer of 1933, Frank Woods and Jack Reid paddled over from their Staney Brae shack to say hello. Sunning on the dock were Mim Fox, and up for a visit, her new friend, Jean Hodge. For the tagalong sternsman and beautiful cottage guest, it was love at first sight.

During the six years before they married in 1939, Jack Reid and Jean Hodge were inseparable — a golden couple in the eyes of their friends who had yet to find mates of their own. The handsome pre-med student, recently bereaved, was welcomed into the Hodge family's warm and lively household at 5 Scholfield, where he was admired by Jean's parents and adored by Jean's sisters — Kay, Dede, Marg, and Val. The Scholfield house, entrancingly full of life and music, became Reid's second home.

Jean Hodge, Foot's Bay, mid-1930s.

In 1935, two years after he and Jean met, Reid graduated from University College with his bachelor of arts and embarked on the three-year medical portion of his biological and medicine sciences program. Jean, now graduated from Central Tech, rented a "studio" in the attic of a house on Bloor Street where she sculpted, painted, did linocut printmaking (Christmas cards and personalized bookplates were specialties), and practised the violin.

During first-year medicine, Reid became close friends with classmate Wilfred "Bill" Bigelow, whose world-famous discoveries after the Second World War in the uses of hypothermia and electrical heart stimulation would pave the way to open-heart surgery and the development of the artificial pacemaker. Bigelow, the son of a country doctor, native of Brandon, Manitoba, and a self-confessed plodder as a medical student, marvelled at Reid's photographic capacity to absorb course material and score consistently high marks while keeping up an enviable extracurricular schedule of tennis, theatre-, concert-, and movie-going with Jean (Reid's entertainment budget augmented by $25 blood donations), dinners at 5 Scholfield, visits to Jean's Bloor Street studio, and summer holidays at Foot's Bay, where Jean became part of the scene, discreetly lodged at the Foxes' cottage or at Georgia MacKenzie's hotel. Old photos give a sense of those summers of romance: Jack and Jean sailing in Professor Dadson's dinghy, sunning on the beach, snuggling on the steps of the shack in the evening as Jack reads aloud by lamplight — poetry that he admired and novels such as *Tristram Shandy* and *The Forsyte Saga* that became favourites of hers, as well.

When apart, they wrote each other often, signing off with pet names of a provenance unknown: "Stephanie" for her, "Michael" for him — soon shortened to the "Steve" and "Mike" they used in their private correspondence ever after. In Toronto, Reid made a habit of leaving little love notes for Jean to find in his absence — ephemera of courtship that she preserved in an envelope that must

Country outing, late 1930s. Jean and Jack, Ruth Jennings (back to camera; would marry Bill Bigelow in 1941), and Bill Bigelow (shadow photographer).

have held one of them — addressed, in Reid's rakish handwriting, to "Miss Stephanie Hodge, Most Privately." Sometimes the note was just a torn corner of paper with *S* on one side and "I love you" or "I adore you" or "Hurry back" and *M* on the other. Other times they could be whimsical: "For Little Stephen, on account of it's Wednesday, and this day with new moon is the most loving yet." Or sappy:

My Dear Steve:

Violets, my darling, because
To me violets mean softness and
Sweetness and exquisite loveliness,
And to me also, softness and
Sweetness and exquisite loveliness
Mean only you.

Or maudlin:

My little one, I love you so
Without you I could never go
Along my way
Through dark by day
To find no happiness.

Or sentimental:

My Dearest Steve,

You stand, totally oblivious of me, talking with interest & animation. You are so very pretty. How soft
and warm.

Days with you pass like the slapping of water against the hull of a ship. So rapidly it flies, so sweet each moment.

Let us keep each lovely moment a memory of ecstasy and a promise of tomorrow.

— Michael[1]

Jean's last letters to Jack at Foot's Bay were written in October 1937. A polio outbreak in Southern Ontario that summer — nearly 4,000 people were stricken, the majority in Toronto — required Reid and his fellow medical students to forgo their usual three-month break and help out during the emergency. Because of it, the start of the 1937 medical school year was delayed. When the epidemic died down at the end of September, Reid went north to spend several weeks alone at the Foot's Bay shack in what turned out to be a spell of extraordinary second summer weather: sunshine and warm temperatures during the day, pleasant coolness at night; Lake Joseph, empty of boats, silent except for the wind and waves; the surrounding shores dotted with blazes of red, orange, and yellow against the green pines. He paddled, fished, read, wrote poetry, and revelled in his luck — an off-season escape he remembered and recommended, should others have the chance, all his life. It was his last holiday at Foot's Bay.

Reid and his classmates graduated in medicine the following spring. He and three close friends — Bill Bigelow, Gordon Gray, and Bruce Charles — began their junior internships at Toronto General Hospital that June, a month that saw another important development: Harry Reid's second marriage, on June 29, 1938, five years after the death of Olive.

It was a midlife union with a history. Harry Reid first met Eva Bastedo in 1903 when, at age 18, he left home in Innisfil to apprentice as a typesetter at Bracebridge's *Muskoka Herald*, the newspaper co-founded in 1878 by his uncle and namesake, Henry "Harry" Oaten, and David Bastedo, Eva's father. Medical doctor, newspaper publisher, sheriff of Muskoka District: David Bastedo was one of the town's most prominent citizens. Eva, eldest of his eight children, was both privileged in her upbringing and accomplished as a pianist and church organist, talents that took her to Toronto to study music at the Royal Conservatory in 1906 — about the time Harry sought his fortune there as a printer.

Whether or not Eva and Harry's departures for Toronto were connected, they went their separate ways once there. In 1907, Eva met Andrew Cridland, a Jamaica-born Englishman studying at the University of Toronto, and following a protracted courtship, married him in 1915, three years after Harry married Olive Gibson. Cridland, who became Toronto sales manager for the Canadian Kodak Company, died in 1935 at the age of 50, leaving Eva childless, financially comfortable, and owner of a home backing onto Grenadier Pond in High Park, not far from the Reids' house on Humber Trail.

It remains unknown if Harry and Eva's marriage in June 1938 was an old flame rekindled, or simply the obvious step for two old friends from the same small town, now widowed in their adopted city. Whatever the case, 79 Humber Trail was sold, Harry joined Eva at 9 Grenadier Heights, and the marriage proved a contented one, their wedding day presaging by a year the long-awaited nuptials of Jean Hodge and Jack Reid — celebrated at long last on June 20, 1939, right after he finished his junior internship.

When it came to their wedding, Reid's singular style and *savoir-vivre* led to unusual stipulations. Bill Bigelow (Reid always

Jack and Jean's wedding reception, June 20, 1939, in the 5 Scholfield garden.

called him "Willie") served as Reid's best man and later recalled with amusement his first duty on the morning of the day: insert a new blade in Reid's Schick Injector Razor and have a shave before passing the razor to the groom. Reid maintained that a Schick blade's smoothest performance came with its second shave, not the first, and he wanted his wedding day to be perfect, start to finish.

Instead of cavernous St. Paul's Anglican Church on Bloor Street East, where the Hodge family had been occupying a pew for nearly 20 years, the wedding took place at St. John's Anglican in York Mills, a more modest stone church built in 1844 on the heights of Hoggs Hollow, north of Toronto, where it had been discovered by Jack and Jean on one of their Sunday drives. The wedding day turned out sunny and warm, the reception was in the garden of 5 Scholfield, the honeymoon a motor trip to New York City, and home, for their first year of marriage, an apartment on Spadina Road a few blocks north of Bloor Street, an easy walk to the Toronto General Hospital where Reid began his senior internship two weeks after they were married. Two months later, the Second World War began.

The likelihood of an international conflict had been growing for years. Reid's generation, born in the Great War period and growing up in its aftermath, entered adulthood watching the unchecked rise of Nazi Germany: Adolf Hitler's dictatorship in 1933; Germany's rearmament, beginning in 1935; reoccupation of the Rhineland in 1936; annexation of Austria in 1938; occupation of Czechoslovakia in 1938 and 1939; Hitler and Mussolini's "Pact of Steel" — the "Rome-Berlin Axis" military alliance — announced in May 1939.

Discussions at 5 Scholfield of these world-worrying events had some insider knowledge. Jean's older sister, Dede, who majored in languages at the University of Toronto's Trinity College and became fluent in French, served with Canada's legation at the League of Nations in Geneva from 1934 to 1939, witnessing first-hand how the Western Allies' policy of appeasement played into Hitler's and Mussolini's hands. Only after Germany's invasion of Poland, with which Britain and France had a binding alliance, were the Allies pushed to declare war against Germany on September 3, 1939. Canada's declaration came a week later.

The onset of a world war was an unsettling set of circumstances in which to begin a marriage and proceed with career plans. But throughout much of Reid's senior internship at Toronto General Hospital — the nine months from September 1939 to May 1940 — not much happened on the war front. Hitler was preoccupied in Eastern Europe, consolidating Nazi control of Poland and Czechoslovakia and planning the surprise invasion of Russia he would unleash in June 1941. Britain and Western Europe, anxious to increase their war preparedness, bought time by adopting a defensive position once the European armies and the British Expeditionary Force had been deployed along the eastern borders of France and Belgium in September 1939.

While Reid and his medical friends must have discussed what impact the war would have on their personal lives and medical training, most of them, Reid included, had already planned at least another year of training following their senior internships. With the war in suspended animation, most of these plans went ahead. What is intriguing in Reid's case is that he chose to do his medical residency in Vancouver, where he had no professional connection, rather than in Toronto, where he was highly regarded by the university medical hierarchy and where Bill Bigelow and his other friends remained.

Whatever the attraction, by the time the Reids moved west in June 1940, the so-called Phoney War had ended with a bang. That May, Nazi Germany launched a massive assault of 800,000 soldiers and airmen against the Western Front, attacking Holland, Belgium, Luxembourg, and France all at once. The four countries — most stunningly France, thought to have the strongest army in Europe — collapsed in a matter of weeks under the Nazi blitzkrieg. By late May, the British Expeditionary Force and remnants of the French and Belgian armies — 340,000 soldiers in all — had to be evacuated from Dunkirk on the French coast and ferried to Britain, leaving most of their weaponry, tanks, vehicles, and other *matériel* behind. On June 10, 1940, Italy declared war on Britain and France, confirming the Axis alliance. On June 22, France formally capitulated to the Nazis, and 1.5 million French soldiers surrendered, most without firing a shot. When the Reids reached Vancouver just after their first wedding anniversary, all of Western Europe was under Axis control, with only Britain and the Commonwealth remaining in opposition. Operation Sea Lion, Hitler's scheme to invade Britain, was due to launch in September. For this offensive, the Nazis needed control of the English Channel and the skies above it. The Battle of Britain — the famed three-and-a-half-month air war of July 10 to October 31, 1940, when the Royal Air Force stymied the Nazi Luftwaffe and held off the German invasion — was about to begin.

3

Canada's Turn to Help:
The "C" Force Mission

In July 1940, the Reids rented a flat in "The Pasadena," a two-storey, California-style apartment building near the corner of West 11th Avenue and Hemlock Street, a 10-minute walk to Vancouver General Hospital, where Reid was doing his residency.

Jean found life in Vancouver an adjustment. Reid was busy at the hospital, often day and night. She was far from family and friends, and the sometimes endless grey or rainy days could be dispiriting, much like the war news. A fear of heights inherited from her father made the looming North Shore Mountains an unsettling barrier rather than an inviting prospect (even driving across the newly opened Lions Gate Bridge took a summoning of nerve). On her own much of the time, finding ways to make new friends didn't come easily. Extremely happy in her life with Jack yet not entirely at home in Vancouver, Jean kept house, tried new recipes, wrote letters, went for walks, and painted.

For Reid, this residency year seems to have been entirely positive. Work at Vancouver General was a stimulating change. The dramatic locale — ocean, beaches, mountains, and sky — offered a sense of openness and freedom that the gentler, insulated countryside of Southern Ontario lacked. The more relaxed West Coast life, after the provincial stuffiness of Toronto, appealed to him. Medical colleagues who liked to extol to newcomers the virtues of the setting — the ocean playground, the rarity of city snow, year-round golf, Vancouver festooned with cherry blossoms in March — were in Reid's case soon preaching to a convert.

Chief among the friends he made in Vancouver during his residency was Dr. Lyall Hodgins, founding partner of The Clinic, a private medical facility established on Seymour Street in 1937 whose doctors had privileges at Vancouver General Hospital. Hodgins, whose clinic was the first of its kind in western Canada, became a close friend and mentor of Reid, and by the spring of 1941, a prospective partner in practice. Although Reid was planning to enlist in the Royal Canadian Army Medical Corps after his residency, Hodgins offered him a job at The Clinic, a position that would be waiting for him whenever he returned from his war service. When the Reids left Vancouver for Toronto in June 1941, "J.A. Reid, M.D." had been added to The Clinic's letterhead, Hitler was invading Russia with three million Nazi troops, and the United States was about to place an embargo on all oil and gasoline exports to Japan following Japan's occupation of French Indochina. If the embargo remained in place, Japan's warlords planned to strike south from China and take control of oil-rich North Borneo, the Dutch East Indies, and everything in between.

Reid was one of a number of University of Toronto medical graduates of 1937 and 1938 who signed up for the Royal Canadian Army Medical Corps in August 1941. Bill Bigelow was another, just back from his honeymoon in Manitoba after a July wedding in Toronto where, tit-for-tat, Reid had been his best man. Other friends were Gordon Gray, originally from Edmonton; Torontonian Bruce Charles; and William Mustard from Clinton, Ontario, who, like Bigelow, would be instrumental in the postwar advancement of open-heart surgery with his development of the heart-lung machine.

The five-week medical officer's training course was conducted at Lansdowne Park in Ottawa. A four-page photo spread published in Toronto's *Star Weekly* in September 1941 featured Reid's class of about 30 novice RCAMC lieutenants going through their paces at Lansdowne earlier that month. The pictures show the men in their newly issued khaki shorts and shirts in a variety of poses: attending a lecture on military law, assembled around a sand table of miniaturized terrain being instructed in battle tactics, evacuating mock wounded by stretcher through a trench they had dug themselves, ogling the camera wearing helmets and gas masks, and — hidebound military protocol — learning how to manipulate and salute with an officer's swagger stick. The rest of the magazine was filled with similarly upbeat stories on the current Canadian and British war effort: the Canadian 3rd Division disembarking in England, pictures of the latest in London air-raid shelters, a British channel gun doing "a spot of shelling" of the occupied French coast, "war dogs" being trained to transport ammunition strapped to their flanks in battle conditions, a bevy of laughing British "farmerettes" harvesting a bumper crop of wheat on the Sussex Downs.[1]

Britain, leader of the Commonwealth, and by the summer of 1941, the island fortress standing alone against Nazi-occupied Europe, would be the initial destination of almost all the armed forces, aircraft, and other war *matériel* shipped or flown overseas from Canada during the Second World War. But as Reid's class at Lansdowne Park was going about the business of becoming medical officers bound for Britain with the rest of the Canadian Army, decisions were being made in London and Ottawa concerning the menace to British holdings on the other side of the world, decisions that would mean other plans for two of the "graduates."

Japan had been on the attack in the Far East for 10 years. Its invasions of Manchuria in 1931 and China in 1937 were first steps in establishing the Japanese-conceived "Greater East Asia Co-Prosperity Sphere," ostensibly a union of Asian states to counter Western imperialism and achieve regional self-sufficiency, in reality Japan's guise to impose its imperial domination over the entire Far East and gain control of the resources — oil, rubber, tin — that Japan's industries and war machine badly needed. "It is Japan's mission to be supreme in Asia, the South Seas, and eventually the four corners of the world," boasted Japanese General Sadao Araki in 1935.[2]

The scale of atrocities and barbarism committed by the invading Japanese troops during the subjugation of Nanking in 1937, when up to 300,000 Chinese civilians were butchered over a period of six weeks, showed the viciousness of Japan's intent. Its refusal to ratify the Geneva Convention after signing it in 1929 and its resignation from the League of Nations in 1933, after the league's unanimous condemnation of the occupation of Manchuria, revealed Japan's contempt for world opinion.

Throughout the 1930s, Britain monitored the defence status of its bases at Hong Kong and Singapore in case war with Japan broke out. Singapore, a massive, well-fortified naval and military installation that had been under improvement since the early 1920s, was considered a fortress stronghold. The 100-year-old Crown Colony of Hong Kong, a tiny British holding on the coast of China, 1,600 miles northeast of Singapore, was another matter.

A 1935 British defence report made by Major-General Frederick Barron, inspector of fixed defences, listed Hong Kong's obvious vulnerabilities. The colony was open to attack from the rear either across the Chinese frontier or by an enemy landing by sea on Hong Kong's mainland territories. Its only airfield was inadequate and was located on the mainland in an exposed position. Rainfall reservoirs built in the late 19th century sustained Hong Kong Island's water needs, but all food and other necessities were imported by ship or by ferry from the mainland, supplies that could be cut off quickly by an attacking force. The Hong Kong garrison of four understrength infantry battalions — fewer than 4,000 soldiers — wasn't enough to protect Hong Kong Island as well as man the 11-mile northern defence line on the mainland. And because of distance, the likelihood of timely support from Singapore or Britain should an attack on Hong Kong occur was highly questionable in the first case, practically non-existent in the second. Barron's report summed up the Hong Kong defences as "deplorable" and stated that the island of Hong Kong would be "easy prey ... and that in the face of a determined attack by land or sea the fortress could not hold out even for the arbitrary period before relief."[3]

In response to the report's findings, some modernization of Hong Kong's mainland defences was approved in 1936 and partially carried out the following year. But the recommendation to reinforce the garrison with two more infantry battalions wasn't, a War Office decision Hong Kong's commanding officer, General Arthur Bartholomew, concurred with: two extra battalions, in Bartholomew's view, would have no appreciable effect on the outcome in case of serious attack. Bartholomew submitted his "Report on the 'Unrestricted' Defence of Hong Kong ..." in July 1937, advising that to mount a reasonable defence would require the installation of 15-inch coastal guns, increasing the air garrison from its current five aircraft to five squadrons (120 aircraft), and bringing troop strength up to a full division of 15,000 infantry.[4] With the present garrison, wrote Bartholomew, "chances ... of [Hong Kong] effecting a prolonged resistance even in the best circumstances seem slight."[5]

By 1938, the British chiefs of staff concluded that Hong Kong wasn't a defensible asset, downgraded its status to "outpost" (meaning, if attacked, its only purpose was to delay the enemy as long as possible), and would have reduced the garrison from four battalions to two to minimize losses should Hong Kong fall, if such obvious defeatism and loss of British prestige hadn't been seen as unacceptable. The garrison's status quo of four infantry battalions was therefore retained.

Disagreement with this change in Hong Kong policy was soon brought forward by two optimistic British commanders on the ground: Major-General Arthur Grasett, a Canadian in the British Army who succeeded Bartholomew as commander-in-chief, China Command (Hong Kong), in November 1938, and Air Chief Marshal Robert Brooke-Popham, who became British commander-in-chief, Far East, in October 1940.

Once in situ, both men judged that Hong Kong's capacity to hold off an attack would be substantially enhanced — quite possibly for the several months required to deliver a relief force by sea — if the garrison was increased by two battalions, as previously considered. Grasett based his case on a much more positive assessment of Hong Kong's mainland defences than his predecessor's, coupled with a low opinion of the fighting quality of Japanese soldiers. Brooke-Popham, who was similarly scornful of Japanese fighting capability and bullish about the strength of Singapore after its reinforcement by Australian troops, thought "an extra battalion or two" would boost morale of the Hong Kong garrison as well as that of the colony's 1.5 million Chinese (half of them recent refugees from Japanese-occupied China), demonstrate Britain's commitment to the Chinese government of Chiang Kai-shek, and show military resolve to Japan. Indeed, Brooke-Popham looked upon both Singapore and Hong Kong as bases for the eventual launching of offensive operations should Japan declare war.[6]

Responding to these proposals in January 1941, British Prime Minister Winston Churchill would have none of it:

> This is all wrong. If Japan goes to war with us there is not the slightest chance of holding Hong Kong or relieving it. It is most unwise to increase the loss we shall suffer there. Instead of increasing the garrison it ought to be reduced to a symbolic scale. Any trouble arising there must be dealt with at the Peace Conference after the war. We must avoid frittering away our resources on untenable positions. Japan will think long before declaring war on the British Empire, and whether there are two or six battalions at Hong Kong will make no difference to her choice. I wish we had fewer troops there, but to move any would be noticeable and dangerous.[7]

So the matter rested for another eight months, until August 1941. That month, as Reid and his colleagues began basic training at Lansdowne Park, General Grasett stopped in Ottawa on his way back to Britain after being replaced through a routine change of command in China. There he met with Major-General Harry Crerar, an old classmate from Toronto's Upper Canada College and Royal Military College in Kingston, Ontario, who was now chief of general staff for Canada. The subject of their discussions was the military situation in Hong Kong, about which Grasett remained confident ... if the garrison were reinforced.

There is no official record of Grasett and Crerar's Ottawa talks, but by September 3, Grasett was back in London remounting his arguments to the British chiefs of staff in favour of sending two battalions to Hong Kong, and — thanks to his discussions with Crerar — suggesting that Canada might be prepared to supply the troops. In keeping with policy, the first reaction at the War Office was negative. But Grasett was convincing enough to inspire second thoughts. By September 10, the chiefs of staff were drafting a proposal to Prime Minister Churchill recommending that two battalions be sent to Hong Kong, after all.

The reasoning for the about-face was laid out in the War Office memorandum presented to the prime minister. Whereas in 1940 reinforcing Hong Kong "would only have been to throw good money after bad," the position in the Far East had changed. British defences in Malaya had been improved, and Japan had "latterly shown a certain weakness in her attitude towards Great Britain and the United States."[8]

Secondly, the chiefs of staff were now of the belief that a small reinforcement of one or two battalions "would increase the strength of the [Hong Kong] garrison out of all proportion to the actual numbers involved" and have "a great moral effect in the whole of the Far East."[9]

Also to be considered was Britain's relationship with the United States, which had recently reinforced the Philippines: "A similar move by Canada would be in line with the present United States Policy of greater interest in the Far East," wrote the chiefs of staff, suggesting an opportunity for alignment with the United States that Churchill probably saw as a valuable precursor to the military co-operation he looked forward to evolving once the Americans finally entered the war.[10]

Underlying this assortment of benefits, and likely the crux of the matter, was the boon of achieving them without committing more British troops — already stretched thin and earmarked for elsewhere — if Canada was willing to supply the battalions.

Churchill was swayed. On September 15, he approved the proposal to reinforce the Hong Kong garrison, contingent on Canada's participation.

On September 19, the day Reid's class finished basic training at Lansdowne Park, a formal request for troops was telegraphed from Britain to Canada. The Canadian government, it seems, was predisposed. After a short discussion on September 23, Canada's Cabinet War Committee, including Prime Minister William Lyon Mackenzie King, agreed in principle to send two Canadian battalions to Hong Kong. As Charles Power, Canada's associate minister of national defence, said later: "I do not think there was ever any question really, or any discussion between General Crerar and myself, as to any reason why we should not take it on."[11]

As for military or diplomatic intelligence that might have weighed against Canada's decision in view of Japan's draconian strategy in the region, especially the sudden threat to Hong Kong if a Japanese attack were launched from occupied China, Power said that he "took it for granted that the [British] military authorities had assessed all that."[12]

Colonel James Ralston, Canada's minister of national defence, was in Los Angeles when the British request for troops was discussed in Cabinet. Response to Britain was delayed by a day so that the defence minister could be shown the telegram and be consulted. When Ralston received the British proposal by messenger on September 24, he was also informed that "[Canada's] War Committee are prepared to accept [Britain's request] … and that [Canadian General Staff] see no military risk in dispatching Canadian Battalions for this purpose."[13]

That evening, Ralston spoke by telephone from Los Angeles with General Crerar in Ottawa. If there were military reasons to question or even to turn down Britain's request, this was the time — and Crerar's duty — to give them. Himself long in favour of Canadian troops taking an active role in the war, Ralston now learned that Crerar had "definitely recommended [to the Cabinet War Committee] that the Canadian Army should take this on."[14] After their conversation, Ralston added his consent, reassured that his own leaning to commit troops to action was now held by the Canadian prime minister, by many fellow Cabinet ministers, and by Canada's top military brass. Other Commonwealth countries were already in the fray — Australians in Libya, New Zealanders in Crete, South Africans in Abyssinia. "It was Canada's turn to help," said Ralston.[15]

On September 29, Prime Minister King cabled to the Dominions Office in London that his government agreed to provide two infantry battalions for garrison duty in Hong Kong. In Ottawa, the scramble began to put together what was now designated as "C" Force.

Reid's class completed its training 10 days before Canada and Britain secretly confirmed the "C" Force mission. The class's intensive five-week course, with days beginning at 6:30 a.m. and ending at lights out after evenings of book study, had finished off with some field training — living in bell tents on the shore of the Ottawa River while going on route marches and battle manoeuvres in the neighbourhood. Informal pictures somebody snapped of their life under canvas were preserved in a wartime scrapbook by Jean Reid. They show her husband, Jack, Bill Bigelow, and Gordon Gray pitching a tent under trees by the river; men stripped to the waist having their morning shaves at outdoor washstands on the shore of the Ottawa River; lineups of Reid and his friends waiting for inspection in the woods in full battle dress, field kits piled neatly at their feet; the men lunching in the shade of a mess tent, then lounging on the grass of a sunny meadow during a cigarette break; trucking home from manoeuvres in the back of an open troop carrier; more gag shots in gas masks; a picnic in the woods to which wives and girlfriends had been invited. The impression is almost of summer camp.

After their return to Lansdowne Park and "graduation," the new medical officers were given a choice: proceed to Camp Petawawa, north of Ottawa, to await posting to Britain, or stay on for a two-week course in tropical medicine being offered at Lansdowne. Reid and Gray opted to take the course and therein lies their tale. Among the myriad decisions made by Canadian military planners preparing "C" Force for overseas deployment was the directive issued in early October to attach two medical officers to "C" Force Brigade — one extra medical officer for each battalion being sent. In view of Hong Kong's semi-tropical climate, two junior officers from the group taking tropical medicine at Lansdowne Park were the obvious men to pick.

The course finished on October 3. On Sunday, October 5, newly minted Captain Reid RCAMC was enjoying a post-training weekend leave with Jean at her family home in Toronto when a telegram from the office of the army's Director General of Army Medical Services (DGMS) in Ottawa was delivered to the door of 5 Scholfield. The telegram said that Reid's weekend leave had been recategorized as embarkation leave, this embarkation leave

Yousuf Karsh portrait of Captain John Reid, Ottawa, September 1941.

was now terminated, and he was to report at once to DGMS headquarters for foreign duty at a semi-tropical station overseas. After a flurry of goodbyes, Reid was on the train to Ottawa that night. The morning of his 28th birthday, he reported to National Defence Headquarters on Wellington Street. As he soon learned, Gordon Gray had received an identical telegram: the two weeks of tropical medicine training had sealed both their fates: they were being deployed to Hong Kong.

The battalions selected for "C" Force by General Crerar and Defence Minister Ralston were the Royal Rifles of Canada and the Winnipeg Grenadiers. Both battalions had just finished tours of garrison duty outside Canada — a year in Newfoundland protecting the Gander airfield for the Rifles, 16 months in Jamaica guarding German prisoners of war for the Grenadiers — "experience," Crerar told Ralston, that would be "of no small value to them in their new role."[16] Crerar also noted approvingly how representative of the country this first Canadian contingent to go into action would be: battalions from eastern and western Canada as well as representatives of French Canada, as many of the Royal Rifles were.

Like Reid and Gray, the Rifles and Grenadiers, barely home, had been hurriedly recalled from leave and were warned to prepare for immediate service overseas. Gordon Gray was assigned to the Royal Rifles as junior medical officer under Captain Martin Banfill, the Rifles' medical officer, and sent to Valcartier Camp, Quebec, where the battalion was regrouping. Reid was ordered to proceed by train to the Grenadiers' headquarters in Winnipeg and report to Major John Crawford, "C" Force's senior medical officer. Sworn to secrecy after the DGMS indiscreetly revealed where they were going, Reid found himself in an uncomfortable position upon reporting for duty:

> The Senior Medical Officer of the force-to-be was cursing and swearing under his lack of knowledge of our final destination. Where, indeed, was it? How semi-tropical? Would there be a hospital? Prime considerations in requesting the proper medical equipment. Alas, the young, innocent, junior officer, imbued with the code of all the gallant officers of fiction, though considerably nonplussed at the vital information imparted to him while not to his senior, kept his lips sealed....[17] I believe we finally left with enough supplies to keep our force going in the middle of the Sahara, even tho' beset by bacteriological warfare.[18]

After two weeks of frenetic preparations, the battalions were dispatched to Vancouver for embarkation — the Rifles from Valcartier on October 23, the Grenadiers from Winnipeg on October 25. The troop trains — two for each battalion — arrived at the Vancouver docks in Burrard Inlet on the morning of October 27 where the troopship SS *Awatea* and its escort, the armed cruiser HMCS *Prince Robert*, awaited them. After what Reid recalled as the "ordered confusion" of embarking through a damp, cool afternoon and evening, the two ships weighed anchor at 9:00 p.m. and sailed into the mist.

Aboard were 1,975 military personnel and two nursing sisters, plus baggage and equipment, but none of their mechanized transport. Through a series of bureaucratic snafus, the force's armoured carriers, light and heavy trucks, and water tankers only began arriving at the Vancouver dock area the day after "C" Force sailed. The 212 missing vehicles were eventually put on a third ship, which for security reasons was rerouted via Australia and Manila and not scheduled to reach Hong Kong until the end of December — a month too late as it turned out. Come the battle, the Canadians' lack of transport would badly hamper the movement of troops and supplies and add immeasurable hardship during the 18 days of fighting.

The voyage carrying "C" Force to China took 20 days. The New Zealand–based ship *Awatea* (Maori for "Eyes of the Dawn") was a modern ocean liner dubbed "The Greyhound of the Tasman Sea" for its speed and grace in plying the New Zealand–Australia run, prior to its conversion to a troopship in 1940. Built in 1936 to carry 566 passengers in comfort, the *Awatea* was now crowded with more than three times that number of soldiers (the *Prince Robert* carried the overflow of 109 Royal Rifles).

Once at sea and still in the dark about their destination, the men were kept busy with daily rounds of calisthenics; parade and boat drills; unarmed combat; arms drills with Bren guns, mortars, and anti-tank rifles; and the usual fatigue duty. Sleeping quarters for the men — hammocks slung in the holds above and below the tables where they ate — were cramped and fetid, their main diet, mutton. Reid's only recorded complaint was of zealous New Zealander stewards banging on officers' stateroom doors at 6:00 a.m. to drop off mugs of undrinkable sweet tea, even though breakfast wasn't served in the officers' mess until 8:30. Such was the divide between officers and other ranks during the voyage.

They reached Pearl Harbor on November 1. Under strict security, the Canadians weren't allowed shore leave. Instead, the U.S. port authorities arranged for a hula dance to be performed by local women on the long dock beside the ship — "swaying, graceful, guitaring, lei-bedecked maids from heaven,"[19] said Reid, maids for whom the men went wild — whistling and cheering from the *Awatea*'s packed decks and portholes, tossing down cigarettes and money in soldierly appreciation.

In the letter Reid wrote and posted to Jean during the stop at Hawaii, he joked about the secrecy and censorship "C" Force was blanketed under: "At present, re the old cartoons, 'we are living on a ship!'" He then turned to personal matters, his first concern being her health. Shortly before his departure, they learned that Jean was pregnant, and now "my very worst moments are due to lack of news of you," he wrote. Of the trip, he told her that he saw several of their West Coast friends, including his medical clinic mentor, Lyall Hodgins, during his few free hours in Vancouver before embarkation, "all of which left me somewhat homesick and with the feeling that I should turn the corner to 1385" (The Pasadena, 1385 West 11th, their Vancouver apartment building in 1940–41). He reported that he and Gordon Gray, with whom he was bunking, were working in the ship's hospital — "as many as 40 patients at once" — and that on the third day out they had a death and burial at sea, "my first, and I hope my last" (the deceased, Rifleman David Schrage, was a severe diabetic who had hidden his condition and overdosed with insulin).[20]

Otherwise, shipboard life was confining and monotonous, free time given over to reading and movies — "*Joy of Living*, of which I have never heard, and *The Story of Vernon and Irene Castle* (Astaire & Rogers) with a war ending of great sadness which was of poor psychology." Reid further reported that Gordon Gray was under the weather with a cold and sinus infection but was otherwise ready for anything: "He has the most amazing collection of goods, including a can of coffee, a can of spaghetti, an Xmas cake, box of Life Savers, chewing gum, etc. If we are ever marooned on a tropical isle we'll buy our way to a kingship of the native tribe with the goods."[21]

Reid was so taken with what he could see of Hawaii from the ship — "even more beautiful than Vancouver" — that he wondered if he and Jean should move there, "after this is over." Then, knowing how desperate Jean would be to know where he was, he sneaked in two clues, missed by the military censor, as to where "there" was: "Even if we stay put [in Vancouver after the war] a winter cruise will be the stuff. Nothing like a good pineapple plantation for winter rejuvenation." (The Hawaiian Pineapple Company, founded by James Dole in 1901, was the largest pineapple producer in the world.) Then, clue number two: "Well, honey, I'll close. Remember all my good advice, freely given, and till the near future I toss you a lei and bid you ... [word effaced by the censor], Mike."[22]

The *Awatea* and *Prince Robert* left Pearl Harbor for Manila on November 2. That evening, Brigadier John Lawson, "C" Force's commander, revealed to his officers their destination. He also divulged the latest news received by the ship: Washington and Tokyo were at diplomatic loggerheads, and the situation in the Far East was rapidly deteriorating. War with Japan, said Lawson, could break out while they were still at sea.

General Hideki Tojo, Japan's aggressive minister of war who in September 1940 signed the Tripartite Pact forming an alliance with Germany and Italy, became prime minister of Japan on October 18, 1941, nine days before "C" Force departed Vancouver. In taking power, Tojo pledged his government's commitment to the "new order in Asia." Infuriating Tojo and his war party were the continuing embargos on oil and other industrial necessities imposed by the United States and Britain in response to Japan's invasions of China and French Indochina, embargos that made the need to target the rich oil fields in the Dutch East Indies, where rubber and tin were also plentiful, the order of the day. All that stood in Japan's way were the British bases at Hong Kong and Singapore and the American naval and air force installations in the Philippines and Hawaii. Given the latest news to reach the *Awatea*, the question was not if but when Tojo would make his move.

The morning after telling his officers they might have to fight their way ashore, Brigadier Lawson disclosed to all the assembled Rifles and Grenadiers the secret that Reid had kept to himself for a month. In announcing their destination, Lawson warned what to expect on arrival. As Reid relates, it sounded much more than the simple garrison duty they had been led to expect:

> At sea again, and a dress parade. Sunny decks. Men sitting packed shoulder to shoulder, so no inch of deck is visible. The Brigadier: "Men, it is time to say to you that we are going into a zone of danger, a place of imminent war against odds. The people will be strange to you, the language unknown. Anyone in the place may be an agent of the enemy. Soldiers we must be now, and from now on. From here in, what you do enhances or diminishes our peril. We are going to Hong Kong."[23]

After the brigadier's talk, weapons and unarmed combat training became keener, discipline smarter, anticipation brighter, Reid said. Unknown to him was the puzzlement among some of the Royal Rifles line officers upon learning that a Japanese attack on Hong Kong might be imminent.

Three months earlier, a number of Rifles officers had attended a course at the Royal Military College in Kingston given by

Colonel Richard "Dicky" Dewing, Britain's General Staff officer in Singapore. In his discourse on the Far East situation, Dewing stated explicitly that Hong Kong wouldn't be relieved in case of war. In light of Dewing's comments, wondered these Canadian officers, were they being sent to the slaughter? Or did Canadian reinforcements signal that a new defence policy had promoted Hong Kong from outpost to fortress status, with more men and resources on the way? In Singapore, Air Chief Marshal Brooke-Popham, Far East commander-in-chief, believed the latter was the case. His memo reflecting this assumption was sent to the British chiefs of staff in London while "C" Force was crossing the Pacific. On November 6, the War Office set Brooke-Popham straight: "Our policy regarding defence of Hong Kong remains unaltered. It must be regarded as an outpost and held as long as possible."[24]

In other words, aside from the two Canadian battalions now en route, Hong Kong would receive no further reinforcements or relief. In case of an overwhelming attack, the colony would be sacrificed, "C" Force along with it.

Although the *Awatea* was steaming straight for it, the war still seemed far away. As they pushed across the Pacific, the air was growing warmer and the men changed to tropical uniforms — shorts and short-sleeved shirts. So far, no enemy presence threatened their passage. Riding the lazy ocean swells, the *Awatea* kept a rhythm that Reid enjoyed: the long pitch, slow roll, easy toss and after-roll of a ship in motion, with the endless *swish-swish* of the bow wave, where dolphins and flying fish rose and dived, rose and dived, keeping pace: "The nights were as imagined — sweet salt air, the sky a star-field of flowers."[25]

The *Awatea* and *Prince Robert* reached Manila Harbour in the Philippines on November 14. After a halt of a few hours to take on oil and water, they proceeded northwest escorted by HMS *Danae*, a British cruiser ordered out by the British Admiralty as anti-submarine protection "in view of altered circumstances"[26] heralded by the increasing belligerence of Japanese diplomatic communiqués. As they steamed into the South China Sea, its name recalled "the old tales, old pirates, old romances" of Reid's boyhood reading — the Henty sagas and the stories of adventure and derring-do in his *CHUMS* magazines. They were now a day from their destination.

On Saturday, November 15, the men were told that letters written on board would be immediately posted home via "Her Majesty's Transport" when they reached Hong Kong. That evening, Reid wrote a two-part letter, its first section giving his general news for family consumption. Here he described the trip's good weather, ship hospital work, and books read (*Turning Wheels* by Stuart Cloete, *Present Indicative* by Noël Coward), and not read (Galsworthy's saga — "I picked out but could not pursue as it brought too great a nostalgia for our times reading it together"). He demonstrated his prescience in stocking up a thousand cigarettes at the shipboard rate of 10 cents per pack ("that should hold me until shipments from home begin to arrive"), and described the clouds of flying fishes they were seeing ("this port being noted for them"), as well as the porpoises "rolling and playing about the ship." Reid then confessed the relief they would all feel when they got to dry land — "the confinement does become wearing."[27]

Having acknowledged that "this note will be useless of any purpose as to informing you of our arrival, for I hope to have cabled you long ere this gets home," he then appends a private note for Jean:

> And here, my love, is a little extra addition for your eyes alone. I've been achingly lonely for you for what seems an interminable period. It's now a month since I kissed your tip-tilted nose on a

Saturday night. I keep, all in all, in a numbed emotional state. I work, talk inconsequentials, but rarely scratch below the surface.

The army I still remain detached from. Now and then you get a glimpse [of its appeal], as on Nov. 11 when the veterans of the last war had a little get-together [on the *Awatea*] and when they appeared at dinner we all stood and sang, "Old Soldiers Never Die, They Only Fade Away": a strong sentiment that touches you for a moment.

For the rest I remain the outsider.... And perhaps this is best as my philosophy has always been essentially individual — group toughness as to fighting does not come naturally to me.

Also in my most heart-rending moments [thinking] of you, I find it is the unguarded moment that catches me out. Always, of course, you are in my mind and in my heart. But I saw the show *Irene* with Anna Neagle. I saw *My Favorite Wife* with Cary Grant and Irene Dunne. Little things, but suddenly I see how you and I sat and laughed and watched them together. And then the sweetness of our life together becomes so enveloping that it is almost, for the moment, too dear to remember.

Also, I find more & more at night, after getting into bed, my mind's eye wanders over afternoons and nights ... so many scenes and moments and beauties together. And I must face then the unutterable loneliness of not having you with me. All is well, always, if we're together. Otherwise, [life] is just a passing shadow to be endured, leaving no impression.

I miss you physically, but as in that last week, its importance seems little. It's the sight of you, to hear your voice, to talk to you, to watch you, to be near you that is so very great in its meaning.

I've consulted long with the guiding spirits and whatever way I do it, it works out that I won't be long and it will be in happy circumstances that I come to you again.

My Darling, are you well? You must be for I take counsel of it daily. And A.J.? [Their baby, to be named Anthony John.] That, too, I find in counsel will go so well.

Sometimes I could weep for not being with you now in the flesh. How I'd love to be, want to be. But, my dear, all else is with you always, day & night at every moment, knowing your thoughts, telling you mine.

You'll be as you are, I know. Sweet, true in the ways of keeping yourself, the way I love you. Keep being my sweet ... and dream a little now and then. Talk to me in the windy corners and in the quiet nooks. And look for me to come around one of those corners before too long has gone, for I'll be back to you soon, never doubt that.

And always, my dearest, I love you with all my heart, my body and my soul, and I love you beyond all telling and beyond all imagining.

Kisses my sweet, kisses and kisses & many more.

— Your Michael[28]

That night, a farewell dinner was held aboard the *Awatea*. At tables of 12, the officers and men mixed and mingled as they rotated through the mess hall for a feast not to be forgotten: "Potage Sydney, Braised Ox Palates Bordelaise, Roast Ribs Beef au Jus, Roast Haunch Mutton, Red Currant Jelly, Garden Peas, Cauliflower en Crème, Roast & Boiled Potatoes, Cold Roast Beef, Salad, Strawberry Jelly, Compote of Fruits, Ice Cream Biscuit, Apples, Oranges, Cheddar Cheese, Biscuits, Coffee."[29]

According to the autographed menu card that survived, Reid sat with Major John Crawford and the two "C" Force nursing sisters — Kay Christie and Anne Waters — among others. Printed at the top of the menu card was "A Personal Message from the Commander, officers & all Members of the Crew of H.M.T. *Awatea*: We extend to the Officers, N.C.O.'s and Men of H.M. Canadian Forces on board, our Best Wishes for your future welfare; and on the eve of your landing, we desire to express to you our Maoriland Farewell: KIA ORA! (Good Luck)."[30]

Early in the morning of Sunday, November 16, 1941, they reached Hong Kong. As Reid describes, whatever the rumours had been, there was no need to fight their way ashore:

> Three weeks out of Canada, on a glorious morning, sweeping in around the long, narrow channel leading into Hong Kong's perfect inner harbour — the basin for the King's fleet. Escorts ahead and astern, the white jackets of Imperial sailors showing on their decks, their gun mounts and barrels gleaming,

and in the middle the fat *Awatea*, her decks lined with cheering Canadian troops.

Sailing in, Hong Kong Island was to the left, with Victoria Peak crawling upward from the island to the sky. At water's edge a dozen tall buildings — the Hong Kong Bank, and the squat Hong Kong Hotel. To the right, mainland Kowloon, a hive of activity. Beyond it, the hills of the New Territories rising higher and higher, all the way to the border with China.

"Welcome, welcome!" cried the cheering crowds on the close hillsides. "Welcome, welcome!" roared the Royal Air Force, circling slowly over us at ship funnel level. All three of the 1927-vintage Vickers Vildebeest biplanes chugged round again and again, each pilot, scarf a-flying, tilting his wings and reaching out as though to grasp our hands. Hong Kong! — like the sound of bells, or the voice of a Chinese gong — Hong Kong! Who could defeat us with a welcome like this.

To the Kowloon side for docking. On the piers cheered the populace. Sampans, strange smells, people teeming, children running. A rush down the gangplanks laden with kit, our line of troops drawn up, numbered off (eyes darting to the Eurasian maids in their high-throated dresses, slit up the thigh), and the files move out — a serpentine two thousand men, heads up, chins out, each in his heart invulnerable.[31]

Canadian troops arrive in Hong Kong, November 16, 1941.

The "Vibration of Asia": The Battle of Hong Kong

M arching through Kowloon in full battle kit to the tunes of a military band and Highland pipers, the Canadians gave the salute and were reviewed by Major-General Christopher Maltby, Hong Kong's general officer commanding, then proceeded to their quarters in the Nanking Barracks of Sham Shui Po Camp.

Built by the British Army on the west shore of Kowloon Peninsula in the 1920s, Sham Shui Po consisted of long white concrete, barn-shaped barracks lined up in neat rows between spacious avenues, with a parade ground to the west of the barracks, and right on the shore, two imposing four-storey structures called the Jubilee Buildings, which housed camp administration and officers' quarters. The barracks were surrounded by grass with neatly trimmed verges. Palm trees dotted the camp. Immaculate now, for many of the Canadians these barracks would later become their war-ravaged prison for nearly four years.

Training for the Canadian battalions began a few days later. Considering them undertrained and inexperienced troops, General Maltby assigned them to reserve positions in the southern half of Hong Kong Island — the Royal Rifles in the southeast quadrant, the Grenadiers in the southwest. Each day they were ferried over from Kowloon for offensive and defensive exercises, running up and down the hot November hills of their respective sectors. Off-duty, there was opportunity for officers and other ranks alike to explore the city and attune themselves to what Reid calls the "vibration of Asia":

> One million extra inhabitants out of China. It bugged a Canadian's eyes. Shops, meek or elegant, loaded with all the "treasures of the Indies." Silks and jade, tourmaline and jasper and myrrh. Bargaining, in heat and jabber, for a tapestry. Being conducted into high cool salons for pearls. From, "Buy, buy, buy — best buy!" to "Only a thousand pounds, sir, and a bargain."
>
> Men on the town: "Big Canadian — two bitty, four-bitty, six-bitty!"
>
> Receptions for officers by the trading rajahs. Girls of an elegance unknown to prairie farmers. English girls with throats as graceful as serpents. For, after all, the Eurasian competition brought out the best in a girl.
>
> Driving through the town, stamping the floor to brake — not able to believe the crowds would part, the British chauffeurs sure they would. And, sure enough, a melting of crowds ahead and a closing in behind, like a ship at sea.
>
> A stroll in evening. Sidewalks full, and here on one of them a figure so ravaged that skin defined only bones, and he was, of starvation, dead.[1]

Reid and Gray were also seeing a different side of Hong Kong from the men. Again selected because of their tropical medicine training, they were assigned to Bowen Road Military Hospital on Hong Kong Island the day after arrival, Reid as an internal medicine specialist, Gray as a surgeon. It meant living out of barracks, first in Hong Kong's famous Peninsula Hotel, then in an apartment the pair rented on the slope of Victoria Peak, near where the hospital was located. It also meant an extra out-of-barracks pay allowance and a life of luxury that included three servants, housekeeping services, meals prepared, an ever-replenished liquor cabinet, and a car and driver. Reid itemizes the setup:

> The Peak, spire of the island of Hong Kong. The higher up, the more expensive. The spot of the elite. For those who would never climb these exalted heights an alpine lift jerking from bottom to top and back again giving a glimpse of the mansions of the rich.
>
> And so to this place, halfway up, with all the beauty of the fleet's basin before us. An apartment with a balcony. High and easy rooms. A major-domo to take the orders each morning: "How many to tiffin? How many to dinner? And shall we have frogs' legs *au français*, snails, *pâté*, *salade au Chine*, a nice guinea fowl? Or, sir, as you please!"
>
> A body servant to do, make, and wait, to serve, tend, and care, to lie asleep inside the front door to open it. And when asked, "Where is your family?" the reply — "Kowloon side, sir."
>
> "Then go to them, don't wait up for me."
>
> "But, sir!"
>
> An amah living behind the back door to starch each shirt so that the air passed under and over in

that hot climate. So cool, good starch, and always there.

In the apartment above, a New Zealander who was a helpful guide. In the next apartment, cheek by jowl, the happy moans of a Eurasian so beautiful and so newly married to a lieutenant of the Middlesex regiment.

Hong Kong![2]

Reid and Gray's work routine was equally privileged. Hospital duty at Bowen Road was generally mornings only, followed by afternoons and evenings to explore and do as they liked — a life of indulgence, Reid later joked grimly, that would have done them irretrievable harm had circumstances allowed them to keep it up until the end of the war, instead of turning them into prisoners. Recognizing the dangers of a louche life, Reid took up rugby, a new game for him, to keep in shape.

The addition of the Canadian battalions to the garrison caused a shift in the Hong Kong defence plan. General Maltby, the 30-year veteran of the British Army in India who replaced General Grasett as China Command's commander-in-chief in July 1941, initially chose a concentrated island defence. If the Japanese attacked, he would abandon the lightly held mainland defence perimeter and withdraw to Hong Kong Island where his combined force of 12,000 men could be deployed to maximum effect. But the Canadian reinforcements changed his mind. The mainland would now be held as long as possible.

Under the revised strategy, Maltby split his command into two brigades of three battalions each, plus support elements. The Mainland Brigade, commanded by British Brigadier Cedric Wallis and consisting of the 2nd Battalion Royal Scots and two Indian Army battalions — the 5/7th Rajputs and the 2/14th Punjabis — would defend the so-called Gin Drinkers Line, a partially completed defence complex roughly six miles north of Kowloon made up of pillboxes, dugouts, redoubts, and entrenchments that snaked 11 miles across the southern portion of the New Territories from Gin Drinkers Bay in the west, to Tide Cove in the east, then southeast to Port Shelter.

The Island Brigade, commanded by Canada's Brigadier Lawson, was made up of the 1st Battalion, Middlesex Regiment; the Royal Rifles; the Winnipeg Grenadiers; and the 2,000-strong Hong Kong Volunteer Defence Corps. It would provide "Home Defence" on the island.

It was a lot of ground to cover for a garrison of 14,000 men. Even with the addition of the two Canadian battalions, both brigades were seriously undermanned for the duties expected of them. Senior Canadian officers assessing the defence situation, most of them decorated veterans of the storied Canadian Corps in the First World War, were disconcerted. Lieutenant-Colonel William Home, commanding officer of the Royal Rifles, writes:

> How even the thought that the Island could be defended without fighters of the Air Force is beyond one's conception. The one belief that was current after checking up on the detailed defences was simply that England did not expect war with Japan in the immediate future. Any other belief can only lead one to the impression that those in authority were sublimely unconscious of what it was all about....

All [Canadian] officers were soon wondering what conceivable difference to the defence of Hong Kong two battalions and a Brigade Headquarters could make.[3]

Company Sergeant Major George MacDonell, "D" Company, Royal Rifles, made his own assessment: "When I arrived in Hong Kong and began to appraise the British defence and the resources available to implement them, I began to wonder. First of all, from a tactical point of view there seemed to be no plan to fortify and occupy the high ground in the centre of this mountainous island."[4]

Major Maurice Parker, MacDonell's company commander, shared this concern. A week or so after the Royal Rifles were deployed in the southeast quadrant of Hong Kong Island, Parker put MacDonell in charge of a reconnaissance mission to explore the route running from Tai Tam Tuk Reservoir, south of Mount Butler, to Pok Fu Lam Road on the west coast of the island (Parker was himself reconnoitring the terrain east of the reservoir). MacDonell writes:

We assembled and, equipped with compasses, binoculars, and instructions, climbed to the elevation required and surveyed and marked the route we could follow to Aberdeen and the highway to the west. We were careful to mark all water catchments, barbed wire, and any pillboxes or defensive works we came across. At the end of the reconnaissance, I went over our findings with the Major in detail. The answer to his question concerning anything that would deter an enemy from moving across the same route from Mount Butler was summed up by me as, "practically nothing." The British had no preparations to garrison or hold the high ground of the island. We never saw a single British soldier or any serious, man-made impediment to an invading force moving west from Mount Butler to Aberdeen. Within a few weeks, that is exactly what the 229th Japanese Regiment did to split the island defending forces in two.... This failure to consider the importance of the high ground became one of the first issues of tension and serious disagreement between the British and Canadian high commands of Hong Kong.[5]

Although MacDonell's last comment had the benefit of hindsight, it didn't help at the time that the British showed a general attitude of presumption, which the Canadians found objectionable. In Reid's words:

Relationships with the British soldiers [were] not too good in Hong Kong. We didn't get on too well.... The British are the British wherever they are and believe themselves best and the Canadians didn't think so. Before the war the British were talking about the Canadians as colonials and that's a bad start with any Canadians to call them British colonials. We got on with individuals, mind you, some of the British doctors I met, well, I wouldn't want to meet a better chap anywhere, but the overall picture is that the men didn't get along with them, nor the officers either.[6]

This British sense of superiority, according to MacDonell, extended to the enemy: "The British believed the Japanese soldier was inferior. We heard from them that the Japanese had very poor eyesight and that they couldn't shoot infantry weapons accurately and their pilots, due to the same optical weakness, couldn't put their bombs on target. Above all, not to worry, the Japanese couldn't fight at night."[7] Compounding the sense of complacency were British intelligence reports stating that only 5,000 poorly trained, badly equipped Japanese troops were stationed north of the New Territories.

These bromides would soon be seen for what they were. Massing across the border in Japanese-occupied China, just 25 miles north of Kowloon, was the Japanese 38th Division, 60,000 battle-hardened troops plus artillery, air force, naval, and combat engineering components. The 38th Division's orders — part of Tojo's master plan to be carried out simultaneously with attacks on Pearl Harbor, the Philippines, and Malaya — were simple: "The main objective of the Hong Kong Operation is to capture Hong Kong by destroying the enemy forces."[8]

On Saturday, December 6, 1941, the garrison and civilian elite of Hong Kong, still unaware of any serious threat, indulged in the usual assortment of weekend recreational activities. At the Happy Valley Racecourse, east of the city of Victoria, crowds of Europeans and Chinese thronged to watch the horse races. Members of the Jockey Club and their guests socialized in the racecourse bar over gin gimlets and whisky sodas. At the Cricket Club, the Middlesex Regiment put on a rugby match. That evening, a large, festive party at the Hong Kong Hotel rolled on until 4:30 a.m., while across Victoria Bay in Kowloon the Peninsula Hotel was the setting for the "Tin Hat Ball," a Chinese charity event aiming to raise at least £160,000 toward the cost of Allied bombers, a present from the people of Hong Kong to Britain.

The next day, Sunday, December 7, the Canadians had been in Hong Kong exactly three weeks. British military historian Oliver

Lindsay described the colony's state of readiness that Sunday evening as, in the slang of the time, the balloon was about to go up: "Nobody in Hong Kong knew what the Japanese were up to, what their intentions were, or of what they were capable."[9]

Meanwhile, back in Ottawa, General Crerar was showing renewed interest in "C" Force's location and present circumstances. In a memo to underlings, he suggested that the British War Office be asked to provide a map of Hong Kong, its Defence Scheme Papers, and information on artillery forces there. Said Crerar: "We should be kept 'up-to-date' on Far East, especially Hong Kong, in view of our particular military commitment there."[10]

Coming more than two months after he recommended sending Canadian troops, Crerar's memo suggested a disturbing ignorance of and belated curiosity about Hong Kong and its situation. His staff must have scratched their heads over his request. Most of the information Crerar was asking for had been available at Canadian National Defence Headquarters all along.[11]

Sunday, December 7, Reid remembered as "a day of soft sun, beauty everywhere." He was orderly officer at Bowen Road Hospital that day, which meant being on duty both morning and afternoon. When he was relieved at 4:00 p.m., it was, in local parlance, "time to seek the Peak" for a cooling bath and spot of tiffin. Instead, he learned that battle orders had been issued at 11:00 a.m. Reid's were: "Proceed at once to Wong Nei Chong Gap, prepared for action."[12]

This wasn't the first alert since the Canadians had arrived. Over the previous two weeks, the entire garrison had been ordered out to their assigned defence positions three times due to short-lived "flaps." Hong Kongers had laughed: "The balloon has been going up here for years," they said. "Pay no mind." General Maltby was of the same opinion. Despite ordering battle stations, his message to London the morning of December 7 showed little concern. Based on the latest intelligence received, reports of Japanese troop movements at the New Territories border "were certainly exaggerated," Maltby said, the activity very likely a ruse to cover up [Japanese] numerical weakness in South China.[13]

Maltby may be forgiven. The faulty intelligence he received that day, on a par with the misinformation his execrable intelligence organization had been providing all along, went on to say that the reports [of a Japanese buildup] "have the appearance of being deliberately fostered by the Japanese, who, judging by their defensive preparations around Canton, appear distinctly nervous of being attacked."[14]

Another false alarm? As Reid packed his field gear that Sunday afternoon, he recalled the adage, "In war, be as comfortable as possible," and this time included a roll-up mattress in his personal kit. By midnight, he and his medical unit had travelled south by truck from Victoria to Wong Nai Chung Gap in the centre of the island, where Brigadier Lawson's Island Brigade Headquarters and two medical dugouts were located. An hour later, on new orders, Reid and his unit moved farther west to Wan Chai Gap, close to Winnipeg Grenadiers Headquarters, where he and his men ended up spending what was left of the night in a vacant hillside mansion stripped of everything down to the hardwood floors. Thanks to his mattress, Reid's couple of hours' sleep were reasonably comfortable. But at first light — 5:00 a.m., December 8 — the unit's radio crackled into life. The news was a shock: "Japanese have bombed Pearl Harbor."

In Hawaii, east of the International Date Line, it was 11:00 a.m., December 7, 1941. Three hours earlier, just before eight in the morning, Hawaii time, 353 carrier-based Japanese fighters, bombers, and torpedo planes had attacked Battleship Row and Pearl Harbor's surrounding naval and air bases without warning, let alone a declaration of war. Sunk or badly damaged were all eight battleships of the U.S. Pacific fleet, as well as three destroyers, three cruisers, a minelayer, and an anti-aircraft training ship. One hundred and eighty-eight aircraft were destroyed on the ground. Casualties: 2,403 Americans killed, 1,178 wounded. All in 90 minutes.

Simultaneously, the Japanese were launching attacks on Manila and Cavite Navy Yard in the Philippines, Kota Bharu in Malaya — and Hong Kong.

No flap, then. This was it.

The Battle of Hong Kong had three phases: the loss of the mainland (December 8–12), the siege of Hong Kong Island (December 13–18), and the invasion of the island that ended with the colony's surrender (December 18–25).

The ground over which the battle was fought was extremely rough going. On the mainland, the terrain north and south of the Gin Drinkers Line was mountainous, sparsely populated, uncultivated territory largely covered with dense, scrubby vegetation. Hong Kong Island, irregularly shaped and roughly three miles wide and 11 miles long at its southernmost point, was dominated by jagged chains of mountainous ridges rising between precipitous valleys whose steep slopes were cut by ravines and deep gullies and covered with the same tough scrub as the mainland. A single narrow road followed the twists and turns of the island's coastline, while interior routes were generally confined to the canyons between the mountains. The island's most strategic corridor was the series of linked roads running down its centre from Happy Valley in the north, through Wong Nai Chung Gap, to Repulse Bay in the south.

Under such adverse conditions, outnumbered five to one, Hong Kong's defenders were to have little chance of holding positions or reforming cohesive lines of defence for any length of time during the 18-day battle. Counterattacks were inevitably costly, and whatever ground they regained was soon lost once more. The Japanese forces, after a decade of fighting in China, were tough, experienced, well-led troops, indoctrinated since birth to die for the emperor. Controlling the air and sea over and around Hong Kong from the first hours of the battle, supported by heavy artillery and mortar fire, and employing ground tactics that combined fanatical frontal assaults with infiltration and flanking manoeuvres in order to slide around garrison strong points and push on, the Japanese either divided and overwhelmed defending units, or isolated them

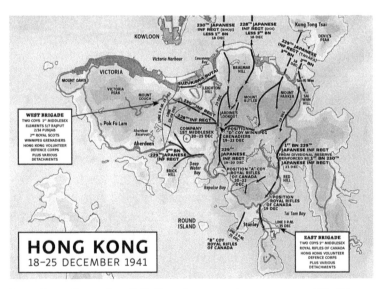

Hong Kong, December 1941. For a larger version, see pages 456–57.

in fragmented pockets of resistance often out of touch with their commanders and out of reach of fresh supplies, water, and ammunition. The defence of Hong Kong, for all of the bravery, fierce response, and endurance of its garrison, was, by the numbers, a lost cause from the beginning.

The opening attack on Hong Kong was launched in the pre-dawn hours of December 8 with thousands of Japanese infantry and support units pouring across the Chinese border into the British New Territories. At 8:00 a.m., as Japanese ground forces moved south toward the Gin Drinkers Line, the Japanese air force launched unimpeded bombing and strafing raids over targets in Kowloon and Hong Kong Island, knocking out the tiny British air force as it sat on the ground at Kai Tak Airport, then going after military installations, naval and civil shipping in the harbour, fuel depots, and Sham Shui Po Camp, where they believed the Canadians were still in barracks.[15]

Several hours before the bombing began, Reid's medical unit was ordered to move south from their overnight position at Wan Chai Gap to Aberdeen Reservoir where "C" Company of the Grenadiers was dug into its assigned defensive position. After finding quarters for his men and setting up his aid post, Reid strolled out into the brilliant Monday morning sunshine. Looking up at the distant sound of engines, he spotted his first enemy action, which had a dreamlike quality: "Strangely, a plane, then another and another, drifting lazily overhead. Strangely, the Rising Sun on the underside of the wings. Strangely, long, oval objects falling, falling from the sky, then fountain bursts — earth, rock, trees spurting skyward."[16]

Too extended, too lightly manned to stop the thousands of Japanese troops sweeping down from the north, the British mainland defences north of Kowloon were smashed with a speed that stunned General Maltby, who was directing operations from his Fortress Headquarters bunker south of Victoria on Hong Kong Island. Smashed, too, in the first 24 hours of battle were the myths of Japanese combat inferiority, poor vision, shoddy equipment, and an inability to operate at night.

Shing Mun Redoubt, the British defensive position considered the pivotal stronghold that would enable the Gin Drinkers Line to hold out for at least a week, was overrun before midnight on December 9, only 40 hours into the invasion. With the redoubt's collapse, the whole line began to crumble, the defenders forced southward as they fought savage, uncoordinated rearguard actions while carrying out bridge, road, and communications demolitions to slow the Japanese advance.

The mainland retreat became a rout. At noon on Thursday, December 11, Maltby ordered a complete withdrawal of British forces to Hong Kong Island, a touch-and-go manoeuvre successfully carried out largely because the Japanese didn't fully grasp and exploit the swiftness and totality of the British mainland collapse. By midnight, December 12, the mainland defenders, including more than 50 wounded, had been ferried to the island, leaving behind 67 dead and 27 soldiers prisoners of the enemy.

The outlook for the colony had quickly become perilous. In only five days, the invaders had swept south from China more than 25 miles, leaving a shattered Gin Drinkers Line in their wake. The entire New Territories, from the Chinese border to the Kowloon docks facing Hong Kong Island's north shore, were under Japanese control.

Now the island siege began. For the next six days, from the morning of December 13 until the evening of December 18, Hong

Kong suffered constant aerial bombing and artillery shelling from the mainland. British military and strategic sites — coastal defences, artillery positions, and anti-aircraft gun emplacements — were all targeted and found vulnerable. The garrison's guns returned fire, knocking out enemy gun installations, ships, and aircraft, but the Japanese had the reserves to quickly replace them. No part of the island escaped Japanese bombardment. The garrison would lose 54 killed and 38 wounded to bombs and shells over the six days and nights before the Japanese invaded the island.

Much worse was the suffering of the Chinese population trapped on the mainland. In Victoria, throughout the siege, screams and wailing could be heard night after night coming across the water from Japanese-occupied Kowloon. During the Battle of Hong Kong and its aftermath, an estimated 4,000 Chinese civilians were butchered by the Japanese, 10,000 raped.

As communiqués arrived in distant London detailing Hong Kong's rapidly deteriorating situation, the War Office, the British government, and the prime minister could do no more than offer the colony prayers and words of encouragement. Churchill's were sent via telegram to Sir Mark Young, governor of Hong Kong, on December 15: "We are all watching day by day and hour by hour your stubborn defence of the port and fortress of Hong Kong. You guard a link long famous between the Far East and Europe. We are sure that the defence of Hong Kong against the barbarous and unprovoked attack will add a glorious page to British annals. All our hearts are with you in your ordeal. Every day of your resistance brings nearer our certain victory."[17]

Twice during the six-day siege of the island, the Japanese demanded that Hong Kong surrender. Twice Sir Mark Young rejected the demand, the second time on December 17. The official communiqué from Young to the Hong Kong garrison and the colony's civilian population was unequivocal: "The Governor has today received a letter from the Japanese Military and Naval Authorities repeating the suggestion that he should enter into negotiations with them for the surrender of Hong Kong. In his reply, His Excellency has declined absolutely to enter into any negotiations and has notified the Japanese authorities that he is not prepared to receive any further communications from them on the subject."[18]

At 9:00 p.m. the night of Thursday, December 18, with a chilling rain falling and visibility down to zero due to the smoke of a burning paint factory and the bombed-out oil tanks at North Point, the Japanese launched a sea invasion of Hong Kong Island's north shore. The final phase of the battle had begun.

After the mainland withdrawal on December 12, General Maltby had reshuffled his mainland and island brigade elements to form two island brigades — West Brigade, commanded by Brigadier Lawson, and East Brigade, commanded by Brigadier Wallis. The dividing line between the defence sectors was the series of roads weaving north-south through the island via Wong Nai Chung Gap, where Lawson and the West Brigade staff had their headquarters. After the Japanese secured beachheads on Hong Kong's northeast shore, it was down this natural fault line and over the high ground flanking it that they swiftly punched south, aiming to split the defenders, bottle up those east of the divide, then drive west the length of the island with Victoria in the north the main objective.

The morning of Friday, December 19, only 12 hours after their shore assault had overwhelmed the island's north shore pillbox defences, Japanese troops reached Wong Nai Chung Gap and surrounded Lawson's Brigade Headquarters. Fatefully, Lawson had already recognized his position's vulnerability and was only hours away from shifting headquarters to Black's Link, farther west. Now it was too late. Rather than be trapped like rats, Lawson signalled to General Maltby that he and his six remaining staff were destroying sensitive documents and equipment before leaving the bunker to fight it out — a better chance of survival than waiting for Japanese grenades to roll down the ventilation shafts.

Pinned down by machine-gun fire in a ditch across the road from Lawson's headquarters, Sergeant Robert Manchester of the Grenadiers saw the brigadier and his men burst out of the bunker and swing right, running along a path beside a cliff that outlined them perfectly. The Japanese machine gunners shifted fire from Manchester's ditch to the easy targets skirting the rock face. Peeking over the lip of his ditch, Manchester saw the result: "They hit the seven with a terrible barrage of machine-gun fire. The brigadier did not have a chance to shoot one gun, let alone two."[19] Lawson and his men were cut down within seconds.

In the north-central and eastern portions of the island, it was a day of bitter fighting everywhere. By 10:00 p.m. on December 19, 591 Hong Kong defenders had been killed in less than 24 hours, 65 Winnipeg Grenadiers and 16 Royal Rifles among them. That night, Sir Mark Young sent a message to all His Majesty's Forces in Hong Kong: "The time has come to advance against the enemy. The eyes of the Empire are upon you! Be strong! Be resolute and do your duty!"[20]

There was an air of unreality in the governor's exhortation to advance. By daybreak on December 20, the Japanese controlled the whole northeast quadrant of Hong Kong Island and had penetrated south of Wong Nai Chung Gap to within sight of Repulse Bay on the island's south shore. The Japanese now controlled the centre of the island. From here on, East and West Brigades would never succeed in linking up again and defensive coordination began to fall apart. Orders issued from Maltby's Fortress Headquarters were out of date before they could be delivered, let alone acted upon. Reinforcements sent to shore up weakened positions were ambushed by Japanese who had already taken or bypassed the reinforcements' objective. Severed communications added increasingly to the chaos, prompting staff officers from Fortress Headquarters to undertake reconnaissance outings, only to be killed or wounded in the field. These losses of headquarters staff were irreplaceable, leaving a widening gap in the chain of command. It only got worse. On Sunday, December 21, Governor Young accepted the grim truth presented to him by a beleaguered General Maltby, and telegraphed the Admiralty in London at 5:00 p.m.:

> Military situation is now as follows: Enemy hold key positions in hills and G.O.C. [general officer commanding, that is, Maltby] advises that we are very rapidly approaching a point at which only remaining resistance open to us will be to hold for short time only a small pocket in the centre [of the island] leaving bulk of fixed population to be overrun. I feel it will be my duty to ask terms before this position is reached. If H.M. Government feels able to give assent please cable single word ABILITY repetition ABILITY. Governor. Ends. 0521Z/21.[21]

The Admiralty's reply to Governor Young didn't include the word *ability*. Instead, it re-sent a new message from Prime Minister Churchill, followed by the stated wishes of His Majesty's Government:

> Your message 0521 has been received. It crossed a message from the Prime Minister, who is temporarily out of reach, as follows:

[Churchill] Begins:

"To C. in C. and Governor of Hong Kong. The eyes of the world are upon you. We expect you to resist to the end. The honour of the Empire is in your hands." Ends.

[Admiralty continues]:

In spite of conditions you and G.O.C. are facing, the difficulties of which are clearly understood, H.M.G.'s desire is that you should fight it out as in Prime Minister's message.[22]

And so they fought on.

Throughout the six-day siege of the island, Reid's medical unit remained in position with the detachment of Grenadiers who were protecting the emergency naval base at the fishing village of Aberdeen on the south coast and Aberdeen Reservoir directly north of it. Bombing and shelling from the mainland had been sporadic. But once the Japanese were lodged on the island and began pushing south and west through its centre, artillery fire north of the reservoir intensified as the enemy approached. In his postwar short story "The Captain," Reid gives a version of what it was like at his aid post on Monday, December 22:

This was the third night. Even though he was snug in a hillside dugout he shuddered every time the shells came over: Banshee wail, cacophonic soul-splitting explosion, shudder and shake.

The shaking was the more embarrassing. Lighting a cigarette became a game of concealment of the hands against the incredulous eyes of the other officers, more so against the tough stare of the weathered medical sergeant who wore the ribbon of decoration for indifference to life under fire in the Great War.

For the twentieth time that night the doctor bent under the rough, board table as though a high wind were blowing in the still, smoky dugout and lit a match to his fag. "Almighty God, make this a dream or make me a man," he groaned, and straightened up again.

Artillery was pounding around the clock, but daylight and sunlight worked an atavistic transfusion of courage. By day, hope flared again, by night the paralyzing, uncontrollable forces took over.

That morning he had been able to make a full inspection of the lines, see that the arrangements for evacuation of casualties were clear, concise, and expedient. Their salient was quiet then, and even though every exposed second he quaked at the beautiful sniper's target he must present, he had been able to put one foot before the other without betraying his fear.

That evening, the awaited contact with the enemy had been made. On the ridge across the little valley in front of his company aid post the star-shells had begun to flare. The squirting lines of tracers spouted like the Roman candles of his boyhood fireworks, and the snarl and growl of machine guns had mixed with the high clatter of small-arms fire to swell and fade and swell again in a noisy crescendo.

In the dusty gloaming the first casualties had been carried in. Young Anderson with most of the left side of his face gone. Bautski, pale and quiet with a small blue puncture in his upper belly. James, walking-wounded, still staring in disbelief at his sagging, unmanageable right forearm.

In bursts he had been busy and concentrated and forgetting, but with each pause the fearful fantasy had welled again. Impossible that men were doing this voluntarily to each other, and that he was there, and that some impersonally fired shell could at any minute smash him to a broken, crying, pitiful fragment.[23]

Reid didn't have to imagine the worst. The previous morning he had seen two British officers, who were calmly watching the enemy shelling from the hillside above their dugout, "disappear in an upflung mound of dirt" — both men obliterated by a direct hit. By December 22, Mount Cameron, several miles north of Reid's aid post, had become the linchpin of West Brigade's defensive line as the Japanese forced their way from the east. The position was held by only 100 Grenadiers, reinforced by a platoon of 30 Royal Engineers — all that could be spared. After raining Mount Cameron's defenders with artillery and mortar fire, the Japanese attacked during the evening with 1,000 troops. The Grenadiers and Royal Engineers fought back ferociously, but a Japanese breakthrough on their right flank threatened to encircle their position and forced their withdrawal northward to Wan Chai Gap. In his postwar debriefing in October 1945, Reid recalls the confusion of this night:

[We were] still at Aberdeen Reservoir. This hill [where we had our aid post] continued to Wanchai Gap. That part was held by the British and Canadians at Wanchai Gap on our left flank. During the night we heard a lot of firing on this hill. We phoned [Grenadier Headquarters, northwest of Mount Cameron] to find out what was going on. They said, absolutely nothing — everything's under control and quiet. In about ten minutes we got a call [from Grenadier Headquarters] in a great hurry and as soon as the phone was off [the hook] someone said the Japs are coming, we're falling back on Mt. Gough, northwesterly, and for us to get up [to Mount Gough] any way we could … we would try to make a last stand there, then they banged down the phone. We picked it up again to ask, what's this all about? Nobody was there.[24]

Mount Cameron fell to the Japanese in the early hours of December 23. Except for Stanley Peninsula, where the Royal Rifles and the rest of East Brigade were cut off but still holding out, the Japanese now controlled the whole eastern half of Hong Kong Island, including the north-south corridor down the centre to Repulse Bay. West Brigade's entire defence line from Leighton Hill in the north of the island to Bennet's Hill in the south was under intense attack. On this day, another telegram was sent to Governor Young by Prime Minister Churchill:

There must be no thought of surrender. Every part of the island must be fought and the enemy resisted with the utmost stubbornness. The enemy should be compelled to expend the utmost life and equipment. There must be vigorous fighting in the inner defences and, if need be, from house to house. Every day that you are able to maintain your resistance you help the Allied cause all over the world, and by a prolonged resistance you and your men can win the lasting honour which we are sure will be your due.[25]

With Mount Cameron overrun by the enemy, the Grenadiers north of the Aberdeen Reservoir, now dangerously exposed, were ordered to pull back to Aberdeen Village on the coast, Reid's medical unit with them. On the morning of Tuesday, December 23, Reid deposited his wounded at the Aberdeen Naval Hospital and took stock of what he should do next.

At the beginning of hostilities, all of the garrison's field ambulances, including the Royal Canadian Army Medical Corps, were reorganized as the Combined Field Ambulance led by Lieutenant-Colonel Lindsay Ride of the Hong Kong Volunteer Defence Corps, with the Grenadiers' Major John Crawford as second-in-command. During the last three days of fighting, the Combined Field Ambulance Headquarters had been on the move and was out of touch with many of its medical units. When Reid finally made contact late on Tuesday afternoon, he was ordered to Pok Fu Lam on the west coast of the island. As he describes in his postwar debriefing, believing his short-lived military career was about to end, he persuaded the Field Ambulance Headquarters otherwise:

> I hadn't been in the army a very long time and I asked the British Colonel if I could be assigned somewhere else.... I had just got into the army and here I was in Hong Kong only a few days and the war was almost done and I asked him if there wasn't something I could be doing. There wasn't anything to do at Pok Fu Lam and there wasn't going to be.

He phoned back.... They said, okay, you go to the
War Memorial Hospital. That was on the Peak ... so
I went over there and gave anaesthetics for a day.[26]

The Casualty Clearing Station at War Memorial Hospital
was dealing with civilian wounded as well as a stream of British,
Canadian, and Indian military casualties. Shortly after the invasion
of the island, the hospital's water supply and electrical system had
been knocked out, although engineers from a scuttled British ship
managed to rig a small dynamo to produce power for the operating room. Reid was a welcome addition to the medical team. Dr.
Annie Sydenham, the hospital's chief anaesthetist, later reported:
"We benefited from the assistance of [Captain Reid] ... as he knew
his own men and was able to give them confidence and cheer."[27]

Reid remembers the night of December 24 as the oddest of
Christmas Eves:

In the basement of the hospital, whose floors above
lay ravaged by shell fire, by the flickering lamps in
the darkness gathered a various group: nurses and
volunteer nurses, the few daughters of the well-
placed who had clung to Hong Kong despite the
signs that the "balloon" was really going aloft this
time, patched wounded, medical orderlies, officers,
and the odds and sods drifting in from the hills —
to all came the sudden realization of Christmas Eve.
Pots of jam were brought out, loaves of bread, tins
of plums, strong hot tea, and — almost surrepti-
tiously — a song: "Silent night, holy night," rising
stronger, louder, fuller till every voice took it up.
For an hour all the old sweet airs [were sung], faces
gleaming, smiling, tear-dropped but buoyed by

the general British "thumbs-up," till finally fading,
most slumped left or right in exhausted sleep.[28]

By dawn of Christmas Day, the remaining elements of West
Brigade were hemmed into the western third of the island, while
those of East Brigade were trapped on Stanley Peninsula in the
southeast. In Victoria that morning, the *South China Morning Post*,
somehow still operating amid the battle, published its penultimate
wartime edition with the headline: "Hong Kong Is Observing the
Strangest and Most Sober Christmas in Its Century-Old History."[29]
Governor Mark Young broadcast a Christmas message to the colony: "In pride and admiration I send my greeting this Christmas
Day to all who are fighting and all who are working so nobly and so
well to sustain Hong Kong against the assaults of the enemy. Fight
on. Hold fast for King and Empire. God bless you all in this your
finest hour.... Let this day be historical in the grand annals of our
empire. The Order of the Day is to hold fast."[30]

Practically the last action of the Battle of Hong Kong was a
suicidal attack ordered on Christmas morning by Brigadier Wallis,
commander of East Brigade, to retake Stanley Village, a position at
the top of Stanley Peninsula recently overrun by the Japanese. The
unit chosen for the mission was "D" Company of the Royal Rifles,
a force by now reduced through casualties to 120 men. Although
Wallis promised artillery support for the attack, none materialized,
and at 1:00 p.m. on Christmas Day, Company Sergeant Major
George MacDonell and two other platoon leaders led their men
across open ground in a wild charge that by its sheer fierceness
succeeded in evicting the larger enemy force from parts of Stanley
Village while inflicting heavy casualties. But greatly outnumbered
by Japanese reinforcements, who began to encircle them, and targeted by a sustained artillery barrage, the Rifles were soon ordered
to retreat by Major Maurice Parker, "D" Company's commanding

officer, a tricky withdrawal by twos and threes, while MacDonell and Sergeant Lance Ross provided covering fire with their Bren guns before barely escaping themselves. Twenty-six Royal Rifles died during the action. With the 75 who were wounded, "D" Company suffered 84 percent casualties in the attack on Stanley Village. For all the men's heroics, nothing was gained.

On the west side of the island, General Maltby had reached the same conclusion: holding Hong Kong was hopeless; fighting on only meant pointless loss of life, followed by inevitable defeat. Maltby's final dispatch to London ended: "At 3:15 p.m. [Christmas Day] I advised his Excellency the Governor and Commander-in-Chief that no further useful military resistance was possible and I then ordered all Commanding Officers to break off the fighting and to capitulate to the nearest Japanese Commander, as and when the enemy advanced and the opportunity offered."[31]

The official surrender of Hong Kong to the Japanese took place at 4:30 on Christmas afternoon. Reid heard the news and its after-effect half an hour later:

> The white flag went up about four in the afternoon. Now isolated pockets [of resistance] only, snarling hedge-hogs, but separate. About 5 p.m. the NOISE faded away, little and lesser noises, fewer and farther and, finally, still, still silence, even movement suspended from that hour.
>
> With the silence [came] a bee-hive of thoughts buzzing in the brain: Hong Kong — how strange; home — so far and unreal; only small boats left, and where to go?; friends lost, found, and unknown. Fundamentally, a sense of de-personalization, as though floating in a limbo and seeing, but not fully comprehending, reality.[32]

Prisoners of War: False Hopes as Contagious as Dysentery

On Boxing Day morning, a gathering of the survivors began, grimy groups of Allied soldiers filtering down from the hills and moving along broken roads past shot-up trucks and cars, shattered buildings, the debris of battle. Orders were to concentrate at Murray Barracks, the old British cantonment in Victoria, after stacking or burying weapons. The men were hungry, thirsty, exhausted. Wounded limped along with help; others were carried on makeshift stretchers. Some were already suffering from dysentery after drinking bad water in the hills. It was a bleak march. Robert Hammond, a captured American missionary being transported by the Japanese from Victoria to Stanley Internment Camp via Happy Valley and Wong Nai Chung Gap Road, describes the havoc the surrendering soldiers passed on their slow march north:

> All around us, and especially down in the valley, were hundreds of British and Canadian soldiers lying

> where they had been killed…. We were riding along
> now on a road that had seen tremendous bloodshed,
> and all around was evidence of a battle having been
> fought, burnt lorries, soldiers' equipment, helmets,
> shoes and clothes scattered everywhere.[1]

Scenes of carnage littered the island. In the 18 days of fighting, the Hong Kong garrison had suffered 2,113 killed or missing and 2,300 wounded, a casualty rate of 30 percent. With 290 dead and 493 wounded, the two Canadian battalions had suffered a casualty rate of nearly 40 percent.

Reid rejoined the Grenadiers at Murray Barracks on December 27. Here he helped with the wounded, escorted a truckload of severe cases up to Bowen Road Military Hospital, and returned with medicines, blankets, and a group of discharged patients, many still in need of medical attention. Back in barracks after 18 days of battle and the shock and disbelief at surrender, all these men, if only briefly, were again in familiar surroundings, with access to quartermaster's stores of food, cigarettes, blankets, and underclothing. For the last time, said Reid, there was "jam and biscuits in every mouth."[2]

Two days later, on a cold, clear morning at year's end, their lives as prisoners of war really began. Japanese soldiers — "rough and ready, cocky conquerors … cookie-cut for war,"[3] in Reid's words — marched the long line of captured soldiers from Murray Barracks down through the business section of Victoria to the harbour esplanade and ferry docks. The city was a zone of devastation after the weeks of bombing, shelling, and the recent street fighting. Bodies floated offshore. The harbour and bay were dotted with destroyed shipping, the sunken vessels showing only their funnels. In batches, the prisoners were ferried to the Kowloon side, where six weeks earlier the Canadians had run down the *Awatea*'s gangplank in spick-and-span tropical uniforms and formed up for the march to Sham Shui Po Camp while bands played, people cheered, and General Maltby bid them welcome. On December 30, 1941, it was the same march to Sham Shui Po, but in an altered world.

Kowloon was war-wrecked. Away from the dock area, the prisoners wound their way through streets spilled with rubble while silent Chinese paused for their passage. Some stared stolidly at their vanquished protectors, some jeered, some wept, many barely glanced at all. Trying to cope in the remains of the bombed and burned-out city, the inhabitants and thousands of refugees had little interest in the fate of the defeated foreigners. The Chinese now faced a brutal Japanese occupation in which many were already starving to death.

For Reid, the march to Sham Shui Po brought one happy discovery. As they passed the barracks compound of the Rajput and Punjabi Indian regiments, where an assortment of Allied prisoners was being held, Reid spotted his colleague, Martin Banfill, waving through the wire. Banfill, medical officer for the Royal Rifles, had been written off as dead when the island was invaded 11 days earlier. Instead, here he was returning the thumbs-up to his passing comrades.

Yet Banfill was badly traumatized. Before the battle, he had been put in charge of the main Army Medical Store established in the Salesian Catholic Mission in the northeast of Hong Kong Island, close to Lei Yue Mun Gap where the invasion crossing was made on the night of December 18. Early in the morning of December 19, Japanese soldiers surrounded and captured the mission, killing two unarmed ambulance drivers as they did so. The mission nurses were sent away unharmed. But after confiscating personal valuables, the Japanese marched Banfill and his male staff to a large drainage ditch on the hill behind the mission and lined them up along its edge. Anticipating the worst, Banfill pleaded with the Japanese officer, who spoke some English, that they be taken prisoner. The officer replied, "Order is, all captives must die." In the next few minutes,

21 medical staff, eight of them Canadians, were bayoneted, shot, or beheaded, and dumped in the ditch. Banfill, forced to the ground with a rope around his neck and a Japanese soldier's boot pinning his head to the earth, saw the shooting, stabbing, and beheadings, and heard the chatter and laughter of the Japanese that accompanied the shots and blows, the cries and screams of his dying men. Banfill was spared temporarily because he was to be interrogated about minefield locations. During the massacre, several of his staff, though wounded, survived by playing dead beneath the bodies of their lifeless comrades, later crawling to safety. Although Banfill expected to be killed at any moment as he was marched around barefoot that day, his promised beheading never came. When it was clear to his interrogators that he knew nothing about minefields, he was spared by an officer named Honda, interned in the Indian barracks with other stray prisoners, and later moved to Sham Shui Po to join the Canadians there.

As in the invasion of China in 1937, the killing of unarmed or disarmed captives was commonplace Japanese behaviour throughout the Battle of Hong Kong. Incidents got worse toward the end. On Christmas Day, just before the surrender, St. Stephen's College on Stanley Peninsula, which had been converted to a 400-bed emergency military hospital, was overrun by Japanese troops who shot and stabbed the medical staff, bayoneted to death more than 50 wounded British and Canadian soldiers in their hospital beds, and gang-raped and murdered the nurses.

Equally grisly discoveries were made a few days later by Major John Crawford. On December 29, the day before the prisoners were moved from Murray Barracks to Sham Shui Po, Crawford and Lieutenant-Colonel Lindsay Ride, the Combined Field Ambulance commander, were allowed out to search for wounded soldiers. In the centre of the island, they came upon three separate groups of garrison troops who had been captured near Wong Nai Chung

Gap toward the end of the fighting. All 82 men had been executed by bullet or bayonet, many with their feet bound and hands tied behind their backs.[4]

Passing through the gates of Sham Shui Po Camp on December 30, 1941, the captured Grenadiers faced a scene of utter desolation. Bombs and shells had shattered the walls and roofs of the barracks, leaving gaping holes. The avenues and parade grounds were pockmarked from explosions and littered with garbage, the rubble of battle, and the remnants of ransacking by Chinese scavengers who had overrun the camp after the surrender, stripping and looting the compound of everything combustible or of use. Furniture, doors and windows and their frames, pipes and faucets, electrical fixtures and fittings, toilets, even plaster and lath from the walls were ripped out, leaving gutted shells of buildings through which the wind blew unimpeded. Into these hulks, several thousand Canadian and British soldiers were herded to live and sleep on concrete floors still strewn with debris and open to the elements. Yet, in these first days of capture, says Reid, even amid the disarray, squalor, and desperation, false hopes were as contagious as the dysentery:

> Now followed three weeks of disorganized apathy and acute starvation, with rumours the only full ration. For the men's wounds and the spreading dysentery already acquired in the hills, treatment was confined to hot and cold water. A little polished rice each day and a belly-gnawing hunger that

denied sleep, as did the unregulated flow from the protein-poor kidneys. Still, always, the rumours: the rejuvenated American fleet was just over the horizon, with the Japanese in full flight; the British navy was steaming north from Singapore, striking fear to the heart of Tokyo; the Chinese were on the move coastward from Chungking; the Americans had swept the enemy from the Philippines. It would all be over in February![5]

Instead, things got worse. Three weeks after the Grenadiers arrived at Sham Shui Po, the Japanese reorganized the three main Hong Kong prison camps, dividing the Allied prisoners according to nationality. The Indian troops were concentrated at the Ma Tau Chung refugee camp in Kowloon, the British troops and members of the Hong Kong Volunteer Corps were brought together at Sham Shui Po, and the 1,685 Canadians who had survived the fighting were consolidated, with a number of Royal Navy personnel, at North Point Camp on the harbourfront of Hong Kong Island, east of Victoria. As prisoner transfers began, a group of Canadian soldiers being treated for wounds and sickness at Bowen Road Military Hospital on the Peak was discharged en masse and marched to North Point Camp through downtown Victoria. William Allister, of the Royal Canadian Corps of Signals, was one of them:

> We made our way down into the city and marched in a straggling line through the streets, no longer crowded but bleak, neglected, their lifeblood drained away. We looked around us: war damage everywhere. The buildings, still standing, watched like mourners at our wake, empty, desolate. We staggered under our loads, straining, feeble, sweating.

The passers-by looked away, taking no satisfaction in these bedraggled, dull-eyed, unshaven creatures, former masters. Strange it was to pass down these broad streets again with their hint of bygone days — but what contrast. On that first triumphal march we were jaunty, full-bodied, our blood roaring with explosive energy, delight, shock, excitement, and the crowds were teeming with bustling life.... Now they were cautious, eyes averted as they glided out of the path of these guards, with their volatile tempers and their Greater East Asian Co-Prosperity Scheme. Fear was in the air around us and a prescient awareness of horrors to come ... of days when they would be eating their own babies.[6]

The Grenadiers at Sham Shui Po were ferried back to Hong Kong from Kowloon on January 23. The main body of the Royal Rifles reached North Point Camp on December 31, having been marched over the hills from Stanley Peninsula, where they surrendered on Christmas Day. More appalling conditions than those faced by the two battalions at North Point are hard to imagine. The camp's ramshackle wooden huts, originally set up as temporary shelter for about 300 Chinese refugees, had been badly damaged by shelling during the invasion. Now they were to serve as accommodation for more than 1,700 prisoners of war, with up to 175 men crammed into huts meant for 50. The entire camp area had previously been used as a dump, first by the British in Victoria, then by the Japanese who stabled their horses and mules there after they invaded the island, leaving huge piles of manure and the carcasses of dead animals wherever they fell. Littered among the dead animals and in the ditches were the decaying bodies of murdered Chinese.

Sergeant Les Fisher, an employee of the Hong Kong Telephone Company and member of the Hong Kong Volunteer Defence Corps, the local auxiliary militia force, was in North Point with the Canadians:

> The wooden huts were a scene of indescribable filth, with rubbish and excreta, both horse and human, lying in all the huts and odd corners. The hot sun had brought out clouds of flies and we had to set to and clean the place up with no brushes and water. It was a heartbreaking and filthy job.... Our latrine was the sea wall, a cold place at night, and rather tricky; the idea was to fasten your belt on to the fence and strap-hang over, otherwise you fell off the edge.[7]

Rifleman Ken Cambon of the Royal Rifles, who was suffering from severe dysentery, almost did:

> There were no facilities of any kind. In the absence of plumbing we squatted on the sea wall, holding on to a wire fence. I was one of the first to get dysentery and spent some of the worst hours of my life hanging on to that fence. Truly, this was the lowest ebb. There were still many bodies floating in the bay. I was holding on to the fence, very weak with fever, nauseated and racked with the cramps that only bacillary dysentery can create, when I glanced down in the water to see a bloated face drift by.[8]

Besides the millions upon millions of flies, the camp was infested with lice, fleas, and bedbugs hosted by the previous occupants.

Food was a twice-daily cup of boiled rice or barley laced with mould, maggots, and mouse droppings, and soup of rotten "greens" — a watery mess that Reid described in his diary as "boiled versions of plants similar to our hardier and hornier roadside weeds." Ever hungrier, the men resorted to rats, snakes, and seaweed. In such circumstances, beginning to establish something approaching livable conditions was a daunting task. Depression was an impediment. A British medical officer noted the early tendencies of men giving in to defeat at both North Point and Sham Shui Po: "For the first month demoralization was complete. There was no open insubordination but a sullen apathy, shown particularly in disregard of personal cleanliness and appearance…. At this stage there were no working parties for the Japanese, and the men would spend their days lounging around the corners of the huts, the only subject of conversation being food."[9]

Lieutenant Harry White of the Winnipeg Grenadiers explains the challenge of keeping up spirits during the three weeks the Canadians were at Sham Shui Po in January 1942:

> We are working hard to get things organized but a lot of the men are letting go — their morale has broken and discipline is difficult to enforce. With the Canadians it's not too bad as we Platoon Officers are working pretty close with our men and on the whole getting cooperation. There is a little mutinous talk but we shall bring them around. It's quite a job trying to make some men realize they must do certain things for their own good.[10]

With the impact of the battle, defeat, imprisonment, and weeks of starvation, some couldn't cope. For Signalman William Allister, now at North Point Camp, one such casualty haunted him:

Every hut had its fill of bizarre histories, of tragedies, of minds hovering on the brink. Some had already passed over the edge. Morgan, a young Royal Rifle, tall, heavy-set, raised in luxury, was one of these. He wandered over the camp, digging out small clumps of earth and grass to eat. I watched him with pity, horror, and envy. He would not survive, but he had escaped.[11]

As indicated by one Canadian who survived, hunger of this order can't be imagined:

I wouldn't have believed I could be so hungry. I'd chew grass, weeds, anything I could find. I would have stolen food from my friends if they'd had any, and that was the worst thing you could do except, maybe, stealing drugs.

We all had diarrhea or dysentery or both a good deal of the time and knew that rice and barley could go through you practically untouched. One day I was in such bad shape that — I'm going to tell this as quickly as I can to get it over with — I cupped my hands under a man squatting with diarrhea, caught the barley coming through, washed it off as best I could, and ate it. Later I saw some other men doing this now and then but it didn't make me feel any less ashamed. I didn't feel ashamed while I was doing it, though. I was too hungry to feel anything but hunger.[12]

What helped the majority of the men adapt to incarceration under these conditions was the gradual reassertion of the routines of military life, daily discipline within a chain of command under officers they knew. George MacDonell, the Royal Rifles sergeant major who led the astounding charge that took Stanley Village on Christmas Day, describes the stiffening of morale:

> After the pell-mell of battle and the anxious days of waiting after the surrender, it was almost a relief to once again live the structured life of a soldier. Soldiers woke to reveille, took part in morning muster, had breakfast, took part in sick parade, evening muster, and then to sleep at the last post — and that is what we did. We were hungry, terribly hungry, and at the mercy of a savage and arbitrary enemy. But we not only believed in our cause, we believed in each other. We were nothing like criminal prisoners. We had done nothing dishonourable. Quite the opposite. We had held up honourably under a terrible onslaught and had damaged the enemy.[13]

By early February 1942, six weeks after the surrender, conditions were being improved. Two latrines in North Point Camp were repaired, and Royal Engineers imprisoned with the Canadians cleared a well to provide water. Medical care, albeit with almost no medicine, was organized and overseen by Major John Crawford, who also kept the medical records. Reid took sick parade for the Grenadiers, and Martin Banfill did the same for the Royal Rifles, between them seeing 200 to 300 men per day. Aside from the constant, gnawing hunger, it was dysentery and skin troubles from bites, scratching, and infection that were the most common complaints during the first months of imprisonment.

Initially, more serious medical cases were transferred to Bowen Road Military Hospital, which had been kept open by the Japanese with its original Allied medical staff. But at the end of January, the Japanese ordered the Canadians to set up a hospital in a dilapidated warehouse on North Point's grounds. Gordon Gray was given the almost hopeless task of running what the men soon called the Agony Ward. Measuring about 11 by 14 yards, with a leaky roof and a makeshift stove that produced more smoke than heat, the hospital had few beds and no facilities. Meant for a dozen dysentery patients, it often held upward of 40, many lying in several inches of water if it had been raining and "in complete darkness each night, with scenes indescribable in the light of dawn,"[14] says Reid. The only treatment the doctors could administer was trying to flush out the patients' systems using warm water with a small dose of Epsom salts from a supply they bought "through the fence" by bribing Japanese guards. Lieutenant Ralph Goodwin, a New Zealand motor torpedo boat naval officer who was wounded during the battle and imprisoned with the Canadians, paints a grim picture of what patients faced:

> The dysentery hospital at North Point was a shocking reflection on our captors. That noisome place of healing was situated in a stone stable near the waterfront. The floor was of cobblestones, ventilation and light were provided by two very small windows and a small door, and the interior was always in deep gloom. Two four-gallon cans were the only conveniences provided. Four or five patients were always clustered about each of those inadequate receptacles, needing to use them at the same time, and the place reeked with the stench of ordure which ran among the cobbles and fouled the blankets of the men lying on the ground. It was a horrible place, and repeated requests were made for better hospital

quarters. There were several large empty buildings just outside the camp which would have been suitable, but the Japanese cared nothing for our condition and every request was refused.[15]

Said Rifleman Ken Cambon: "Thank God I had my [dysentery] attack before there was a hospital."[16]

In the absence of significant treatment, the medical orderlies gave Agony Ward patients the only care they could offer: carry them out into the daylight and with rags and water wash them clean as well as they could.

– 6 –

Believed to Be Alive –
Joy Overshadowed: The Home Front I

When Jack and Jean Reid returned to Toronto from Vancouver in June 1941, prior to his enlistment, they moved in with Jean's family at 5 Scholfield. For a brief spell, it was like the old days for Jean. All five sisters were home again, chatting and laughing together as they used to after returning from girlhood summers at Camp Tanamakoon in Algonquin Park. Val, the youngest, was still at university. Kay and Marg, both working, hadn't left the nest yet. Dede had a job in Toronto, having returned from Geneva with the rest of the Canadian delegation after the League of Nations suspended political operations just before the war.

Another change in the family was the retirement of Jack Hodge earlier than expected. Disagreement with Dun & Bradstreet's head office about the effects of the war on business had prompted him to resign at the end of 1939, age 60. Unaffected were Eva's activities — her music and volunteering with the Women's Auxiliary of St. Paul's Church doing good works for the community and the local war effort.

There were weddings in view in June 1941, the original dates sped up by wartime: Bill Bigelow and Ruth Jennings (she would become Jean's closest friend) in July; Dede Hodge at the end of August to Bill Latter, a Quebecer from Richelieu introduced to her by League of Nations friends; and Marg Hodge in early 1942 before her fiancé, Gordon Roy, also from Quebec but met on the tennis courts in Rosedale Park, was posted to Britain with the Canadian Military Engineers.

Like Jean, Marg would stay at home when her husband left for Britain. With Dede's move to Chambly, Quebec, following her marriage, and Reid's departure overseas in October 1941, those remaining at 5 Scholfield were Jack and Eva Hodge and four of their five daughters. This would be the status quo at the house until the end of the war four years later.

The wartime scrapbook that Jean began in September 1941, just before Jack's departure, didn't get very far. It starts with the *Star Weekly* article showing Reid and his colleagues in the medical officer course at Lansdowne Park, followed by the several pages of private snapshots taken during their field training.

When "C" Force's secret destination hit the news after its arrival in Hong Kong in mid-November, Jean pasted in a succession of stories about the Crown Colony and the Canadians' disembarkation and deployment there. These clippings have a newsreel excitement to them: stirring copy, dramatic vistas of Hong Kong and its harbour, pictures of marching troops, of gunnery practice, of shore defences at the ready — all topped with upbeat headlines: "Big Colony in Orient Thrilled by Arrival," "Troops Ready for Anything at Hong Kong," "Chinese Cheer."[1]

Among the Hong Kong coverage Jean included a human-interest story about Mrs. J.K. Lawson, formerly Miss Gussie Wilson of London, Ontario, now a plucky volunteer at the Ottawa Red Cross blood donor clinic, mother of two young boys, and wife of Brigadier John Lawson, "C" Force commander. Datelined November 17, 1941, its headline reads: "'Daddy's Off Boat' Rejoice Hong Kong Brigadier's Sons: Long Weeks of Waiting Finally over for Lawson Family." Mrs. Lawson is quoted: "The boys are simply thrilled ... [they] didn't know where their daddy was going, but did know he was on a 'boat' and now they know he is safely off it.... They are still very excited.... I thought word would never come. It seemed such a long time, while the ship was on its way."[2]

Jean, now several months' pregnant, must have shared Gussie's relief.

On November 26, Jean received a telegram from Reid saying he had arrived in Hong Kong safely. After that came an airmail letter, the first of three from him to reach Canada before all mail from Hong Kong ceased. The next clipping in her scrapbook is datelined "Hong Kong, December 8," and is the last one pasted in: "Canadians Face Imminent Action at Hong Kong."

The December 8 news story reported that there were "ineffectual" air raids on the Crown Colony by a few Japanese planes, one of which was shot down by British gunners. Troop formations of 300 to 400 Japanese had been observed across the Chinese border from Hong Kong's New Territories. Damage and casualties from the air raids were said to be slight. There was no hint of concern in the report, though Japanese assaults by land were believed to be imminent, "meaning," the correspondent continued, "the

Canadian contingent here will be the first of the Dominion's land forces to go into action [in the Second World War]."[3]

One week later — after Pearl Harbor, the Japanese sinking of the Royal Navy's warships HMS *Prince of Wales* and HMS *Repulse* in the South China Sea (Britain's principal naval assets in the Far East), and the attacks on the Philippines, Malaya, and Hong Kong — Jean's scrapbook becomes a jumble of loose clippings:

> December 15 — "Canadians in Thick of It as Main Japanese Attack Launched at Hong Kong"; December 17 — "'Quiet Night' at Hong Kong Reported as City Shaken by Concussion of Gunfire"; December 20 — "Hong Kong's Gallant Stand Against Encircling Masses Continued on Island Peaks"; December 22 — "Defenders of Hong Kong Still Hold Half of Island Is Last Word at Ottawa"; December 22 — "Waves of Attacking Japs Storm Hong Kong Lines but Garrison Hanging On"; December 23 — "Canadians Hold Fast to Mountain Posts ... Lawson Killed."[4]

And on December 26, the *Globe and Mail*'s muted report of the surrender: "Hong Kong Resistance Ends."[5]

At Camp Niagara, where Jean had been invited by Bill and Ruth Bigelow, who wanted to comfort and support her as this bleakest of Christmases approached, the worst had already been faced. On December 22, Jean clipped an Associated Press (AP) report from London that said three belated communiqués had just been received from Hong Kong, sent two days after the Japanese invaded the island. Based on their contents, British authorities refused to speculate how long resistance could last. For Jean, "how long" didn't matter now. Above the byline of "J. Wes Gallagher," AP's London correspondent, ran the subhead: "No hopes held."[6]

As abruptly as the Battle of Hong Kong erupted, then ended 18 days later, news of it practically vanished from Toronto newspapers. On December 27, the day after the surrender was announced, speculation about "C" Force in the *Globe and Mail* had moved to page four as other stories took precedence: with the United States now in the war, Winston Churchill was meeting with President Franklin D. Roosevelt in Washington, D.C.; after Washington, Churchill was going to Ottawa to address the Canadian House of Commons on December 30; the Soviet army had smashed Nazi lines in Russia; Hitler was preparing an offensive in the Near East. By December 29, there was only one small reference to the Hong Kong disaster — an article on page three about Ottawa's request for help from the Swiss in obtaining a Canadian casualty list.

When Hong Kong coverage resumed in January, it must have appalled anyone with a relative or loved one caught there. British newspapers were now stating that the Crown Colony wasn't a serious strategic loss to the Allies, indeed, had never been considered a position to be held if the Japanese attacked. These revelations, which contradicted the original assurances from the British War Office of Hong Kong's importance and defensibility, were an embarrassment to both the British and Canadian governments, which tried to recast their actions in a more favourable light.

Prime Minister William Lyon Mackenzie King followed the British lead. He neither protested the apparently pointless Canadian losses at Hong Kong nor — as even the *Times* of London saw fit to say in an editorial while the battle was still raging — did he demand greater Canadian say in future British deployments involving Canadian forces.

After Churchill's address to the Canadian House of Commons on December 30, 1941, five days after the surrender, King recorded in his diary: "[Churchill] spoke feelingly of Hong Kong, saying he was not sure at first about sending Canadians, on the theory that if war did not come, they would not be needed, and if war did come, it would be a difficult place to hold."[7] After Churchill's speech, Prime Minister King and the members of his War Committee were reported by the press to be "subdued and appreciative."[8]

Meanwhile, the Dominions Office in Britain sent an official note of condolence and commendation to Canada for its role in the battle: "The defence of Hong Kong will live in History as yet one more chapter of courage and endurance in the annals of the British Commonwealth."[9]

In offering the condolences of the Canadian government to the country, and especially to the grieving families and friends of "C" Force members, King embellished his homage by comparing the Canadian defenders of Hong Kong to Adam Dollard des Ormeaux and his handful of French militia and Huron warriors who, in 1660, were annihilated at the Battle of Long Sault trying to repel 700 Iroquois warriors, but in doing so saved Montreal.[10]

What Jean Reid made of such triumphalism is unknown, but Canadian opposition parties weren't satisfied. In January 1942, George Drew, the Conservative Party leader in Ontario, began to ask probing questions about the preparation and equipping of "C" Force, questions that were taken up by the press: Why were so many undertrained soldiers attached to the two "C" Force battalions at the last minute? Why did mechanized transport fail to go with them? Was the Canadian government misled by Britain about the nature and circumstances of the mission?

In a long speech in the House of Commons on January 21, four weeks after the surrender, Defence Minister James Ralston did his best to explain the sequence of events and reasons in favour that led to the Canadian contingent being sent to Hong Kong. Ralston's summary wasn't enough to satisfy Drew and other critics, who kept hammering away for clearer answers. Both federal opposition parties now called for a parliamentary inquiry into "C" Force, to which King agreed. But in February, the prime minister backed away from establishing an all-party inquiry and instead appointed Sir Lyman Duff, chief justice of Canada, as a one-man royal commission.

The appointment of Duff temporarily stalled some of the political outcry, but the British and Canadian governments couldn't stifle stories leaking out of the Far East about the brutal treatment and appalling conditions already being endured by the Hong Kong prisoners. In mid-February, an AP story reported that 5,000 prisoners in Kowloon were being badly maltreated and that dysentery was rampant in the prison camps. On February 19, Ottawa received a cable from Britain on the state of the Hong Kong prison camps, based on testimony of escapees: "Conditions undoubtedly deplorable and Japanese completely callous. Doctors unable to treat many cases of dysentery owing to absence of medical stores. No proper arrangements for cooking, feeding, or sanitation." The cable also revealed that after the battle "there were many authenticated cases of brutality, including murder of prisoners and nurses and rape of nurses."[11] On February 24, Vincent Massey, Canada's high commissioner in London, cabled Ottawa further details of atrocities and of the "studied barbarism employed [by the Japanese] with the object of breaking [the prisoners'] morale."[12]

The British and Canadian governments would have preferred suppressing these stories, but confirmation of Japanese atrocities by British officers who reached safety in Chinese-held Chongqing, 670 miles northwest of Hong Kong, made secrecy impossible. On March 10, Anthony Eden, Britain's secretary of state for foreign affairs, rose in the British House of Commons to confirm the rumours: British and Canadian soldiers had been shot, bayoneted, and beheaded by the Japanese after surrendering; Asiatic and European women had been raped, some murdered; wounded soldiers had been murdered in their hospital beds.

Because Japan never ratified the 1929 Geneva Convention, which included regulations for the identification and treatment of prisoners of war, hair-raising reports such as Eden's were almost the only news to reach Canada about the Hong Kong situation for nearly a year. Only in October 1942 did the Japanese provide Ottawa with a partial list of casualties, augmented by names brought back to Canada by civilians repatriated from China by ship. Even so, news of some "C" Force soldiers didn't reach family members until 1943. In this respect, Jean Reid was fortunate, thanks to Lieutenant-Colonel Lindsay Ride, commander of the Hong Kong Field Ambulance in which Reid and his fellow medical officers had served throughout the battle.

An Australian by birth and professor of physiology at the University of Hong Kong since 1928, Dr. Ride spoke some Mandarin and Cantonese and had many Chinese connections. Shortly after the surrender, he made use of them. On January 9, 1942, 10 days after he and Major John Crawford made their fruitless search for survivors on the battlefields of Hong Kong, Ride and three trusted associates escaped from Sham Shui Po and made their way through Japanese lines to Chongqing, the provisional capital of China and the Allied Command Headquarters in the region. Here Colonel Ride — "The Smiling Tiger," as he was nicknamed — formed the British Army Aid Group (BAAG), a division of the British Directorate of Military Intelligence (MI9), and set up a network of agents and Chinese guerrillas operating in southern China and Hong Kong to gather intelligence, help POWs escape, and smuggle medicines and other supplies into the prison camps.

Among its duties, BAAG compiled the names of incarcerated Hong Kong civilians and British and Canadian POWs culled from the recollections of prison camp escapees and refugees from the occupied Crown Colony who managed to reach Chongqing. These names were passed on to contacts in Australia, and on March 3, 1942, the *Melbourne Argus* published a partial, unconfirmed list of Hong Kong prisoners. The *Argus* story was spotted by Mrs. C.M. Forrest of Victoria, British Columbia, who passed it on to the *Daily Colonist*, her local newspaper, because several Canadians were on the list. Their names were published in the Toronto papers on May 7, 1942.

Stipulating that the report was based on the hearsay of escaped officers and refugees and not entirely reliable, the newspapers said that Captain "Jack" Reid of Toronto and Captain Gordon Gray of Edmonton, graduates of the University of Toronto Medical School and currently RCAMC officers with "C" Force, were believed to be alive and prisoners of war in Hong Kong. Major John Crawford of Winnipeg, "C" Force senior medical officer, was also among those accounted for. As father of the Toronto officer mentioned, Harry Reid was interviewed by the local press, and a follow-up story on Reid's background and medical training appeared in the paper the next day together with his picture — the smiling studio portrait in uniform taken by famed photographer Yousuf Karsh before Reid left Ottawa (see page 47).[13]

Jean's relief must have been immense. But her joy was shadowed by a sadness she was shouldering without him: the loss of their unborn son through miscarriage that winter.

Part II:
1942–1945

The Secret Medical Diary:
The Bitterness of Playing God

By the end of May 1942, the Canadians at North Point Camp had been on a starvation diet for five months. With rations of about 1,000 calories per day, weight losses were dramatic, and the consequences of prolonged malnutrition and severe vitamin deficiencies — wet and dry beriberi, pellagra, edema, and skin infections — were widespread. More than 40 percent of the prisoners had contracted malaria. Dysentery, a debilitating scourge from the beginning due to contaminated food and water as well as contagion from flies and the cramped conditions in which the men lived, was rampant and recurrent: "We had nothing to treat it," said Reid. "Magnesium sulfate and some bismuth. Totally inadequate."[1]

Signalman William Allister describes something of the physical and mental deterioration afflicting him and those around him by spring:

We seemed marked for the seven plagues of Egypt. A disease called pellagra brought open, running pus sores to many parts of the mouth and body. One of the curses produced red, swollen testicles, dubbed "strawberry balls." Another turned them into huge, melon-sized monstrosities called "Hong Kong balls." Wet and dry beriberi stymied the medics. Men developed "electric feet" — painful nerve shocks in the toes that continued relentlessly day and night.... It progressed in stages. First came the pain-filled sleepless nights, which produced exhaustion and lack of appetite. In time, at the middle stage, the misery gradually drove men mad. They could neither eat nor sleep. Finally they wasted away and died.

A hut was set aside for the advanced stages, again dubbed Agony Ward. Their gaunt figures bent double on the floor, weaving and bobbing and rocking back and forth in pain, like penitents at the Wailing Wall, rubbing their tortured toes and weeping, made a haunting sight. I had never seen grown men cry. It roused pity, disgust, horror, fear — fear that this was awaiting me. When we visited a friend and recognized the mad, faraway look in the eyes, we knew it was a matter of time.[2]

In spite of the sickness and debilitation of the prisoners, the Japanese instituted slave labour in June 1942, beginning with the enlargement of Kai Tak Airport by levelling an ancient Chinese burial mound ("pick and shovel work, knocking down a mountain and taking it away in baskets," as Reid depicted it).[3] Alternating between Royal Rifles and Grenadiers, work details of 200 men per day would get up at 4:00 a.m., breakfast on bad rice and greens, and be ferried to Kowloon, where they slogged for 10 to 12 hours, often in miserable weather, with no more than a bun for lunch. Slowness or not understanding orders provoked the three "B's" — guards using their boots, bayonets, and rifle butts to punish the men. They were like zombies on returning to camp at night, stumbling around in a daze.

Following the universal system, POW privates worked, NCOs supervised, and officers didn't work, the exception being medical officers. In March, again according to the Japanese system, POW officers had begun to be paid, but most of the money was held back by the Japanese to pay for clothing, toilet articles, and food that the prisoners never received. With the money that did filter down, Reid proposed that a food fund be set up to alleviate the effects on the slave labour work parties: "The men were getting very bad and I suggested that we take some of our money and buy food for the sick men, and all the officers contributed a relatively small amount ... there were seventy or eighty officers and we could usually get as much as we could spend. We bought food and established a sick mess and fed them special diets."[4] The supplier was a Chinese merchant the Japanese allowed into the camp.

In June, when the slave labour program began, a man might be chosen to go out on a work party every third day. But as the summer of 1942 wore on, the Japanese doubled the daily quotas, forcing more and more of the seriously ill men to work, sometimes until they dropped. Royal Rifle Geoffrey Marston was stricken with severe dysentery in July 1942 and subjected to treatment conditions worse than ever, due to the callousness of the Japanese:

> Committed to the camp's ramshackle hospital, which reeked with indescribable stench, I was helped

to a cot and lay huddled on it wet with rain that was seeping through the rotted roof. Next to me lay a very young-looking comrade who was labouring for breath. I was certain that he was deteriorating more and more into a state of no return. I shuddered when I thought his next breath could be his last....

The atmosphere was frightening. Patients were tottering at a snail's pace along a narrow aisleway to reach a closed-in quarter at the end of the ward that was used as a toilet. Those unable to muster the strength to leave their so-called beds lay in their own muck. Dirty, blood-stained pieces of toilet paper littered the floor.

Mustering enough strength to pay a toilet call, I reeled back from the awesome stench of the room containing nothing more than five old peanut oil cans that were in constant use, and those who couldn't control their body functions had to use the floor. Cakes of excrement and pools of urine lay everywhere.

The filth proved a Mecca for rats which were scampering about in large numbers. We were deathly afraid that they would attack our buttocks, thereby devouring chunks of flesh. Time and again, orderlies tried to stave them off with long sticks to keep them from coming nearer.

The next day, the downpour had gotten heavier and never let up. The roof began to leak like a sieve causing flooding to the depth of six to eight inches. Bricks were brought in to elevate the cots.

In the meantime, our officers confronted the Japanese and sternly requested that they repair the decayed roof and provide better toilet facilities, but the Japanese were adamant in refusing to do so and declared in anger that if they were further bothered, all prisoners would be subjected to a cut in food ration.

The rodents, which were swimming around the floating muck, tried to clamber on our beds. Some succeeded and began attacking the flesh of patients. But they didn't feel it. The flesh was dead.

The lad next to me expired. I watched as the orderlies taped his eyes and stuffed his mouth and rectum with cotton wool and wrapped the remains in a blanket, then placed it on a stretcher and took it away.

Our overworked doctors and orderlies worked feverishly almost around the clock trying to save those who were still clinging to a shred of life. Without any source of medications, their only alternative to combat the disease was no intake of food for several days to stabilize the intestines. Only tea was given several times daily.

Our Padres spent every minute of their time trying to comfort us.... On the third day, I could feel my strength rapidly declining. I couldn't raise myself off my bed. I was growing weaker and weaker. The room was spinning like a top with the sounds around me gradually diminishing.[5]

Pressed by the camp doctors, the Japanese transferred Marston to Bowen Road Military Hospital before it was too late.

As work party numbers rose, so did sickness rates and susceptibility to infection. On August 7, 1942, Reid looked down a sore throat and saw a dirty greyish membrane: the first case of diphtheria among the Canadians at North Point Camp.

"Here," Reid later wrote, "was a true nightmare."[6] A highly contagious bacteria that thrived in cramped, unsanitary living conditions, diphtheria could kill either by infecting and swelling the throat tissues to the point of strangulation or by the toxin it produced inside the body, which impaired nerve functions that controlled swallowing, heart action, and movement of the arms and legs, ultimately causing death by heart failure. Before the discovery of diphtheria antitoxin in the 1920s, the disease killed thousands a year. Ironically, the antitoxin, discovered by a French scientist at the Pasteur Institute in Paris in 1924, had been perfected, tested, and mass-produced at Toronto's Connaught Laboratories beginning in 1926, just a few blocks from where Reid and Gordon Gray trained as doctors 10 years later. By then, Ontario schoolchildren were routinely being vaccinated with the antitoxin, achieving almost 100 percent effectiveness. But for many of the men at North Point the general use of the diphtheria antitoxin had come too late: nearly 600 of the Canadian prisoners — Grenadiers raised in rural Manitoba and Royal Rifles from the isolated Gaspé region of Quebec — had never been inoculated.

Given this susceptibility, the North Point diphtheria outbreak was swift and deadly, largely because Captain Shunkichi Saito, the Japanese doctor in charge of medical oversight of the Hong Kong POW camps, refused to accept that the malady *was* diphtheria and withheld antitoxin. Diphtheria complicated by acute dysentery, which most of the men had, was a lethal combination. Of the 79 Canadians who contracted the disease in August and September 1942, 38 died. Dr. Saito always carried a piece of rubber tubing for punishment purposes, lashing any prisoner — officer, NCO, or other rank — who broke camp rules or otherwise provoked him. His hysterical reaction over the diphtheria outbreak was to line up the doctors and medical orderlies on parade and hit them in the face for "allowing" so many men to die. The sight of the diminutive Saito reaching up to strike Major Crawford, who stood six foot five, was remembered by many.[7]

At the end of September, with the diphtheria epidemic still spreading, the Japanese shut down North Point Camp and transferred the Canadians, diphtheria patients included, to Sham Shui Po on the mainland. By now, the diphtheria bacteria was attacking every physical weak point. In men so rundown and plagued with sores, the result was not just diphtheria of the throat but diphtheria of the nose, diphtheria of the scrotum, diphtheria of the penis, and diphtheria of the leg and foot where open ulcers were perfect breeding grounds for the bacteria.

In early October, the Japanese began to panic at the Sham Shui Po death rate, and a visiting Japanese senior officer ordered Saito to provide anti-diphtheritic serum to the camp doctors. Shortly after, additional serum was bought on the black market by Major Crawford, using officer funds. Some of the Chinese camp workers — actually members of Colonel Ride's BAAG group — managed to smuggle in some more. Still, the supply of antitoxin was far too little for proper dosages. Confronted with 248 new diphtheria cases in October, Reid said the doctors were in a terrible position: "I remember one night after we got the antitoxin we had to go into the long ward among the men with diphtheria and we had only a small amount of antitoxin and we had to use it where it would do the most good. We would say this one is too late, this one will, this one won't: just playing God in a way you don't want to play God anymore, signing life and death warrants."[8] Reid admitted: "Playing God ... was one of my bitterest moments."[9]

After the Canadians were moved to Sham Shui Po, the diphtheria patients were isolated in a windowless old building with up
to 200 sick men lying on the concrete floor. Sergeant Lance Ross,
who on Christmas Day 1941 had covered the retreat from Stanley
Village with Sergeant Major George MacDonell, was one of them.
He wrote in his diary for October 11 and 12, 1942, while in the
"diphth hospital": "Can hardly write so sick. Tonsils are as big as
eggs. Can hardly breathe…. Three died last night."[10] Private Frank
Harding of the Grenadiers saw the infection as a death sentence.
When Reid told him he had diphtheria, Harding almost despaired:
"I looked at the electric wire fence and I considered putting an end
to myself. I don't know why I didn't do it, but I didn't. That's the
lowest I've ever been."[11]

But enforced rationing of the serum led to a happy discovery.
After a few weeks of treatment, Reid and his colleagues found that
even a tiny dose of serum tipped most patients to the safe side. Of
the 380 men stricken with diphtheria between October 1942 and
January 1943, only 20 died, a much lower mortality rate (5 percent) than in August and September 1942 when, without serum,
the death rate reached 48 percent of those infected.

Later in October, the doctors negotiated with the Japanese
to reorganize the medical setup. Diphtheria patients were moved
into Sham Shui Po's Jubilee Buildings, where they were more isolated, with Martin Banfill in charge. Gordon Gray continued to
look after the dysentery hospital, and Reid took sick parade for the
Grenadiers as well as running the "general" hospital, with up to a
175 patients at a time.

Although the pool of available prisoners was much reduced,
the Japanese continued to demand work parties through the worst
of the diphtheria epidemic. Trying to protect these overworked and
enfeebled men was a continual frustration for the medical staff, as
Reid describes: "The men went out to work before daylight, came

back at night when it was dark. You couldn't examine them or look for 'diphths' and prevent them spreading [the disease]. That was really goddamn bad. The Japanese demanded a work party of a certain size. We graded the men a, b, c, d, and e and it was just a matter of starting at the top and getting enough for the work party and a lot of sick men had to go to work."[12]

Yet, paradoxically, Crawford and Reid later concluded that the diphtheria outbreak had also saved lives: "Routine pharyngeal swabs of the camp population began in October 1942 and revealed a great many diphtheria carriers. These were isolated and forbidden to go on work parties by the Japanese who had a great personal fear of the disease. These men continued on the usual diet but did no work, and thus exhibited a universal weight gain and improvement in the general state of health."[13]

Aside from the diphtheria epidemic, by November 1942, 10 months of malnutrition and vitamin deprivation had worn the men down in a bewildering combination of ways. Dysentery, boils, and skin ulcers were universal complaints. Neurological symptoms such as paraesthesia (tingling, pricking, or burning sensations of various parts of the body) and ataxia (lack of voluntary coordination of muscle movements — staggering gait, for example) were routine. Vision afflictions included night blindness, corneal ulceration, and optic atrophy, the last sometimes causing permanent loss of sight. Auditory impairment and cardiac changes were also on the rise. Tachycardia, a heart condition typically defined as a resting heart rate of 100 beats per minute or more, was so common that a rate of a 130 was required for a man to be exempted from work parties.

Three-quarters of the men had parasitic worms of one kind or another, sometimes to a horrifying degree. Hospitalized for a parasitic infestation, Grenadier William Ashton was told by an orderly that he passed more than 180 large worms in his stool while recovering. Although the rectum was the usual exit point, Royal Rifle Walter Grey disgorged worms out of his mouth that were over a foot long. Royal Rifle John Stroud witnessed men "with worms coming out of their mouths like spaghetti.... Some actually choked to death on the worms."[14] The doctors lacked any significant anti-parasite treatment.

Yet there were medical "victories." At the end of November, a supply of fish oil containing units of vitamins A and D came into camp, and to the doctors' delight the corneal ulcers cleared up almost overnight. And after killing 58 Canadians, the five-month diphtheria epidemic finally subsided in early 1943, a natural burning out of the infection for lack of susceptible men.

In the medical diary he kept secret from the Japanese through the war, Reid presents a composite of the physical and mental health of the Canadian prisoners of war at Sham Shui Po Camp at the end of 1942, 12 months after the surrender at Hong Kong:

> Rifleman X is not so well as some of his fellows, but much better than others. He can and does go on work parties, at least part of the time. He is very thin, having lost 20 percent (on average, 36 lb.) of his former body weight, and he appears about 50 years old, though his real age is 30.... There are cracks at the corner of the mouth and patches of dermatitis in and around the nose. He has a deep ulcer on the calf of the left leg. His tongue is sore, smooth and red, with a deep furrow down the centre. Two teeth are chipped from biting on pebbles

in his rice, and several other teeth are grossly carious so that he has difficulty in chewing his food.... He complains he cannot read ordinary print, but he can make out newspaper headlines. Bright sunlight causes excessive lacrimation.... He complains of constriction, like a band, around his chest.... His history includes malaria with two relapses [and] he has just recovered from one of several attacks of diarrhea. He states that both lower extremities are numb from thigh level to the toes.... The right great toe is deformed where a tropical ulcer has healed.... He staggers in the dark, but manages moderately well in the daytime.... He has some numbness of the hands, especially the finger tips.... Nocturnal frequency of urination ... has disturbed his sleep for so long that he regards it as an integral part of his existence.... He ... does not appear greatly concerned over the usual anxieties of life.[15]

This was the median state of health of the Canadian prisoners when the Japanese announced on January 11, 1943, that nearly half of them were being shipped to Japan to work as slave labourers for the rest of the war. The Japanese ordered that only one officer, a medical officer not a line officer, would accompany the Canadians. Major Crawford was to stay at Sham Shui Po; thus it was Banfill, Gray, and Reid, the three junior officers, who drew straws for the command. Reid "won." The selection process of the men going with him was equally slapdash, indeed, farcical.

Signalman William Allister: "We lined up for a fitness test — we must be able to work in Japan. We were each instructed to walk across the road. Those who made it were pronounced physically sound, A-1 category. Even Blacky [Lance Corporal Georges

"Blacky" Verreault, Royal Canadian Corps of Signals], who dragged himself across with a cane, passed with honours."[16]

Over the next week, those selected were isolated from the other prisoners in a fenced-off area of the camp, subjected to a battery of primitive diagnostic tests, and vaccinated for dysentery, typhoid, and cholera. Meanwhile, fellow prisoners pooled their resources: "Everyone [got] a present from a Canadian left behind," Reid later wrote, "usually some article of clothing to ward off Japan's winter cold. A cloth cap, a suit of underwear, a treasured duffel coat."[17] Dr. Martin Banfill describes the departure of Reid and his contingent from Sham Shui Po Camp on January 19, 1943:

> It was a most spectacular morning when they marched away. I'll never forget it. It was a gray dawn, and they had these 650 [men] out [on the parade ground], and the Japanese had issued them these white gloves. We thought that was very remarkable — you could see who the people were who were going ... perhaps it was ceremonial. They formed up inside the gate and [Reid] said "Quick march," and they started to whistle "I'm Ninety-Five," the Royal Rifles' march-past. They walked jauntily out of the camp into the coming dawn whistling this very catchy tune. That's the last I saw of John.[18]

At the head of his whistling column, Reid was in an interesting state of mind: "I was absolutely green. I didn't know anything about handling men from the line angle or anything else."[19] He added elsewhere: "I still recall the bewilderment in my heart, concealed as well as possible, as we marched out of camp.... I had 660 Canadian troops, with no line officer, and suddenly found myself with considerably more than medical duties to contend with."[20]

Marching away to the docks, Reid was leaving behind medical colleagues and friends with whom he had worked closely, under extreme conditions, for more than a year. He said later that he learned a tremendous amount from his nearly three years in Japan as commanding officer as well as medical officer of his fellow POWs, that he was glad he went. But on January 19, 1943, he was leaving the known for the unknown: "Out the gate and a backward glance at the windowless gray barracks, the double barbed-wire fence, and the sea on the other side, whence the rescuing fleet had not come. Strange to feel a little jab of loneliness at leaving that sad, barren ground. Down through Kowloon for the final time, streets almost deserted now. Only occasional furtive figures hurrying past."[21]

A few hours later, 1,177 POWs — 430 British soldiers, 83 members of the Hong Kong Volunteer Defence Corps, and the 664 Canadians — were herded aboard the *Tatuta Maru* for what the prisoners had dubbed "The Water Jump" to Japan.

– *8* –

Tokyo Camp No. 5:
"You Cannot Win This War!"

By 1942, Japan was in desperate need of workers. Its wars of aggression, beginning with the invasion of China in 1931, had drained the country of manpower after a decade of high casualty rates and the need to garrison the tens of thousands of square miles that Japanese forces had overrun in China and Southeast Asia. At home, disease — beriberi, most commonly — was ravaging the poorly fed Japanese civilian population. In August 1942, the Japanese Home Ministry ordered the importation of POWs from all the occupied territories to work in Japanese mines, manufacturing, stevedoring, and shipbuilding to boost "national defence." This was in direct violation of the Geneva Convention, which stipulated that prisoners of war weren't to be employed in the capturing nation's war effort.

The first Hong Kong draft of 618 British soldiers was shipped from Sham Shui Po to Japan on a freighter in early September 1942. A second draft of 1,816 British soldiers, also drawn from Sham

Shui Po, departed Hong Kong on the cargo ship *Lisbon Maru* later the same month. With no markings to show the ship was carrying prisoners of war, indeed, armed and with a major cargo of Japanese troops aboard, the *Lisbon Maru* was torpedoed by the American submarine USS *Grouper* in the East China Sea off Shanghai on October 1. The prisoners managed to break out of the locked holds as the ship slowly foundered, but many were gunned down by the Japanese guards as they reached the deck. Those who got over the side risked drowning, being shot in the water, or being attacked by sharks before they could be picked up by other Japanese ships. Eight hundred and forty-three British POWs died in the disaster, news that soon filtered back to the Hong Kong prison camps.

Royal Rifle Sergeant Lance Ross, one of the group sent to Japan under Reid, scribbled in his diary *their* chances on the voyage after boarding the *Tatuta Maru* on January 19, 1943: "We are like rats in a trap. Should we be torpedoed, not one would be saved."[1]

Twenty-six-year-old Sergeant Tom Marsh of the Grenadiers, son of a Canadian First World War veteran, collector of military memorabilia since childhood, and a professional soldier since 1934, was older than many of his comrades, and like Reid growing up, a devotee of *The Boy's Own* and *CHUMS*:

> We were poured down the hatch and into the hold like so much coal. There were no bunks, nothing but steel walls and stanchions. We were packed so tight that there was no room to lie down. I sat on the metal stairs that went up to the hatch for the three days it took to get to Nagasaki. Guards were mounted above and kept constant watch over us. We thought of submarines but worried little. We were a miserable bunch. I thought of my boyhood and the stories I had read of the old slavers that sped through

the night with their cargo of slaves battened down
in filthy and stifling holds. I never thought then that
I should live to experience something very similar.[2]

This trip to Japan was bad, but not as bad as on one of the
decrepit freighters the Japanese later used for POW transports,
roundabout voyages to evade American submarines that could
take weeks to reach the Japanese Home Islands while men were
dying in the holds. Although the prisoners on the *Tatuta Maru*
were packed in like sardines, the ship was a modern ocean liner that
had plied the Yokohama–San Francisco run through the 1930s,
carrying such notables as Albert Einstein and Charlie Chaplin in
luxury across the Pacific. By January 1943, the opulence of peacetime was long gone. As the temperature in the ship's holds rose to
104 degrees Fahrenheit, the stink of hundreds of sweating men
and the stench of vomit and overworked latrines intensified. Still,
Reid counted their blessings: "She was a big luxury liner and this
was one place where we had a stroke of luck. While the men were
in the hold in the ship she went very fast and very straight with
no escort and, from what the Japanese said to me — this was the
first draft after [the sinking of] the *Lisbon [Maru]* — our people
had been notified about this ship because she went hellbent for
election with no zigzagging straight for Japan — just three days
to Nagasaki."[3]

For a brief spell, their luck held. When they disembarked in
Nagasaki on a cold, drizzling January evening, their spirits were
raised by what Signalman William Allister describes as "a story-
book encounter." Instead of the tough, scruffy Japanese soldiers
they were accustomed to in Hong Kong, the Canadians were met
on the wharf by a party of the emperor's Imperial Guards. These
men were taller than typical Japanese, decked out in new uniforms
and smart peaked caps, and commanded by a huge sergeant major

with a red sash and pointed black military moustaches. He asked
for the Canadian officer in command:

> Captain Reid came forward ... the only officer on board.
> He saluted the Japanese officer, who greeted him in ex-
> cellent English. They shook hands. The Japanese stared.
> "Reid? Reid? Can it be true? Don't you remem-
> ber me?"
> Reid gaped in astonishment. "Good God!"
> They had known each other, it turned out, in their
> student days at a Canadian university. They greeted
> each other effusively. A storybook encounter. The by-
> standers, watching joyfully, passed the word along.
> What a break!
> The officer was fairly beaming. "What an odd
> place to meet," he said. "I'm to escort you. Is there
> anything you need? How can I help?" He was
> heaven sent.
> Reid was not slow to answer. "The men are cold
> and hungry. They need food and clothing."
> "I'll look after that." He gave swift orders in
> Japanese.[4]

That night, as the Canadians waited for the train to take them
north, trucks pulled up to the Nagasaki station. Every prisoner
was issued with a thick, warm army greatcoat and five delicious
buns. Allister and his buddies couldn't believe it: "Wondrously
fluffy buns, oval, half a foot long, of pure white flour covered with
a thick sweetened crust, the first sweet thing in ages. We expected
one per man and were startled to get *five*.... Spirits soared. Was this
land enchanted? There were gurgles and giggles and animated talk
as we stuffed our faces with these succulent marvels."[5]

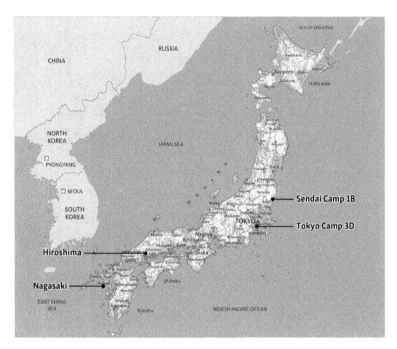

Japan.

Before joining up in 1941, Allister, who grew up in Montreal, had begun his acting career on the local stage and CBC Radio before graduating to zany comedies on the Catskills theatre circuit and advanced drama classes in New York City. Now, warmly dressed, bellies full for the first time in more than a year, he and his pal, Lance Corporal Robert Warren of the Canadian Provost Corps, broke into song under a street light outside the train station, an impromptu concert for the men around them: "I felt transformed as I sang," said Allister, "an instrument giving vent to the collective craving around us. A grand arrival, grand welcome. For one night we were back with the human race."[6]

Reality resumed. Before being herded onto the train, the Canadians were divided into two groups. Along the way, 163 men were to be dropped off for transport to Omine Prison Camp, near Kobe. The rest would continue on to Yokohama. For the Omine Camp detachment, Reid picked out one Rifles section, one Grenadiers section, and a mixed section from Brigade whose NCOs he thought were best able to manage on their own, and wished them luck.

The morning of January 24, 1943, after a 29-hour train ride from Nagasaki and a nine-mile shuttle by electric train, the 500 Canadian POWs under Reid's command arrived at Tsurumi Station, Kawasaki, unloaded, and were marched down a dirt road into Tokyo No. 5 Branch Camp, newly built for these slave labourers in the gritty and barren factory area five miles northwest of Yokohama and a third of a mile as the crow flies from Tokyo Bay. Sergeant Tom Marsh reports:

> All was confusion. The guards gave us no time to
> find our own bags and cuffed us around. At least
> our baggage was put on a couple of trucks, and with
> a Jap officer on horseback in the lead, we marched
> two miles to our new camp. The district was a poor
> one and given over to industry. Everything looked
> dirty and dilapidated. There were bits of rusty ma-
> chinery scattered around and evidently a lot of small
> sheds were used to house machines that did sub-
> contract work for the shipyard nearby. We saw few
> people. Our camp was in a factory yard enclosed on
> one side by a steel works and the other by a refinery.[7]

A squalid, dusty compound measuring 180 by 230 feet, Tokyo Camp No. 5 contained two shoddily constructed, barn-like bunkhouses built of bamboo and plywood to hold 250 men each, a parade square between them, a bathhouse and an area sectioned off for urinals and 24 pit latrines at the south end, and a Japanese headquarters at the north of the camp beside the gate. The bunkhouses had leaky roofs, dirt floors, seven-man platforms covered with 60-by-30-inch tatami straw mats separated by strips of lath for sleeping quarters, and no heating arrangement. Against the cold, the prisoners were issued useless porous blankets made of wood fibre, and for mealtimes a bowl and a cup each, but no eating utensils. Tokyo Camp No. 5 (renamed Tokyo Camp 3D in August 1943) would be home for the next 28 months. The workplace was Nippon Kokan, the biggest shipyard in Japan, located two miles away, a march the men had to make each morning and night. Escape was unthinkable. For Caucasians loose on the Japanese Home Islands, there was nowhere to go.

A bleak prospect. But even so the men could still rise to the occasion. A few hours after they arrived in Tokyo Camp No. 5, Lieutenant Masao Uwamori, the new camp's commandant, ordered the prisoners to muster on the parade ground to hear the ritual Imperial Japanese Army "speech of welcome." It was delivered, says Sergeant Major George MacDonell, by Colonel Kunji Suzuki, officer in charge of all the Tokyo-area POW camps:

> He was a big, fat Japanese in his olive dress uniform,
> polished boots, gold braid, and a great samurai sword
> trailing in its inlaid scabbard at his side. He was an
> imposing figure, oozing authority, as he swaggered
> into camp with his retinue to inspect the guard and
> then to address the assembled prisoners. He climbed
> up on a box placed in the centre of the parade ground
> before us and launched, scowling at us all the while,

into a diatribe in Japanese which his interpreter translated for us. He told us we were prisoners and lucky to be allowed to live. We could be and would be summarily executed for any disobedience to the soldiers of the Emperor. Japan was winning the war on every front and would soon invade our homeland and subject Canada to Japanese rule. After that occurred, and perhaps after twenty years, we may be allowed to go home. We were slaves with no rights, no hope for anything better, and no prospects.[8]

Colonel Suzuki concluded the speech by drawing his sword and slashing the air this way and that to demonstrate the punishment for disobedience. The men were dismissed and returned to the bunkhouses. Within minutes, a wise-cracking Royal Rifle from the Gaspé had the men in stitches as he parodied Suzuki and his

Commandant Masao Uwamori (front row, centre) and Japanese staff, Camp 3D (formerly No. 5), 1943.

interpreter by performing a "rewrite" of the colonel's speech in gibberish Japanese, interspersed with a mangled, French-accented English translation that can only be imagined: "Ho! Japan is losing war! Too bad! Japan make many mistakes! Most shameful behaviour! Apologies for the camp's awful food and terrible accommodations! So sorry for inconvenience!"

Commandant Uwamori and the Japanese guards were mystified by the prisoners' laughter. Later that day, Uwamori summoned Reid to his office for an explanation of the Canadians' behaviour. What was there to laugh at? Were his men insane? Just showing good spirits, Reid assured him, without going into details. Adds Reid: "Then we ... had to sign [a paper saying] that we wouldn't try to escape.... I protested about it ... and I told them when we signed back in our own country we had signed our own allegiance and if we signed this under duress it didn't matter. We would escape if we could. They looked at me as if I was a freak out of a drainage pile."[9]

The predicament Reid found himself in was daunting. The Japanese intent was to extract the most work from the most men with the least amount of food possible. Work quotas were demanded daily and the men, already debilitated by 13 months of captivity and labour in Hong Kong, were now forced to work 12 hours a day, 13 days out of 14 at drudgery of all sorts — from pipe fitting, riveting, and hull painting on high, shaky scaffolding, to lugging cement, welding (without protective goggles), scraping rust off steel plates, and tarring everything from ropes to railway undercarriages. Many sick prisoners were sent out to work, barely able to drag themselves to the shipyard. Those who were slow or complained of illness on the job were often beaten by the guards, who were deaf and blind to the men's obvious weakness and physical impairment.

Aside from the medical kit Reid brought with him from Hong Kong and some rations saved from the voyage to Japan — supplies that were soon exhausted — the only relief he could prescribe for the sick was rest, in other words, exemption from work. Jousting with the Japanese authorities about who was too sick to work, the need for more food, medicines, bandages, boots, and warmer clothes, was a daily exercise in persistence that commenced for Reid on arrival in camp and never ended. From the outset, his daily stock-in-trade was a program of personal persuasiveness and logical negotiation — "probing," he called it. Whoever he was dealing with, Reid's first step was diplomatic: "I always tried to get these Nips to the place where we were fairly friendly — they thought so anyway — and my request would carry some weight and they would do what we wanted them to do. If they didn't like you and you wanted a man off work, it didn't go. If they did and you wanted a man off work, it did, and that's about the size of it."[10]

From the beginning, Reid took every opportunity to exercise his considerable charm and force of character to achieve the ends he was after. During the first month, the Japanese wanted all the prisoners to have their heads shaved. It was February, and Reid said it was too cold for the men to be shorn, and he argued back and forth with the authorities for about a week. In the end, the men were allowed to keep their hair. But through these discussions Reid got on the good side of an army interpreter, an officer with clout, and proposed a bargain to him. Reid said he, the Canadian commanding officer, would shave his own head if the interpreter would get some stoves for the bunkhouses. The interpreter thought this was good fun and agreed. Reid shaved, and the stoves arrived, four for each hut.

In this new setup — a camp of 500 POWs and just one officer, Reid's concern for his men and the relationship he established with them were both appreciated and effective. Early on, before Reid negotiated ways of buying medicines through the Japanese, basic hygiene, rest when possible, and encouraging words were often all he could offer the sick. Twenty-year-old Roger Cyr of the Royal Rifles describes how Reid was soon seen by the men:

> Dr. Reid was a hero to us.... He was a medical practitioner who had no medicines, nothing to work with except his own hands. [He] was an inspiration to us all because he used his personal powers and abilities in dispensation of psychology.... You were sick, and he knew to what extent you were sick ... and he had nothing to make us better with ... nothing other than words ... and you have to appreciate what words mean in this particular context.... An arrogant person would have the tendency to slough you off ... like many other people did.... Captain Reid was an officer and all of the other people in the camp were not [so he] could have stayed aloof ... he could have ... sat back on his officer status, but chose not to do so. He did not establish a difference; he was one of the boys.[11]

Aside from the guards, the first level of the Japanese hierarchy that Reid typically dealt with was the camp's Japanese medical sergeant, a man named Ito, who had to approve any treatment Reid gave his men and okay any men Reid recommended taking off work for medical reasons.

Twice a week, a young Japanese army doctor named Inoue came to the camp to see the "serious" cases, with whom Reid would discuss diagnoses and treatments.

Over these men, the guards, and other camp staff presided Lieutenant Masao Uwamori, Tokyo No. 5's commandant. Semi-conversant in English, educated above the Japanese norm (he had been a stockbroker before the war), and blessed with a degree of humanity out of character for his present position, Uwamori would prove over time to be someone Reid could manipulate and bend to his views and aims. The positive consequences of this influence on Uwamori's thinking would be crucial to the men's survival.

But complicating Reid's job of negotiating for better conditions were the other two tiers of authority: Tokyo's Japanese Army Command, which oversaw Uwamori and his prison camp administration, and Nippon Kokan, the shipbuilding company where the prisoners worked. Often, after he had achieved some understanding with Uwamori and his administration, new orders from army headquarters or from the bosses at Nippon Kokan would interfere with the improved arrangements and take things back to square one so that Reid had to start negotiations once again. This inconsistency in Japanese policies meant Reid never knew what new wrinkle he would be trying to iron out next. But for the men there was no such variety. Each day blended into the next with an unending sameness, starting with the march to the shipyards.

Signalman William Allister, whose artistic eye and sense of humour never seemed to dim, gives this theatrical description:

> Our footwear, often worn-out tennis sneakers with no socks, was pitifully inadequate as we sloshed through icy puddles on the dirt road....
>
> We were issued cotton jackets and pants, our work clothes for the remainder of the war. They must have expected monsters, since all the clothing was so badly oversized we looked like walking tents.... The small men disappeared in a sea of cotton. Marching

135

to work, four abreast, we were a wonderful sight to behold — straggling, bumbling, clumping along as though in time to some dissonant arrhythmic music. Japanese calligraphy — our numbers — adorned us front and back, with numbered ribbons hanging from our hats and waving like banners in the wind. We sailed along, a motley flotilla of gaunt-faced freaks in some tragicomic Oriental festival.[12]

On arrival at Tokyo No. 5, Reid set up two hospitals, one for cases of enteritis (the various gastrointestinal ills), which he located at the lower end of the hut, near the latrines, the other at the upper end of the hut for all other patients. To help with daily hospital care, he selected and trained a group of medical orderlies who became indispensable supports (as he would later write, "No reward is too good for these lads for all the dangers and dirty work that they have done in this war").

Two senior NCOs, Sergeant Major Paddy Keenan of the Grenadiers and Sergeant Major Leslie Shore of the Royal Rifles, accompanied Reid to Japan. Both were British veterans of the First World War, and Shore, a seasoned, reliable, and unflappable non-commissioned officer, became, despite his chronic ill health, a particularly valued support for Reid. Keenan's "theatricality" is what impressed William Allister:

> Paddy Keenan did things in style. He moved in an enchanted aura of untouchable certainty — "I am the very model of a modern major general." When

he strutted down the aisle exuding his special brand
of defiant confidence, the dingy barn with its bare
rafters faded from sight and a broad, immaculately
tended, sun-kissed parade ground unfolded before our eyes. Japan, the guards, the hunger, the
dirt vanished. We stood at attention in our spank-
ing fresh uniforms, rifles correctly sloped, muscles
bulging, bellies full. He was magic; he was home; he
was freedom and derring-do. The present became a
triviality — tough, but only a brief passing phase in
the swashbuckling life of a soldier, and we would
soon be reminiscing about it over a bottle of beer.
Escapist? Completely. But who the hell wanted reality? No actor ever offered a more meaningful daily
performance than our Paddy Keenan.[13]

As a fellow actor, perhaps, Allister appreciated Keenan's performance. Others didn't. The majority of the Canadians saw
Keenan as a pompous, by-the-book NCO who was much too cozy
with their captors.[14]

An unexpected helper in running the camp was Lieutenant
Charles Finn, an American naval communications officer who arrived at Tokyo No. 5 in late January 1943, just after the Canadians.
Finn had been captured after the fall of Corregidor in May 1942,
spent five months as a prisoner in the Philippines, then was summoned for questioning at Japanese headquarters in Manila because
of his communications expertise. In mid-January 1943, he was sent
to Tokyo. His story, says Reid, shines an interesting sidelight on
Japanese incompetence:

[Finn] was at a work camp in the Philippines and was
called in from that camp around October 1942 and

questioned. They were after ciphers and codes and that sort of thing. They kept him around Manila until January and in January he and an Army communications officer were told they were going to Japan for more intensive questioning. They had been questioned by a Col. several times in the Philippines.... The two of them came up on a Japanese ship.... It was a rush business to examine them in Japan on this same communication problem. He came into our camp about a week after we did and they split the two of them up as soon as they got to Tokyo and sent the Army man to another camp. [Finn] stayed in the camp from the end of January [1943] to October 1943 until finally somebody came into camp to question him. They came in and they asked him — they said, "Do you know anything about army codes and ciphers?" [Finn] said, "no, he was Navy." They were disappointed and went away and never questioned him again. That's an example of what they do — take this bird up, see him and forget all about it for a period of nine months, and then question him once very superficially and then that's all.[15]

Ten years older than Reid and an experienced officer from San Jose, California, Finn began alternating with Shore and Keenan as orderly officer and sharing Reid's sleeping quarters, welcome company for Reid, who as commanding officer had been billeted on his own. Reid describes Finn as an unobtrusive, solemn fellow who at first didn't get on too well with the men ("a dour, humourless, pudgy-faced type with hanging bloodhound jowls, black bushy eyebrows, and an impressive officer's cap, which he must have worn to bed, since it was never removed,"[16] was William Allister's early impression of him). But, quiet waters running deep, Lieutenant Finn was an officer the Canadians eventually came to like and appreciate very much. He remained with them until the end of the war.

Reid's routine, like everyone's, started with reveille at 6:00 a.m., *tenko* — roll call — at 6:10, breakfast (a half-ration of rice, a few spoonfuls of beans, watery miso soup) at 6:30, then sick parade until seven, typically 30 to 40 cases per morning, when he would decide, based on the work quota, who, for medical reasons, he thought should stay in camp and who, despite illness, had to go to work. This led to the daily argument — typically an hour or so — with Sergeant Ito and the Japanese medical orderlies about his choices. Once the work party was chosen and marched out of camp, further arguments about the special fatigues the Japanese wanted to assign to the men who remained in camp came next.

Later in the morning and in the afternoon, Reid did camp hospital rounds, somewhere fitting in the two hours of personal labour (medical work didn't count) that he needed to perform in order to receive his daily food ration (he sawed firewood). Pacing the compound and tossing a 12-pound medicine ball with one of the medical orderlies was his physical exercise. An hour's afternoon reading of the medical books he brought with him was his intellectual distraction. When a thought struck him and he could snatch the time, he wrote poems in a small notebook he always carried.

In the later afternoon, Reid took sick parade of those ill in camp and then an evening sick parade for those in the returning work party who required attention, typically 40 to 50 men.

Evenings before lights out at 8:30, he devoted to the practical minutiae of running the camp and the administrative and disciplinary concerns of managing 500 men in these extremely trying circumstances — everything from pooling enough footgear for the next day's work party to dealing with misdemeanours or disputes among prisoners brought forward by their section leaders (for organizational purposes, the camp was divided into 10 sections of 50 men, each with a section leader assigned by Reid).

In the early months in Japan, Reid found that filling the combined role of officer commanding and medical officer complicated his exercise of discipline: "It is very difficult to argue with oneself,"[17] he noted in his diary in March 1943. The approach he developed was a mixture of reason, persuasion, and example:

> Actually, I had no means to discipline [the men], so it came down to doing what I wanted them to do because I wanted it, which built up a very fine relationship.... There's no doubt about it if you are in a place like that the medical officer is the best to have....[18] There were various individuals getting into difficulty and they would be sent up [by their section leaders] to be talked to and straightened out and got on the primrose path again. That had to be done without any [actual] discipline. [The aim was to] to cure them, and leave the section leaders instructed and satisfied with what you had done....[19] My idea at all times [was] to influence the man's future course of action, rather than exert an eye-for-eye principle and I [was] getting unusually good results with some rather eccentric methods....[20] The whole idea was to prevent things from happening.[21]

Malingering by a few individuals was an inevitable consequence of the prison camp circumstances, and in such cases Reid fought every step of the way to meet the work quotas fairly and assert his control within the camp:

> All through this time in Japan you had a little difficulty with a few men realizing if they put on a show for the Japanese the latter appeared to be very sympathetic in the individual case. If a man put on a show for the Japanese, they said, "He must stay in, he can't go to work today." You knew these few men were much better off than a number of others, and those others felt, "Why should I go to work?" When that happened I had quite a struggle with the Japanese, usually. If I said a man has to go to work, he went, otherwise the whole disciplinary system fell apart.[22]

As in every large group, there were a few tough nuts ready to break rules for their own benefit. Tokyo No. 5's assortment consisted of nine such characters — always the likely suspects if belongings disappeared. When this happened, Reid sometimes took a different approach, as Sergeant Tom Marsh relates:

> My friend Allister lost his sweater. Obviously it was stolen. Now a sweater was essential to offset the cold winter. It could not be replaced and meant that the loser would suffer real hardship.
>
> Allister reported his loss to Captain Reid. All Captain Reid had to do was call the nine men of our underworld before him and say, "I know one of you has the sweater. If the one who has it does not return it to Allister before morning, I will turn

the whole nine of you over to the Japs and let them locate the culprit."[23]

By morning, Allister had his sweater back.

Key to Reid's leadership was his choice to be open with the men through the conferences he held regularly with the section leaders and at times with the camp as a whole: "I used to tell the men a great deal of what was going on. They realized what you were trying to do and appreciated the situation.... I told them what I was going to do and also why I was going to do it."[24]

A crucial part of Reid's message to the men as time went on was hope. Sergeant Major George MacDonell, who at 14 years old had coped with the loss of his parents, and three years later, eager to serve his country, had lied about his age to join the army when war was declared, both embodied and admired that optimism:

> Captain Reid always made it clear that we would win this war, that it was just a matter of time, we would succeed, no question about it.... He never, never for a moment, left any doubt. He knew that if [the sicker soldiers] thought he believed we were going to lose this war, they would have died in 24 hours. [They would have thought:] "Why try to stay alive, why put up with this if we're going to lose anyway?" Captain Reid said, "Put up with it. We aren't going to lose. It's just a matter of time. These people will never defeat us...."[25] He told Uwamori that! He told Uwamori, "You cannot win this war."[26]

With several years' experience serving under Canadian Army officers, MacDonell was struck early on in Japan by Reid's ability, with only five weeks of military training and no line (combat) officer training, to assume command and win the respect not only of the men under his care but eventually that of the Japanese. Reid had the calm, self-contained personality of a natural leader, says MacDonell, but also attributed the captain's authority on both

Sergeant Major George MacDonell, Royal Rifles, Camp 3D prisoner photo, 1943. The Japanese took "mug shots" of all prisoners upon arrival in camp.

143

sides of the wire to his strength of character: absolute honesty; absolute fairness in dealing with the men; relentlessness in his efforts to protect them, medically and otherwise; a toughness that under years of pressure never cracked; and the courage to stand up to the Japanese until, in MacDonell's view, Reid was a god not only to his own men, but to the Japanese:

> When an officer is placed in that situation, he can try to be a nice guy. He can pacify these maniacs. He can concede. But Reid didn't do that. He didn't lose his dignity when he talked to them. They admired courage above all else and he wouldn't kowtow to them. He wouldn't flinch. To the Japanese military that was very important. If he had kowtowed to them, that camp would have become a disaster. At least another hundred allied prisoners would have died. And that dignity filtered down to the men. They all walked a little straighter. All that time in the camp, all those Canadians, not a single word was said against him. In fact, if you'd said anything against him — duck! — because something would've happened to you before sundown.[27]

Reid also had the passe-partout, says MacDonell, that has worked with soldiers throughout history — a sense of humour:

> He was not a serious, down-in-the-dumps guy. He was always joking with the people in the hospital. Always understating — "This isn't so bad! We're only temporary guests here!" — always looking for a joke with the troops, never telling us that we were dying of starvation and malnutrition. None of that.

Just the opposite. He was always upbeat and with everything he always saw the funny side. Now, if you want to get along with soldiers, that's the best technique imaginable — to be joking with them, not whining. You never heard him say one thing about how bad it was. It was always, "We're going to get out of here, this isn't the end of the world." Never for a moment letting his real understanding of the situation get through to the troops.[28]

But on occasion, Reid says, he had to be tough:

[Sometimes] the odd man in the long line squatting or lying outside the Medical Inspection Room door broke down in front of you with the words, "Sir, I can't stand it anymore." One rapidly and realistically developed a brutal answer to this, which was to silently point to the perimeter fence and then say simply, "And what are you going to do about it?" Slowly the men would turn. For a little while they would study the fence. Usually, after gazing across the dusty camp square to the barbed wire and armed guards, the tension melted, the shoulders straightened, the glaze left their eyes, and they mumbled, sometimes with a grin, that they supposed they could stand it after all. A few couldn't or wouldn't, and turning their faces to the wall rapidly succumbed. However, almost all, from that [conversation] on, spoke no more of "not standing anything."[29]

A constant nagging issue for the men during the year of imprisonment in Sham Shui Po had been the division of rations, the fear that some men, through working in the kitchen or having a friend who did, might somehow get more than the others (a deeper ladling in the soup pot where the "vegetables" lay, a tighter packing of rice in the bowl). At Tokyo No. 5, a new variable exacerbating these worries was that each day's quantity of rice and soup was affected by the number of sick who were off work: those who couldn't work were assigned only one-half, sometimes one-third rations, a practice, Reid pointed out to the Japanese, that would hinder their recovery and therefore their ability to return to work. But stuck with the rule, the mess system Reid devised as the most fair and reassuring to the men — a system he oversaw himself to ensure compliance — was that all food was pooled at every meal and each man, whether working or off sick, received the same amount, with servings measured out for all to see. This was a stand Reid maintained consistently against direct Japanese orders to put sick men who weren't working on reduced rations: "I would argue how foolish it was.... Then I would say, you have given us the order and if we disobey, please don't look too closely.... [To let the Japanese save face] I promised to feed the sick men the reduced ration, and then of course we didn't do so.... The rice was issued from the kitchen under my supervision and I was always sure it was ... equal."[30]

Reid came to see the Japanese disregard for individual life, their readiness to consign sick men to the rubbish heap, simply as part of their culture of the time, an understanding he took into account in his dealings with them: "They didn't worry too much about men. The cheapest thing they have in their country is manpower. If they have a machine and a man and one has to go, it's the man. With us it's the machine."[31]

A strategy that Reid evolved to increase the food supply was to sell the Japanese on the logic of granting more rations to prisoners doing less work than normal, but enough work to warrant more food than if they were off sick completely. He also instituted "slow walking groups" made up of prisoners who would march to Nippon Kokan at their own slower pace, and once there, do sit-down jobs like sorting nuts and bolts. Variations of this were prisoners who went to work every other day, or every three days, resting up in between. In camp, Reid convened what he called the "anvil chorus," beriberi patients who sat outside on good days and straightened Nippon Kokan welding rods with hammers — hammering away for 10 minutes, then resting for five. All of this limited activity counted as work and brought in more food without doing harm to the sick men involved.

Yet the food battle was constant. Reid's efforts, after rations were further restricted in late winter 1943, causing a sharp downhill course for the men doing heavy labour as well as the patients with severe beriberi, illustrate some of the difficulties he faced whenever he was putting his case to the Japanese:

> I strongly protested this [ration] change to the camp authorities, which involves hours of work because we do not have adequate interpreters here and complex ideas are exchanged only with the greatest difficulty. No change was made. Yesterday I made my last complaint to Dr. Inoue, the Japanese M.O., our conversation being a combination of sign language, Japanese words, English words, and German words.... He at once agreed with me in total and went off in high dudgeon to change this ration, but returned with the information that it was an official order from Tokyo Headquarters and he was powerless to cause any change....
>
> Beriberi under these conditions does not improve with any celerity so it appears our beriberi will grow and our rations diminish and this will

establish a vicious circle. I fear it will be necessary to keep the men [with serious illnesses] working as long as possible in order to keep rations up, for if everyone stayed in camp on one-third rations, the result would be starvation.[32]

This was the balancing act Reid performed as commanding officer and medical officer, day in, day out, for almost three years: weighing all the factors, constantly pushing the Japanese authorities, and each day making his choices and imposing his orders concerning who must work and who would remain in camp or hospital. As a matter of record in case of his own death, he explains his overall approach in his medical diary soon after coming to Tokyo No. 5:

The policy I've always held as the final criterion ... is to consider the main factor is not illness nor even disability that may be more or less permanent but to consider as the main factor the danger to life in the reasonably near future.... Thus my endeavour here is to take back as many men as possible to Canada, whether well or ill, and not to concentrate on complete health. I would rather return five hundred men in various stages of beriberi, which perhaps in future can be cured, rather than to return three hundred men in good health and leave two hundred dead behind.

Such it seems to me has been the Anglo-Saxon philosophy, and it is mine here since I must make the decisions and, I may add, that many decisions have had to be taken by myself ... of an arbitrary nature and which, in the mass, determined life and death for the individuals. This playing of God has

been one of the most arduous labours imposed…. It
is not an enviable position to occupy, and one must
sympathize with a God who makes such decisions
his life work.[33]

The first four Canadian deaths in Japan occurred within a
month of arrival at Tokyo No. 5. The swift-killing maladies —
complications of severe beriberi, acute hepatitis, malnutrition,
pneumonia — show that these early victims and many of the other
men were in no condition to be selected for Japanese labour camps
in the first place. Now another duty, that of chaplain at his men's
funerals, fell to Reid, a role he would fulfill 23 times before the
end of the war. A Buddhist ceremony, by insistence of the Japanese,
always came first:

> When a man died he was placed for a day in a rough
> coffin festooned with presents of sweet biscuits for
> the spirits he was to meet. That night, as the men
> were marched in from work, they were drawn up in
> solemn ranks on the little parade square in the windy
> dark. At the head, on a trestle, rested the body of
> their erstwhile comrade, and then a long, strange
> service was said over it by a Buddhist priest in the
> ghostly light of two lighted candles, interspersed
> with the intermittent striking of a small bronze bell.
> The sense of eerie loneliness and sadness of those all
> too frequent moments I shall never forget.
>
> But the men were restless that they should be
> conducted through death in such a manner and I
> obtained permission to read a short service follow-
> ing the Buddhist performance…. I did it because
> the men were in low spirits, one of their buddies had

died, and to come out and stand in the parade square beside him, cold, sick and hungry, with a Buddhist ceremony going on, flickering lights and tinkling bells and so on — gave them a sort of horror.

I found a few lines, towards the end of the Bible, that surely never have been used for such a purpose before or since, but which seemed appropriate to me. It took me away from that place to stand at the head of my column of men and speak these words in the gusty black of the night. My ceremony wasn't a Christian burial. But to have somebody stand over the body and read a short service. It made the men feel better.

The next morning, four men would be excused from the work party to trot the body on a handcart out of the camp to a far-off hillside where it was cremated. The little boxes of ashes were then shipped to Japanese Headquarters to await the war's end.[34]

By late winter 1943, Reid had persuaded Commandant Uwamori to allow severely ill patients to be taken to outside hospitals for treatment — a Japanese military hospital in Tokyo to begin with, later on to nearby Shinagawa Hospital, an old work camp converted to take POW cases, where Reid sometimes went to consult with the Allied and Japanese doctors. At Shinagawa, certain minor operations could be performed and the prisoners received some level of medication, and occasionally, more food. Shinagawa was "a rubbish heap, more or less," says Reid, but at least it had the basics. His in-camp medical facilities soon lacked even bandages: "How the medical orderlies kept producing something to wrap around a wound was something of a miracle. The men would pick up some cloth from the company and smuggle it in. Every night some man would come in with something picked up outside, cloth or tape or something like that. We lived on that for the rest of the time. They completely stopped by the summer of 1943 any supply of bandage."[35]

Obtaining medicines for in-camp use required another strategy. In 1942, at Reid's suggestion, the officers at Sham Shui Po had pooled their money to buy drugs "through the wire." At Tokyo No. 5, he managed a variation on the theme. Using his own accumulated officer's stipend, Reid persuaded Sergeant Ito and Dr. Inoue to begin buying Atabrine, sulpha drugs, bismuth tablets, and Aspirin at local drugstores for use in the camp hospitals. This trickle of medicine was a godsend. Having established his sources in the spring of 1943, Reid was disconcerted a month later when it was announced that the Japanese medical staff at the camp was being changed. Having nurtured a useful working and trade relationship with his Japanese counterparts, he worried about having to re-establish this groundwork. Instead, the medical staff change worked in his favour:

A new Japanese doctor came to the camp now, Dr. Iino, a 2nd Lieutenant, a pre-war physiologist. He was an older and better informed individual than his predecessor. You might say that — this fellow — I gained his confidence and he really established a precedent of letting me run [things]. Previous to this we had to take all these patients over to the Japanese every day. Now we were beginning to get away from that — to see them in our hospital and take the results to the Japanese for their approval.

With this fellow we began to get more and more on our own. I simply took the men off work and he okayed them, a very simple process. Because of this doctor I got much forwarder in gaining the confidence of the Camp Commandant, which stood us in good stead when it got to the stage of the Japanese doctors coming in and trying to get all the sick men to work. Uwamori would wait until they went away and then say, "Do what you want."[36]

Reid did. By the spring of 1943, he was keeping up to 160 prisoners back from work, two-thirds of them with the excuse of severe beriberi. As well, submitting to Reid's persuasive charm, Dr. Iino, Corporal Hachiichiro Koyanagi (a very helpful camp interpreter), and several of the new Japanese medical orderlies were now buying drugs for him from drugstores in the district or on the black market. Occasionally, Reid would be taken out of camp so that he could make the choices himself. But in the summer of 1943, control of Tokyo Camp No. 5 was shifted from the Imperial Japanese Army to the company administrators at Nippon Kokan, causing a name change to Tokyo Camp 3D (D for *dispatched* from army control). This changeover prompted an entry in Reid's medical diary that indicates the success he was having in winning over the Japanese to his purposes:

> I must make special mention here of Dr. Iino.... He has not only been helpful, but has never interfered with my assessment of sickness, and further has been a good personal friend whose conversation, books, flowers and general tolerance and education do honour to our profession and make a bright spot in my routine here. While we are handing out bouquets, one must go to Lieutenant Uwamori, the Camp Commandant, a sportsman and a gentleman whose regime has been understanding indeed.[37]

At this stage, Uwamori's co-operation became more important than ever. In June 1943, the Japanese authorities instituted a "food conservation" program that would see the prisoners' rations progressively reduced over the next six months. Reid learned from an interpreter that the intention of headquarters was to keep cutting the food supply until they found the least amount the prisoners could live on and still work:

> The first ration cut was in July and in August another and September another and the [men's] weight went down, down, down.... All this time I was protesting and warning [the Japanese] what the next winter would be [like]....[38] It is not the degree of cold that is so serious as the unbroken continuance of the state in unwell men who at no time day after day, week and after week, are warmed through....[39]
>
> During this fall was the time of lowest morale. [The men] were hungry and winter was coming on and they were pretty ill and physically exhausted....[40] I mean this literally. Not the physical exhaustion of home, but that of those days in which a man was unable to stand any longer....[41] I went to the Japanese day after day after day after day, all during the summer and fall, trying to do something about these rations. And the Commandant would go down to headquarters and try to do what he could down there, but we never got to first base until after six months had gone and the men had lost a tremendous amount of weight and the winter was upon us.[42]

Collectively, the camp lost 3,000 pounds in August 1943 and another 1,000 pounds in September, an average of seven pounds per man for men already a quarter to a third below their normal weight. Repeated conferences with the Japanese from headquarters had no concrete effect, and Reid had to gauge carefully how far to push them.

> You got to the stage that if you pushed any harder they were going to put you out of the camp and bring in another doctor. I felt I could look after these men better than some American or British doctor. I pushed as far as I dared, but not to the point where they would take me out and put another in. The Japanese doctors continually tried to send sick men out to work, but the Commandant continued to back my judgment and let me keep in [camp] anyone I pleased.[43]

A measure of Reid's success in keeping sick men back is that the outside Japanese authorities repeatedly complained to Commandant Uwamori that Tokyo 3D's sick rate was consistently much higher than other prison camps. But in December 1943, with the Nippon Kokan company officials and its doctors once again pushing Reid very hard to increase the size of the work party, things came to a head:

> At one point it got so serious the Commandant began to waver in his policy.... One night we finally came to the situation that I felt I could not let go of the thing even although they moved me out of the camp, it was better. So I more or less handed in my resignation to the Commandant [and said] if I couldn't follow my own opinions, that I would take no more responsibility and would do

no more work, and that tossed the thing right back at them. [Commandant Uwamori] thought it over for twenty-four hours and then said, "Okay, you go back." That was the closest we ever came to him backing up the Japanese doctors instead of me.[44]

What Reid couldn't deflect, at least directly, were medical orders that came from Tokyo Area Army Headquarters. In November 1943, a month before the showdown with Commandant Uwamori, an edict was issued by Army Command that all POW cases of beriberi, gastritis, enteritis, neuralgia, arthritis, and rheumatism were to receive moxibustion treatment. This was an ancient Eastern cure-all based on the theory of counter-irritation in which multiple nubs of dried mugwort plant (moxa), or other slow-burning material such as punk or pieces of frayed rope, were placed on a patient's skin above various nerve centres, set alight, and allowed to smoulder down to the skin, a process sometimes repeated over a number of days. Believed to stimulate blood supply below the burn-irritated areas and promote the healing of deeper internal maladies, moxibustion was, as far as the Canadian POWs were concerned, a medically useless form of minor torture, but one most Japanese of the day had received multiple times in their lives as a matter of course — with the scars to prove it.

Proposed as a remedy for the Canadians' ills when they first arrived in camp in January 1943, Reid (as with the men's head shaving) had been able to argue the Japanese out of moxibustion for his men. Aside from the pain, Reid was worried about secondary infections from the burns. This time, Reid was told that if the POWs didn't submit to treatment the whole camp would be punished, which typically meant the men being forced to stand at attention on the frigid parade square for hours on end, even overnight. Fortunately, Reid's apparent acquiescence, some clever on-the-spot dissembling by the men chosen to receive the treatment, and some leniency won by Reid from the Japanese medical staff in charge of applying the moxibustion combined to limit the number of Canadians who underwent serious courses of the procedure:

> This [moxibustion] was done in the Japanese medical offices and our orderlies used to go over there every time and take the men over who were supposed to have the moxibustion treatment. They would get the whole bunch in the room and by our boys [orderlies] going over there [to help] and by the ingenuity of the men themselves, the Japanese [authorities] were happy that it was [seemingly] being done. But of course not one percent of what was supposed to be done was actually done.... The Japanese did want a lot of these cases who were working to take this treatment, but I managed to argue them out of that. As long as they were working there was no treatment.[45]

A few, like Sergeant Lance Ross, weren't so lucky:

> One time they took four or five of us, stripped us completely of our clothes and made us lie flat on our backs with arms and legs out. They came along with this cotton rope and set them on their ends, at, I think, about six points. I had one on each side of my chest, one on each hip, on the side of my stomach,

one on each wrist, one on each ankle, and one on
the centre of my forehead. Before they put them on
they would light them with a match, and you know
how slow cotton burns. They put them on a nerve
centre. And they would let them burn right down
to nothing.

My God, it was awful the pain with it, when the
fire came close to your skin. If you showed any tendency of moving they would holler at you and raise
the rifle butts, and you had to stay there until all the
rope burned away, and then they would let you up. I
had open ulcers and sores for months after.[46]

Christmas 1943 brought a bit of cheer. The men were able to deco-
rate the bunkhouses, put on a holiday show of songs and skits, and
with Staff Sergeant Charles Clark of the Canadian Postal Corps
playing Santa Claus (silly clothes, painted nose and cheeks, an old
red sock on his head), to share the contents of some rare Red Cross
parcels among themselves and a new group of American prisoners
who arrived in camp in pretty bad shape — all this a lift to the
spirits and a testament to the men's resilience.

Music, another balm for the soul, had also found its way to
3D. In May 1943, a shipment of Red Cross food and some YMCA
paraphernalia — checkers and chess sets, baseball mitts, a Ping-
Pong net and bats, carpenter's tools — came into camp. On the
musical side, the YMCA had included a ukulele, several mandolins, three harmonicas, and a second-hand phonograph with records, but no needles. The sports equipment and tools were kept

by the Japanese and given out at their discretion. But the games, instruments, and record player were put under Reid's control. He assigned the ukulele and mandolins to two men who played them well. The games, harmonicas, and record player — once he had scrounged some needles and rigged up the machine with pieces of elastic band and other odd bits to get it in working order — were farmed out in the evenings to different sections, with Japanese say-so. In October 1943, while on an escorted foray outside the fence to buy medicines, Reid found some old recordings of classical music in a local shop, which he began listening to for a soothing hour when his day permitted. William Allister describes the cold night when Reid played Beethoven's Fifth Symphony in the camp's mock concert hall — the cold, empty, currently unused camp bathhouse:

> We brought tiny footstools to sit on, hard on the bony backsides but better than the cement floor. A couple of dozen prisoners converged quietly like a gathering of scarecrows at a witches' sabbath.... What a crew we were. Gray skin marked with dried-up pus sores, pores clogged with dirt, bodies humped forward, bony knees high and sharp, faces gaunt, eyes curious, burning, eager, uneasy. Some had never heard classical music but had come along for the ride. It was certainly the strangest audience Beethoven had ever been played to and the most humbly attentive.
>
> The music began, not softly, not gradually, but loudly, defiantly — a challenge to the gods, the fates. Beethoven linking hands with this little band of lost souls, united in a symphony of survival.... One voice — his, ours, mine — from our deepest

core, sending all our anger charging to the surface: *tn-tn-tn-TOMMM! tn-tn-tn-TOMMM!* Shouting, "I-will-not-DIE! I-will-not-DIE!"

We joined in his leonine roar: "I-will-not-DIE! — I-will-not-DIE! — I-will-not-DIE....!"

I listened, gazing about me at the grimy, flimsy walls, blasted out of sight by the music.[47]

Yet, in the winter of 1944, many would die.

1944: Coping, Communicating, and the Candle Conspiracy

The winter of 1944 was their worst time in prison camp. The cold and wet of the Japanese winter was continuous, and there was no practical alleviation. For six weeks, the coal supply for the stoves was suspended. The bathhouse remained unused for the same reason. Cooking with the fuel supplied — immature peat moss composed mostly of mud — was practically impossible; the interior of the bunkhouses had to be scavenged for scraps of wood to cook with. The men's thin clothes, once wet, never really dried.

Suffering from unrelenting cold, hunger, and the effects of beriberi, tuberculosis, infectious hepatitis, fevers, chronic diarrhea, and countless skin lesions, many of the men now came down with a new, often merciless killer: pneumonia, sometimes compounded by pleurisy. In the four months between December 1943 and April 1944, 14 of Reid's men died, 11 of lung disease. Without sufficient medication, and given the men's frail state, there was almost nothing he could do to stem the tide of infection. On top of this, the camp was hit with an influenza epidemic. Commandant Uwamori, who was personally canvassing local stores to obtain sulpha drugs and disinfectants for Reid's use, issued hundreds of blankets and gave Reid carte blanche to deal with the outbreaks in his own way. Reid's diary entry for March 21, 1944, reads:

> I have now been given a complete free hand in this camp to fight the [influenza] epidemic. I have enlarged the hospital. We have had fires in the stoves for the last two nights when it was cold and wet, which helped considerably, and we have now constant fires in the two enclosed hospital areas in the past week. The epidemic has produced an atypical and interesting picture which I hope to analyse in the future, but not now, as I am rather tired through this period.
>
> Today, Staff Sergeant Ellis's funeral service was held. There was no Buddhist priest. We had our own service with last post and reveille.
>
> This morning is a beautiful early spring morning with blue sky, fluffy clouds and sunshine. One has lived now so long with these boys that their deaths are very trying and haunting.[1]

As a doctor, Reid's frustration must have been great, knowing that every death could have been prevented by proper food and drugs. A hint of the emotional toll the mounting losses were costing him showed up in his medical diary in April 1944 after the death of another section leader.

To replace Staff Sergeant Ellis as leader of number seven section, Reid chose Sergeant James "Jimmy" Emo of the Canadian Provost Corps, a man, like his predecessor, universally well liked.

Although Emo was over six feet tall, powerfully built, and an expert in jujitsu, wrestling, and boxing, it was his grand personality — "Irish personality galore,"[2] according to Sergeant Léo Bérard of the Grenadiers — that kept the men in line. Lance Corporal "Blacky" Verreault agreed: "I never met a more conscientious, straight man and with so many incomparable qualities as Jim Emo had. His kindness was written all over his frank and jovial face."[3]

Reid had likewise been impressed. When recording Emo's appointment as section leader — recommending at the same time that Emo be considered promoted to company sergeant major as of his appointment date — Reid noted in his diary that throughout their entire incarceration, Emo had been "reliable and intelligent and a good leader."[4]

Four weeks after his appointment as section leader, Jimmy Emo, who by the end had lost more than 90 pounds since his capture, was dead from pneumonia and cardiac failure. He was Reid's 20th death in Japan: "This man actually died before the official death, but pulled out of that, and every fifteen minutes had some kind of treatment for three [more] days. I stayed with him all that time. I liked him very much. All we succeeded in doing was getting three days more pay for his wife. That really got me. I was really fed up with things at that time."[5]

"He had to make these decisions, and make'em and make'em and make'em and it was so hard," says Sergeant Robert "Flash" Clayton. "He didn't have anything to help anybody with, and I can remember when Jimmy Emo died, I can remember [Reid] crying. And when Murray Goodenough died he was eighteen years old. He won the MM [Military Medal] in Hong Kong when he was sixteen. He died in December of 'forty-three [of catarrh pneumonia] and [Reid] just cried and cried and cried. What can you do?"[6]

If Reid, as doctor-commander, felt he shouldered responsibility for every death at 3D, it was his men who suffered its gross indignities, a nightmare experienced in all Japanese prison camps where coffins for prisoners were often hideously inadequate. William Allister recounts the night after Emo died:

> Bob [Lance Corporal Robert Warren] told me how he had put Jimmy Emo into the coffin. He was on duty that night, with the huts deep in sleep. He and Paddy Keenan tried to lay Jimmy in the coffin, but it was fully a foot too short. They doubled the legs up at the knees and shoved hard, but the head rose like a live thing as they pressed. Bob had been very fond of Jimmy, recalling the little things: in the tropical heat and thirst of the *Awatea*, for instance, when we were allotted one glass of beer per man, Bob had stood outside the sergeants' mess while Jimmy, typically, passed glass after glass out to his men through the window. No one else did. Now as he lay folded grotesquely in the fetal position, the horror of handling his dead body was too much. The head must be forced down to close the lid. Paddy balked. Bob had to seize the skull and press it with all his strength till the neck seemed to snap and the limp head went down. It was like killing, making him die twice. They closed the lid, but the trauma was never closed down.[7]

All those who survived Japanese POW camps would, one way or another, be physically and mentally scarred for the rest of their lives. Yet what struck Reid during their years of imprisonment was his men's stoicism in the presence of death. Among old army sayings was the maxim that "there are no atheists in foxholes" — everyone gets religion when death stalks close. That wasn't Reid's experience: "Whatever convictions a man may have had, he didn't change them when he was going to die and didn't speak about them when he was going to die. Nobody suddenly became a Christian that had not been a Christian, and nobody was particularly interested in any religion at the end. They just went out without any comments."[8]

Disease and chronic debilitation were Reid's constant medical foes, but serious injury due to beatings by Japanese guards and NCOs was a daily threat to all prisoners of the Japanese, no less at Camp 3D. In trying to curb it, Reid saw the Japanese impulse to inflict physical punishment as their "normal," not only for the military but for the Japanese culture at large: "In the Japanese Army every rank beats every rank below. That's their form of discipline — minor discipline. They beat each other and give each other terrifically terrible beatings. It's a common thing to get [offenders] down and beat them with sticks.... Starting at the Emperor they beat everybody down below them. The last man beats the pig, I guess."[9]

In the case of peasant guards reacting to prisoners seen to be stepping out of line, says Reid, the phenomenon was accentuated: "The Japanese are like a nine- or ten-year-old child to whom you give adult physical strength and adult problems to handle and give him nobody to say, 'Nay.' They had the emotional instability of a child, the lack of perseverance of a child.... They get in a rage when they were obstructed."[10]

At first, Reid's only possible response to prisoner beatings was to protest to Commandant Uwamori. But as their relationship developed and Uwamori's respect and admiration for the Canadian commander grew, Reid appealed more and more to Uwamori's humanitarian side, trying to evoke in him what was the honourable course to take. Uwamori gradually came around, beginning with the transfer out of camp of two of the most moronic and brutal veteran army guards, known to the Canadians only as "Horse Face" and "Moose Face," whose violence often got out of hand. In one instance, Reid risked a beating of his own, or worse, by stepping in when two prisoners were being beaten and kicked, elbowing the berserk guards aside, and carrying the most severely injured soldier to the camp hospital.

Such sadistic behaviour wasn't always something Uwamori could control. In the summer of 1943, three Canadian prisoners were caught trading for cigarettes with Japanese workers at Nippon Kokan, a serious offence since they bartered with Japanese Army clothing — a pair of army boots in particular — that the Japanese workers were later caught trying to sell for high prices on the black market. Trading Imperial Japanese Army property was a criminal offence. Police from outside the camp controlled by the dreaded Kenpeitai, the Japanese version of the German Gestapo, now got involved, and the Canadians who had been caught were badly beaten over several days to make them confess — a situation, Uwamori told Reid, he had to go along with or be replaced as camp commandant for being too soft on prisoners who broke Japanese Army law.

But things improved. By the end of 1943, Reid's protests and appeals to an increasingly compliant Uwamori, who in turn was restricting his staff's unwarranted actions, had succeeded in largely curtailing the random incidents of violence against the prisoners. A serious occurrence in April 1944 gave Reid the leverage to bring beatings to an end, at least in camp.

The infraction was minor. Private Alexander Baraskiwich of the Grenadiers had turned in a torn piece of Japanese Army–issue underwear, worn for more than a year, which he had failed to repair. Three of the camp staff — Corporal Toshitsugo Yamanaka, the chief of the guards, and two vicious privates named Teruo Shebota and Kensako Baba — flew into a communal rage while questioning Baraskiwich in the guardroom, knocked him through a window, punched and kicked him into unconsciousness when he fell down, then began hitting him with a piece of wooden two-by-four. Reid arrived on the scene as the beating was being halted by Sergeant Masuzo Masuda, Uwamori's second-in-command, with the help of the interpreter Hachiichiro Koyanagi, and several prisoners who risked beatings themselves by stepping in. Reid removed Baraskiwich to the camp hospital, stitched his wounds, and kept him off work.

The next day, Reid took advantage of the incident: "I sent a very stiff letter to the camp commandant stating that this form of punishment was simple sadism resulting from uncontrolled rage and requesting the removal of authority for punishment from all camp staff until cases had been referred to him personally."[11]

Reid's intent was to foil the random, reflexive brutality of the guards by enforcing a cool-down period. If guard staff had to ask permission from Uwamori to inflict physical punishment on a prisoner, Reid was confident that Uwamori, a man who found violence repugnant, would refuse the request.

After receiving Reid's letter, Uwamori reacted as hoped. He severely reprimanded the Japanese staff involved in beating Private Baraskiwich and instituted the order that no punishment was to take place in future without his assent. Beatings inside 3D stopped for good.

By 1944, Reid and his men were into their third year of imprisonment. Sergeant Major George MacDonell writes:

> To keep from going mad, I tried to escape the misery of the present, I tried to free my mind from my starving, often lice-covered body by letting it soar back across the blue Pacific to Canada. I fantasized about the warm, well-fed, carefree, sunlit lives I wanted to imagine was the nature of life in Canada, my faraway home. I tried to reconstruct in my mind what my earlier childhood life might have been. I remembered, and relived again and again, the few happy times I had as a child with my mother before we were separated by her illness. Somehow, the paralytic minutes and hours ticked by and another day of captivity was over and, at dawn, another day began. And, as it will, each day passed yet again into another day.[12]

This drab sameness, while living in a vacuum concerning the progress of the war, made keeping up spirits a relentless struggle. Relief was hard to come by. Doctoring the food, says Reid, was one small way to fight the monotony:

> It is impossible to explain to anybody what it is like to eat rice three times a day for three and a half years or so…. The men were extremely ingenious in changing the flavour in that they added anything that could be eaten and some things that we would regard as inedible to put on their rice. One of the favourites was the Japanese-issue tooth powder. One time the Japanese gave us a tub of grease for shoes and that was put on

the rice. Later on we did get some condiments to put
on the rice — pretty rough stuff, too: a bit of curry,
some red pepper, then perhaps a little tooth powder,
mix these all up together and smear that on the rice.
I was afraid it would explode.[13]

There were other diversions. The baseball and Ping-Pong
equipment was occasionally available on *yasumi* ("rest days"),
though the men were often too worn out to play. Cards were a
regular evening pastime. On days off, a few of the men sometimes
put on little concerts or theatrical shows. On the very rare occasions when the Japanese issued Red Cross parcels, Reid encouraged
trading among the men as another distraction.

Private Angus McRitchie of the Grenadiers saw Reid's wisdom:

Now, some people always get stung. There always
has to be, there always has to be a winner somewhere, eh? Some guy might end up, from half a
parcel, he could end up with one and a half; somebody else could lose all his parcel. This, Dr. Reid
wouldn't stop. As a matter of fact he put a board
up, just outside where his little room was, on a post
there. This was the daily market: a square of choc-
olate was worth one package of cigarettes. In some
parcels you got prunes, and in other ones you got
raisins; well, raisins are worth a package of prunes
plus something else.... Dr. Reid felt that even
though the guy was losing the parcel, what he was
going to get out of it wasn't going to do that much
for him anyway, because you only get a little bit. So
he was getting more out of this parcel in trading, to
keep his mind off other things. And it's true.[14]

A very dangerous but highly satisfying morale booster was the sabotage the Canadians pulled off whenever they got the chance at the Nippon Kokan Shipyard — little acts of defiance such as over-drilling rivet holes, taking incorrect measurements, "accidently" cracking moulds, mis-cutting pipe, clogging bearings with iron filing–laced grease.

On January 20, 1944, Staff Sergeant Charles Clark (fresh from his Christmas role as camp Santa Claus) and his accomplice, Private Ken Cameron of the Royal Canadian Ordnance Corps, succeeded spectacularly. Taking the advice of an American naval engineer, recently transferred to 3D, on what building to target, the two set fire to the shipyard's mould loft by means of a lighted candle hidden behind rubbish in a little-used storeroom. They timed the candle to burn down after closing time and ignite carefully hoarded combustibles heaped around the candle's base. Bursting into flames at about 8:00 p.m., the fire quickly spread, destroying the loft, the shipyard's blueprint stores next door as well as the steel shed, the ship outfitting stores, the riggers' lobby, tool rooms, and part of the ship fitters' shop. Nippon Kokan was the largest shipyard in Japan, and its production of escort destroyers and merchant ships — until the fire about 8,000 tons per month — was cut by more than 60 percent for the next eight months, a crippling blow to the Japanese war effort dealt by a pair of cool-headed prisoners conniving right under the noses of the Japanese guards and shipyard staff.

The only downside for the rest of the Canadians — out of the loop, but happy bystanders of the mysterious conflagration — was that the prisoners' mess hall went up in flames with the rest. Until new canteen arrangements were put into place a month later, those on work detail had to return to camp for lunch — an extra march to and fro each day. Like everyone, Reid was in the dark about the fire's cause for a long time. The Japanese never found out. After weeks of sifting and interrogating, the investigation by the Nippon Kokan officials and outside police authorities came up empty.

Finding secret ways to fight back was a tonic for soldiers who had suffered defeat and now been imprisoned for so long. It was a way of denying surrender, of engaging the enemy in spite of being ground down by hunger, sickness, and servitude. But the greatest lift to the spirits was also the rarest — communication with home.

Japanese disdain for surrender, hence for those who did so, along with their rejection of the Geneva Convention, meant that mail, one of the most important prisoner amenities in other theatres of the war, got short shrift in Japanese prison camps. For many Canadian prisoners, this was the cause of the two most wearing psychological stresses they endured in Hong Kong and Japan: years of worrying that loved ones didn't know if they were alive or dead, and once some mail was allowed, the excruciating slowness of letters from home and the frustrating randomness of whose mail got through and whose, through the vagaries of war, got lost on the way.

After the fall of Hong Kong, no mail was allowed out of the Japanese prison camps until June 1942. Even then, only a minority of prisoners were permitted to write, so they had to draw lots for the privilege. Subject matter and length were severely restricted. Because every letter or card had to be censored and Japanese translators were few, mail piled up for months before leaving or after arriving in the camps. The roundabout process of shipping mail through the International Red Cross via internee exchange ships, later in the war by way of Siberia, added to the slowness. If it arrived at all, mail typically took eight months to two years to reach Japanese prison camps from Canada, and a year or more for prisoners' notes to be delivered to recipients back home. In Tokyo No. 5's case, the letters from home distributed to the prisoners in early June 1943 — a batch of 300 divided among about 100 men, Reid among them — was the first mail they had received since their capture a year and a half earlier. It would be another six months before any more arrived.

"The mail situation was so upset that you felt if you got one you were lucky," says Reid. "Some men never got a letter."[15] Equally uncertain, the chance to write home continued to depend on the fluctuating whimsy of their captors:

> [Early on,] we wrote letters on a form, a piece of paper that had been printed. They told us ... that officers could write every week and the men every month [it didn't happen] ... and the next thing they told us that we could write a letter every two months and a postcard every two months. We actually wrote one or the other every four months for the first couple of years, mostly postcards, later on at six-, eight-, and ten-month intervals.... I also got permission to write short notes to the families of those who died in camp.... I don't know whether they got to [Canada].[16]

The other way that prisoners could sometimes send news was through the broadcasting of radio messages that the Japanese instituted in 1942 as a form of propaganda. Japanese sound technicians would come into the prison camps and record prisoners' voices and sometimes their musical offerings. Packaged in programs such as *American War Prisoners Information Hour, Humanity Calls*, and *The Postman Calls*, the recordings were broadcast as part of Radio Tokyo's Overseas Program. The Japanese intent was to show that Allied prisoners were being well treated.

In late June 1943, radio technicians visited Tokyo No. 5 to prepare a segment of *American War Prisoners Information Hour*.

Messages by Reid and about 40 other prisoners were recorded, along with renditions of "Drink to Me Only with Thine Eyes" and "The Band Played On" performed by Tokyo No. 5's band members. Most of the men's messages were brief "hellos" to family. As Tokyo No. 5's "Prisoner No. 1," Reid, who led off this all-Canadian episode of *American War Prisoners Information Hour*, was allowed a longer message. They made the most of these opportunities:

> We were glad to play [along] with them although we realized that it would be broadcast between Japanese propaganda programs. But the attitude I think among ourselves was that Japanese propaganda was so childish that anyone could see through it.... We felt that from our own viewpoint we could get out information by this method.... First of all, conditions in the camp and the people who were there and, secondly, a word to our own relatives which we considered important to us and to them. We made three of these broadcasts altogether over a period of a year. We covered every man in the camp — every name.... We always managed to include in the messages some information about our condition — the Japanese were not very good about picking up that sort of stuff. We got the nominal roll out and sometimes mentioned a man who had died and his cause of death.[17]

The first recording of Reid and his men, broadcast over Radio Tokyo on July 6, 1943, was picked up by more than a dozen American ham radio operators in California, Washington State, Oregon, and as far east as Abilene, Texas. All of these radio operators were private citizens, part of a loosely organized volunteer network called the War Prisoners Listening Post, dedicated to monitoring Japanese prisoner broadcasts and passing on word of POWs heard or mentioned in them to the American and Canadian governments and to the men's relatives directly, if home addresses were given. This time, the volunteer network was delivering more than personal news. Its reports of the Tokyo No. 5 broadcast were the first alert to the Canadian government that a large number of Canadian prisoners had been transferred from Hong Kong to Japan under Reid's command.

Jean Reid was lucky. By mid-July 1943, she had received 14 letters and cards sent by listening-post volunteers who caught parts of Reid's somewhat garbled message. (Canada's Royal Mail also "did its bit": as well as delivering the messages properly addressed to 5 Scholfield, Toronto's postal service correctly redirected letters addressed to "5 Schoolfield," "5 Schalmfield," and "5 Goldfield.") Perhaps the most reassuring news for Jean was in the card from Henry C. Strohm of Los Angeles, California, who only heard Reid giving his name, rank, age, and Toronto address before reception cut out. But until it did, said Strohm, "his voice was strong and clear."[18]

On July 13, 1943, the Canadian Department of National Defence (DND) sent Jean an official summary of Reid's message, compiled from the civilian sources:

Re: Capt. REID, John A.G.
R.C.A.M.C. Attached to Winnipeg Grenadiers

Dear Mrs. Reid,

This Department has received the following information from an unofficial source and consequently is unable to vouch for its authenticity. The message purports to come from your husband, who was taken prisoner of war at Hong Kong.

He states that he is now in a Japanese prisoner of war camp near Yokohama with a group of other Canadian prisoners of war and he sends his love to you and to his parents.

He further states that since their arrival, their general health has exhibited a marked improvement. The men work daily elsewhere and he keeps busy at his own job inside the camp. He states that the following medical orderlies are with him and are feeling fine: Neal, Morgan, Matheson, Melkowski, and Pat Poirier. He then goes on to state that some Canadians still remain in Hong Kong, among them Gordon Gray who was in good health sometime in January when he last saw him. Capt. Reid states further that he is in excellent physical health and has his work, a few books, some Japanese prints, and some music for mental recreation. He states that he recently had his first letter from you which filled a long-felt want and he hopes that some of the letters he has written have reached their destination.

He sends his love to his Dad ... and asks you to extend his best wishes to all his friends and particularly the Vancouver Clinic and the Toronto Medical School.

He further states that you are never out of his thoughts and asks you to keep yourself as essentially unchanged for him as he remains for you.

The message ends with your husband's stating that you have, with the deepest intensity, all his love, always.[19]

Aside from this broadcast, a sense of how Reid was coping can be gleaned from the four letters and three cards that Jean eventually received from him (some after the war), as well as from several references to his personal situation that he recorded in his camp medical diary.

Health-wise, Reid's diary indicated that from early 1943 onward he was chronically plagued with ethmoiditis and tracheitis, which caused headaches and severe night coughing. He referred to recurring numbness of his toes, which he assumed to be beriberi, "but nothing to be alarmed about." An entry in the winter of 1943 described a 24-hour bout of severe abdominal pain that gave him visions of performing a self-appendectomy (mercifully, the pain receded on its own). On December 28, 1943, he noted his weight was down to 143 pounds, "lightest since I was 11 years of age"; he then added, "2 weeks last month [the] worst attack of sinusitis and tracheobronchitis [I] have had. In bed except for necessary duties during this time."[20]

There are several recorded thoughts of home. On March 19, 1943, Reid ended the day's medical entry with: "Today is the 10th anniversary of Mother's death."[21] A year later, on March 17, 1944, his diary entry concluded: "11 yrs. Today, St. Pat's [St. Patrick's Day] since mother ill"[22] — referring to the onset that culminated in her sudden death at 79 Humber Trail two days afterward.

Invariably, his letters and cards to Jean concentrate on reassuring her about himself and his situation, encouraging her to pursue her art and music, and reinforcing his love and need for her. Reid's letter of January 15, 1944 — perfectly hand-printed, like all his missives, to make it easy for the censors to read and approve — is by far the longest he wrote in prison camp and the most revealing of his daily routine and state of mind. At the time of writing, two years and three months have passed since he and Jean last said goodbye in Toronto in October 1941:

Steve, My Dear, Another note to you, following
that of last July [1943]. First, news. I am perfectly
well in mind and body, and mature of mind. For
my part, having obtained a state of reconciliation to
the irreparable loss of your presence, the hours between work have proven a peculiar boon. Books are
few but thus read and cogitated deeply. Goethe in
German and English for broad philosophy, Marcus
Aurelius, Shaw's searchlight on sociology, Wells'
World History, Hebrew Literature in the Bible, a
few great symphonies, Hiroshige's prints, a medical
text. The application of all knowledge in general, as
well as my special work in camp — these hold a lifetime of experience. My ideas become ever broader,
clearer, more coalesced. Xmas [1943] was a true
pleasure for me. The men had a holiday and dis-
played the most amazing enthusiasm and ingenuity
in their decorations. The acme was a paper fireplace,
painted, with lights for coals, candles, and stock-
ings. We had two Xmas trees, carols, and Church
Service Xmas Eve, and on Xmas morn one of our
jovial lads was transformed into a Santa Claus to
give out Red Cross parcels to the men. The parcels arrived Xmas Eve and have been a great treat.
The men also had oranges and cigarettes on Xmas
and their pleasure that day was satisfaction to me,
feeling as I do, like the father of a very large family.
During last autumn I was the joyful recipient of several letters from you, one from Dede, and one from
Kay and your mother. None from Dad yet. All the
mail so far is of late summer and fall 1942. Also got
snapshots of you in [the] garden [of 5 Scholfield]

and one of the McAinish photos which is my pride and joy. This month, mail of 1943 and the first personal parcels we have had, are beginning to arrive in camp. I look forward to mine.

[To] Dad and Eva [Reid]: how goes the bridge and fishing? Are you keeping each other sober and happy till your wayward son gets home?

How is John Cory's golf, my golf clubs, and Eva's roast beef? [Referring to the Hodges.]

Remember me to everyone, Farquhy [Dr. Ray Farquharson, assistant professor of medicine at the University of Toronto and Toronto General Hospital], Bill [Bigelow], Mim [Miriam Fox], and the others. To you, My Darling, I send my constant thoughts and imperishably, all my heart, fuller, with each passing day, of our love. Take care of yourself, and no matter how stiff that upper lip becomes I'll tend to the affair. All my Love, Always, Mike.[23]

Along with the cold and wet and deadly sickness, the beginning of 1944 had one bright spot — the arrival in camp of George Pollak, the man who became Reid's closest friend of the war.

Reid's diary entry for January 9, 1944, 11 days before the shipyard fire at Nippon Kokan, stated: "On Dec. 30/43 two American naval officers came into camp, i.e., Lt.-Commander Dockweiler U.S.N. and Ensign E.G. Pollak U.S.N.R. These are being sent to Nippon Kokan, starting Jan. 2, and so far have spent each day sitting in [the] mess hall there. Came from Headquarters Camp, Shinagawa."[24]

The journey that brought the two Americans from the bombed-out ruins of Cavite Naval Base in the Philippines to Camp 3D, Kawasaki, was a tough one. In early 1942, 10 weeks after the Japanese attacks across the Far East, Dockweiler and Pollak were among 45 specialized naval officers ordered south from the American stronghold of Corregidor to the island of Cebu in the Visayas as the northern defences of the Philippines began to crumble. Leaving Corregidor at the end of February aboard the inter-island steamer MS *Legaspi* — the last American surface ship to escape from Manila Bay — the group sailed at night and anchored among the islands during the day to evade Japanese pursuers. Before departing Corregidor, says Pollak, the betting ran 10 to 1 against their reaching their destination. They beat the odds:

> We arrived at Cebu on a cold, wet daybreak and felt a tremendous sense of relief. Once again we were in the land of fresh fruit, eggs, tobacco, and comparative quiet. We felt that from here we were not completely cut off, we again had a chance. We were tired and worn out from the trip, but expectant and anxious to work. We felt hope again. On the voyage down we had reacquired some *esprit de corps*. We had to take this opportunity and do something. We were no longer part of the completely lost cause of the Bay [Manila Bay].[25]

Their sense of relief and newfound purpose soon evaporated. Three hundred and seventy-three miles south of Manila, they found a disorganized, badly led American garrison seemingly oblivious to the seriousness of the Japanese threat. There was no welcome on arrival, no orders for the navy men's deployment, nor any inclination on the part of Cebu's three bickering army colonels to make use of them in defence preparations, a waste of highly trained personnel who could have provided valuable service had they been allowed to act in their proper capacities.

Prior to Cebu, George Pollak had survived the bombing that levelled Cavite Naval Base on December 8, helped cope with the horrific and chaotic aftermath, then spent six weeks jungle-fighting in the Bataan Peninsula along with the Mariveles Naval Battalion and U.S. Marines in an attempt to halt the Japanese land forces threatening to invade Corregidor, the island fortress still controlling the mouth of Manila Bay. In Bataan, these cobbled-together American units had fought in gruelling mountainous jungle conditions with whatever resources they had, poorly trained, ill-equipped, and outnumbered though they were. In Cebu, Pollak and his group were dismayed by the state of denial:

> The Army in Cebu had no idea that there was a war going on. They were so engrossed in their own machinations that the main purpose completely slipped their minds. They talked a good war, but they were so far removed from reality that we became deeply shocked. Not only did they have no conception of what was happening, but they actively and unpolitely blocked all suggestions and attempts we made to act.... It was amazing how otherwise sane and sensible people would say, "Maybe if we don't say or do anything they will bypass us and leave us alone." They actually believed that the Japs would not bother them, perhaps not land on Cebu. They wanted to think that their little bit of isolated romantic civilization would be able to carry on undisturbed.[26]

Facing this level of negligence and disintegration in Cebu's command structure, the navy men eventually split into small guerrilla groups and prepared to fend for themselves. As Pollak relates, when the war arrived on Cebu's doorstep, the failure of leadership was complete:

> On the tenth of April [1942] Bataan fell and by the next morning the Nips had made several landings on Cebu. The resistance, as we had expected, was almost nil. The house of cards collapsed suddenly and violently. The civilians ran, the Army ran, we ran, everyone ran. There was nothing else to do.[27]

Dockweiler, Pollak, and seven other members of their navy group snuck through the Japanese lines to the west coast of Cebu at night, commandeered several outriggers from local fisherman, and sailed 28 miles across the Tanon Strait to the island of Negros, still untouched by the enemy, where they took to the hills.

Three weeks later, Corregidor fell. On May 8, 1942, two days after Corregidor, the Americans officially surrendered the Philippines to the Japanese. But on Negros, the Dockweiler-Pollak guerrilla band — joined by others on the run and now numbering 26 men — held out until August when, with no chance of rescue, they received orders from American authorities to surrender. If they did not, came the warning, the Japanese would retaliate by executing American prisoners.

Capture now inevitable, Pollak must have thought ruefully of his one chance to escape. In late March, several weeks after Pollak's group reached Cebu, two Australian transport ships arrived in port with food for the beleaguered islands. Pollak was assigned to oversee unloading at the pier and had several conversations with one of the ships' captains, a jovial, bearded Welshman named Llewellyn Evans:

He was the first contact with the outside world I had had since the outbreak of war, and speaking to him was like feeling a breeze cut through the miasmic fog that seemed to hamper our actions and thoughts....

"Why don't you come along," said the captain. "They need engineers down south [Australia] and obviously this set-up is hopeless and useless. Moreover, we stand a damn good chance of making it; the Japs aren't too thick."

I had to refuse, and I can say it was the hardest decision I had to make during the whole war. It was an offer of life. Somehow I would never have felt right if I had gone. Undoubtedly, no one would have ever mentioned the subject, and, if anything, I might have gotten credit for getting out. Yet, I would always have had the feeling of having run away, of leaving the rest of our gang behind, of having disobeyed an order.[28]

Six weeks after they surrendered, Dockweiler and Pollak were among the 1,994 sick and starving American prisoners shipped from temporary prison pens outside Manila to Osaka, Japan, where, after the hellish month-long voyage in which 30 prisoners died, they both ended up in Yokohama-area prison camps — Dockweiler at Omori Camp, Pollak at the prisoner of war hospital at Shinagawa, the rundown facility where Reid occasionally sent patients. After a year in their respective locations as internal administrative officers, they were plucked from Omori and Shinagawa and told that Tokyo Army Headquarters had ordered their transfers to Camp 3D for a new assignment. They arrived the day before New Year's Eve, 1943, escorted in separate cars. It was the entrance of Lieutenant Commander Dockweiler that made an impression on George MacDonell:

> One day in the winter of 1944 I learned that a high-ranking Allied officer was coming to stay at the camp. That afternoon, a Japanese staff car drove up and from it emerged a senior American naval officer, immaculately attired in Navy dress blues. He wore a matching blue naval overcoat over his uniform and he looked as if he had just stepped off the quarterdeck of a battleship. His sleeves were adorned with multiple gold rings of his rank and he had a wreath of gold scrambled eggs on the peak of his impressive cap. He was a small man, about 50 years old, and he stood ramrod straight. He gazed straight ahead, as if his eyes were fixed on some distant object. He gave no sign of recognition, either to those who accompanied him in the car or to the Japanese reception committee at the gate. When he proceeded to enter the gate, the guards backed up quickly and scrambled around him, out to the car, to get his suitcase and sea bag. I noticed that he never attempted to carry his own bag, but stalked into the camp as if he were sleepwalking through an annoying dream. He disappeared into the hut where he was given a small private room with a bed, desk and chair.[29]

Dockweiler and Pollak were a study in contrasts. Lieutenant Commander Edward Dockweiler — in fact, 42 years old at the time — was a career naval officer; a graduate of the U.S. Naval Academy at Annapolis, Maryland; and a third-generation descendant of one of Los Angeles's original pioneer families, a clan by now prominent in California state politics and the law. A 20-year veteran of the navy when the Japanese attacked in December 1941, Dockweiler was in charge of ship repair and construction at Cavite Naval Base, the Americans' main navy yard in the Philippines.

Ensign George Pollak, on the other hand, was a recent volunteer. Twenty-four years old and over six feet tall, Pollak had immigrated to the United States from Vienna with his parents and brother in 1924 and grown up in Chicago, Long Island, and New York City. Offered a commission in the U.S. Naval Reserve in 1940 while still an engineering student, Pollak received his orders after graduating and arrived in the Philippines as a neophyte ensign in August 1941. During the four months before the Japanese attack, he was employed at Cavite Naval Base trying to patch up the station's aging and neglected ships as well as supervising the loading of torpedoes on submarines.

What Dockweiler and Pollak had in common was their professional training. Both held postgraduate degrees in engineering and naval architecture from the Massachusetts Institute of Technology (MIT), expertise the Japanese now hoped to exploit by putting them to work as shipyard engineers at Nippon Kokan. When informing Dockweiler and Pollak of their transfers, Tokyo Headquarters mentioned additional privileges. Their new positions, the men were told, would entitle them to better living quarters, extra food, and a private office at the shipyard.

Upon their arrival at 3D, Commandant Uwamori oriented them personally, then handed them over to an interpreter named Kakuyama to take them to the shipyard and show them around. Dockweiler and Pollak had no intention of co-operating. As Pollak describes, the outcome for the Japanese was as useless as their interrogation of Lieutenant Charles Finn about army codes a few months earlier:

[At Nippon Kokan] The interpreter at first took a very jovial and very friendly attitude toward us, saying, "Well boys, what sort of work would you like to do?" — attempting to give us the impression that everything would be very cordial in their relations with us. Captain [*sic*] Dockweiler and myself answered by saying we neither volunteered nor intended to work in any such capacity.

Kakuyama then questioned Captain Dockweiler and myself as to previous experience and qualifications. Captain Dockweiler stated that he had done only personnel administrative work for many years. I insisted that I had no experience at all in practical engineering work.

At this impasse the Japanese, through the company interpreter, began hinting that the company, which at this time administered and supplied food and supplies for the camp, would take recriminatory action against the whole camp ... if our refusal to work in the shipyard continued.[30]

Back in camp after this stalemate, Dockweiler and Pollak conferred with Reid, who steered them toward a diplomatic response:

We talked the situation over.... My advice to them was to write a polite but firm letter to the Japanese invoking the Geneva Convention about officers, and the fact that the Japanese had said after the Philippines fell that officers would not be required to work and it was contrary to International Law and they didn't want to work with this company — but not to refuse to go out to the company. If you turned a flat refusal in to them, that gave the Nips something to go on for beating them.... When [the] Nips got the letter there was a great gaffufle and the Nips felt they had to send it through to headquarters, which they did.[31]

Pollak picks up the tale:

The result was that Captain Dockweiler and myself continued to go out to the shipyard without doing any actual work for the Japanese. It appeared to be the main concern of Uwamori to get credit for having two working prisoner officers at Camp 3D. The company, on the other hand, had the satisfaction of being able to say [to headquarters] that they had two American naval officers working in their plant, although neither of us did any actual work. It was apparent that the company seemed to think that eventually they could entice, inveigle or force us to perform engineering work since we underwent periodic questioning and badgerings by company officials.... [However] nothing more was said by Uwamori, who seemed to be satisfied of the fact that Captain Dockweiler and myself reported to the shipyard daily.[32]

This bizarre arrangement, which lasted for about three weeks, was an unexpected piece of luck for Staff Sergeant Charles Clark, who had been scheming with Private Ken Cameron about sabotaging the shipyard with a fire. Who better to advise them on the best building to target than the recent commander of Cavite Navy Yard? Dockweiler was brought into the "candle conspiracy" and became the saboteurs' Trojan Horse, concluding from his comings and goings to Nippon Kokan that the mould loft and an adjacent building where ship blueprints were stored would be the most damaging losses for the Japanese: without designs and prototypes of vessel parts to work from, production in the shipyard would be severely curtailed. The candle was planted in the mould loft as Dockweiler suggested, and as related earlier, Clark and Cameron's spectacular blaze of January 20, 1944, delivered the hoped-for devastation.

Ironically, it was the fire — specifically, the loss of the prisoners' shipyard mess hall where Dockweiler and Pollak had spent three weeks twiddling their thumbs — that gave the Japanese a chance to save face in their standoff with the two Americans and quietly "reassign" them in late January 1944.

Pollak goes on to describe the proceedings:

> After the shipyard fire ... Commander Dockweiler and myself were told ... that inasmuch as there was no space available for us at the shipyard, we were to remain in camp for a few days.... No mention was ever made again of Captain Dockweiler and myself going out to work in the shipyard.
>
> After a period of time doing nothing around the camp, Captain Dockweiler and myself were called into Uwamori's office and told ... that being idle was bad for our health and that we must do some work around the camp. We were also informed that non-working officers received only reduced rations while as workers we would be entitled to full rations.... Captain Dockweiler and myself elected to plant and work a small garden in the back of the barracks where we were billeted.... [Our] duties

[also] consisted of assisting the Jap staff in store-keeping, making out various forms for office use, and keeping camp rosters.[33]

As a lieutenant commander, Dockweiler outranked Reid and could have taken over as 3D's internal camp commander as soon as he arrived. Certainly, Dockweiler's performance since December 1941 showed his determination and capabilities in a tight spot — at Cavite, on Cebu and Negros, and as senior Allied officer on the *Tottori Maru*, the Japanese "hell ship" that took the boatload of American prisoners from Manila to Japan in October 1942, a nightmare voyage in which Dockweiler managed to maintain discipline in the crammed, filthy, vermin-infested hold even after the ship was damaged by an American torpedo and mutiny by panicking prisoners became a possibility. But, as Pollak relates, at 3D, Dockweiler left well enough alone:

> Before our arrival at Camp 3D, Major J.A.G. Reid, RCMC [*sic*][34] was senior officer of the camp and he, together with Lt. C. Finn, USNR, performed internal administrative duties. Uwamori dealt with Captain Reid in all matters affecting prisoners of war at the camp. Although Captain Dockweiler was acknowledged as senior officer, the previous arrangement was retained for working purposes and the four of us, i.e., Commander Dockweiler, Major Reid, Lt. Finn and myself divided various necessary internal camp tasks.[35]

Dockweiler was less involved, perhaps, than the others. His contribution to the shipyard fire during his first weeks at 3D had been invaluable. But with Reid in charge, Dockweiler remained somewhat aloof, preferring to stay much of the time in the private quarters made available to him. George MacDonell recalled: "He seldom came out of his cubbyhole. He ate his rice and barley in his cubicle…. He flatly refused to parade for roll call and ignored the Japanese. He did not speak. He seemed unwilling or unable to accept his surroundings and it was apparent that while his body was with us, his mind was elsewhere. He was a very, very angry man, brooding on his fate."[36]

The only time Dockweiler said a word to MacDonell — a chance meeting when the two men were alone in the shipyard mess hall before the fire — Dockweiler vented his frustration at being sidelined so early in the war. MacDonell sympathizes:

> He had spent his life preparing to command U.S. naval forces at sea and, instead, here he sat while all his Annapolis classmates were rising rapidly in rank in the mighty U.S. Navy. He was furious at his fate and could not unbend or adjust to his circumstances. Everybody in our camp, including the Japanese, watched with respect as he strode by and no one wanted to interrupt or antagonize this silent, forbidding figure. I certainly didn't.[37]

Half Dockweiler's age, a wartime volunteer, not a career officer, George Pollak coped with captivity more positively. Throughout the terrible winter of 1944, he discovered in Reid a "comrade-in-arms" he came to respect and like very much:

> Jack had preceded us to 3D. He was the only Canadian officer with a contingent of Royal Americans [sic] from the Quebec backwoods, another of Winnipeg Grenadiers, all via Hong Kong. Jack was their commanding officer, their doctor,

their father confessor, their hero, their disciplinarian, and every other leading role....

Jack had a very busy day. He had to hold sick call before the men went off to work, and he had to argue with the Japanese on how many sick he could retain in camp. He had to go and look after the ones in sick bay, and if he had no medicines he would sit with them and try to cheer them up. He had to look after the usual administrative chores, deal with Japanese orders and complaints, sit in judgement on internal squabbles, make his rounds again in the evening, and so on and on....

Jack was diplomatic — pressing when necessary or possible, but not taking up causes for the sake of causes. Moreover, I think he struck everyone, even the Japanese, by his forthrightness and no-nonsense attitude. At any rate, the Japanese let Jack continue to rule his troops and I am sure in private the camp commander was greatly thankful for the many headaches he was spared thereby....

Every once in a while in the afternoon, before the lads came back from work, there was a lull in activity and he could take an hour to listen to Beethoven. I started joining him in these interludes and there wasn't much conversation needed.... These bits of music — from a different world — were helpful. They sort of kept one in touch with things beyond the immediate dismal scene, and of course music of different sorts affect people emotionally. They take you out of one's surroundings, and that was badly needed at the time. Beethoven isn't really soothing, but he did fill the need, or reflect the feelings....

As I got to know Jack better, he gave me glimpses of his younger days. Of course I greatly admired the picture of his beautiful wife which he carried. And he talked about summers in Muskoka and the group of young people that gathered there and their antics. I think Jack's great charm and attractiveness came largely from his complete lack of affectations. He had considerable self-assurance, but in the best sense of that term....

Of course he was a bit older than I was, and it seemed to me that except for the current unpleasantness he sort of "had it made." And it seemed to me that it was fit that someone as decent as Jack should be in that position. Me, I still had a couple of years and a couple of hurdles to go.[38]

Whatever the hurdles — "current unpleasantness" included — the discipline and devotion to duty that were part of Pollak's upbringing served him well. For Reid, born and bred in Ontario like his parents, the stories Pollak told of his European background and transplanted life in America had a touch of the exotic.

Before immigrating to the United States, Pollak's father and mother were part of a Viennese network of cultured Jewish families, originally from Bohemia, Moravia, and Slovakia, who had established themselves in Austria in the 19th century, intermarried, and over several generations became prominent in business, science, medicine, and architecture.

Two of Pollak's great-uncles were the founders of Hauser & Sobotka, one of the largest breweries in Europe. His grandfather was a physician on the faculty of the Medical University of Vienna. One of his uncles was the designer of the Austrian pavilion at the 1937 World Exposition in Paris. Another had followed Pollak's parents to the United States and become director of chemistry at New York City's Mount Sinai Hospital.

Like Reid, Pollak had a privileged upbringing in spite of the Great Depression. His father, Alfred, was a chemical engineer who had travelled and worked in the United States before the First World War and held a number of patents registered with the U.S. government. A second American sojourn in the early 1920s working for the Fleischmann Company in Chicago convinced Alfred and his wife, Marianne, to settle in the United States permanently. The move to Chicago with their two sons was made in early 1924, and in 1928 the family became naturalized U.S. citizens.

In 1930, Alfred Pollak became a food industry consultant, based in New York City, and moved his family to the affluent community of Woodmere, Long Island, where he enrolled his sons at Woodmere Academy, an elite private secondary school much like Toronto's UTS. Home life was conducted with an old-world formality. As boys, George and his older brother, Martin, were expected to come to their feet, click their heels, and bow when their mother entered the room — a measure of the strictness and reserve that Marianne Pollak maintained during her sons' upbringing.

Education was of paramount concern. Both English and German were spoken in the household (Alfred was also fluent in French and Czech, Marianne in Italian), and Martin's and George's scholarly accomplishments were expected by their parents to lead to solid professional careers. Martin's acceptance at Harvard in 1933, a rarity for a Jew at the time, reflected the success of these aspirations. George, on the other hand, dreamed of becoming a writer. But practicality, in his parents' view, came first. Bowing to their wishes, George's second choice, inspired by his love of the sea, was the U.S. Naval Academy. His third choice was Harvard. Parental control was asserted once again. When George failed to

get an appointment to the academy, his father insisted on his taking engineering at MIT. George submitted. But following his own
lights, not his father's expectations, he registered in MIT's four-
year naval architecture course.

Pollak had entered MIT in 1936 as the darkly handsome, re-
served young man that nature and a regimented, emotionally cool
upbringing had made of him. He soon broke out of his protective
shell. Cocky and brash in this new setting, Pollak spread his wings
academically, at dances with girls from the Seven Sisters colleges, as
"commodore" of MIT's Nautical Association, and at Jacob Wirth,
the old German-style beer hall in Boston, on boys' nights out.

In 1940, when the U.S. Navy came to MIT to recruit engineers
for the reserve, Pollak signed up but elected to stay at university for
another year to complete his master's degree. He had formed a
deep attachment to a beautiful music student from Smith College
and wanted to marry her. Things went wrong. When he graduated
in June 1941 and was asked by the navy his preferences for duty,
Pollak picked, perhaps rashly, the most distant posting with the
best opportunity to see action: the Philippines.

Hearing this part of the story as their friendship grew, Reid
could appreciate the irony of Pollak's impulsive choice, given that
his own bad luck — the posting to Hong Kong — was set in motion
by a brief tropical medicine course he easily might have skipped.
Now, two and a half years after the two men made their fateful
choices in the summer of 1941, chance had thrown them together
in a prison camp in Japan. Their shared imprisonment lasted 15
months — through thick and thin, says Pollak:

> We helped each other retain our sanity and sur-
> vive....[39] In the sort of situation we found ourselves,
> one develops a way of judging other people which is
> quite different from that which is common in more

conventional circumstances. In analogy, it seems rather well established that good peacetime officers are not necessarily good wartime officers, and vice versa. Similarly, in our situation one required complete faith and reliance in one another. If and when that connection was established, it became an enduring one. I admired Jack's capabilities and devotion tremendously.

In observing Jack, I found that he rarely lost his temper. Oh yes, I saw him get angry and such, and I saw him really get to the depths of despair, but otherwise he didn't fly off the handle.

Jack retained his sense of humour. He had an engaging twinkle in his eye which warned of some comic or witty pronouncement. Of course, we all had some sort of black humour, but his was good fun. Jack could elicit a laugh or a chuckle from his troops or from us because of a natural wit and good humour. I mention this sense of humour in particular because I have found that a great many people who find themselves in positions of responsibility entirely lose theirs. Jack took his responsibility for his men as seriously as anyone I have ever seen. But he didn't lose his sense of humour. And the men loved him for both reasons.

By late winter 1944, things were becoming rather grim. Food was minimal, the men were losing weight, the vitamin deficiency diseases were increasing, and the war was dragging on interminably. I shall never forget a cold wet winter night (we were allowed a fire in the small stove in the large hut about three times per winter) when four or five lads were down with pneumonia and Jack had left only one full course [of medicine]. Jack agonized most of the evening, with me as sounding board, on what to do. Do you give each one a quarter of the necessary dose and hope it will pull some of them through? Does one select one or two? And what are the criteria for selection, the weakest or the strongest? One can argue this question from some interesting viewpoints. We went through all of them. I don't think I ever saw Jack as shaken and unhappy as that evening.[40]

Now, at least, Reid had someone to talk to, a friend to listen. And after the terrible winter of 1944, the relief of spring:

April 20, 1944

Steve, My Dear: April came in white and blue, again, bringing you so vividly to me once more. A very busy winter is over, and I remain well, although, despite all philosophy, restless with the rebirth of springtime. Still, the humanity of Beethoven's music; still, enough literature to stimulate the imagination. A few letters, now a year old; perhaps, yet, that parcel you sent. All my deepest affection to Dad, Eva, your family, and all my friends, old and new, old and young. Live your life, Stephen. Keep that sweet retroussé nose into mischief. A bit of the luck of the Irish and all my love, always, Mike.[41]

With spring came warmer weather, slightly increased rations, and an unexpected change of assignment. On May 3, 1944, Japanese headquarters ordered Reid to Shinagawa Hospital, 12 miles north of 3D, to do a six-week stint assisting with the continuing pneumonia outbreak and other serious cases. Reid was unhappy leaving his men under the joint command of Dockweiler and an American major named Edwin Kagy, imported to 3D to replace him as medical officer. But there was no choice. During his time at Shinagawa, Reid got word from prisoners sent to the hospital that things weren't going well under the new leadership, particularly the medical setup of the erratic Major Kagy, who was quarrelsome, bigoted, and distrustful of the men. Reid tried to manage the disintegrating situation from afar:

> I had sent [via] the underground [POWs returning to 3D from Shinagawa Hospital] various orders back to them to keep themselves in hand and not be insubordinate in any way. When I got back to camp, indeed, there had been a great deal of trouble.
>
> This American doctor [Kagy] ... he was a regular Army Officer ... had attained an extremely brilliant standing at medical school and went into the regular army — a very excellently trained medical officer from the point of view of both medicine and surgery....
>
> However, he was a very unstable person emotionally. He had three prejudices: one was the Roman Catholics, one was the American Navy, and the third was the British. During the time he was in camp he would begin a tirade on one or other of the three. All the other officers, realizing that you simply couldn't quarrel in such close quarters, bore with it, and he, realizing that nobody else was

going to quarrel, really let himself go. Two of the American officers were Catholics and two or three were Navy Officers and on good days the Canadians were Canadians and on bad days they were British.

On top of that he had developed from his regular army experience the notion that any man on sick parade was deliberately trying to swing the lead, but I am glad to say the men never forgot themselves and never spoke back to him, but it had already reached the point where a man would be sick and refuse to go on sick parade [see Kagy] and that was a serious thing because you couldn't let a man get rundown under those conditions without treatment.[42]

One of Kagy's patients was Grenadier Angus McRitchie, who was admitted to the camp hospital shortly after Reid was posted to Shinagawa:

I had just gone into the hospital in 3D with pneumonia. [Captain Reid] was transferred out just at that time to somewhere else in the Tokyo area — he was ... considered sort of a pneumonia expert [by the Japanese]. He left our camp and we got an American doctor in, a Doctor Kagy was his name, and with Kagy his motto was to get as many people out to work instead of staying in the camp and you had to go out to work when you weren't well — which was exactly the opposite [of Reid]. Reid's motto was ... try to keep as many people as he could off the work force rather than going out to work.[43]

Reid's personal interactions with Major Kagy had challenges of their own:

> After I got back [to 3D], [Major Kagy] decided he was going to be moved to a new camp. He had been moved fairly often and been at Shinagawa and he and this other doctor, a Lieutenant in the U.S. Navy Medical Service Corps, had had quarrels there heard all over the hospital. [Now] he turned every- thing over to me and waited for the move. He never did move from the camp until the following May when it broke up…. During that time, because of the difficulty with the men and because the men got on so much better with myself, I maintained all the medical work in camp and he … treated such Japanese as came around for treatment, which took that nuisance off my shoulders. I would consult him and we went on that way fairly satisfactorily for a whole year.
>
> For quite a while he deliberately tried to bait me the same as the others. I never lost my temper and finally I think he actually got to a place where he liked me as well as he ever liked anyone in his life and the arrangement was satisfactory with me. While I could keep control of everything there were a certain number of things which he could do better than I could and he did them when [such cases] came along. Dockweiler kept on with some administrative duties which he had [taken on] while I was away. The disciplinary duties fell back on my shoulders because I had so much influence with the men….

> Getting things done satisfactorily in camp with-
> out having blow-ups was great training for a diplo-
> matic career.[44]

Commandant Uwamori was the biggest beneficiary of Reid's diplomacy. The prisoners, Uwamori admitted, were much happier and better disciplined with Reid back in charge.

Reid's return to 3D coincided with signs of the war's changing fortunes. By the early summer of 1944, cracks were appearing in the Japanese picture of total victory, heralded by silver specks moving high through the skies over Japan — American B-29 bombers photographing future targets. The situation at sea, apparently, was equally ominous for the Japanese. Prisoners working on the docks reported many Japanese ships limping into port with torpedo and bomb damage from American attacks. Reid had first-hand knowledge of the changing climate: "It was July ... I was told by the Japanese medical orderly that now a new order had come from headquarters. Previously when prisoners died it was very good, but now very bad. At the time there was a definite change in mind of the Japanese, though it didn't result in any effectual changes."[45]

In response to the increasing threats, Commandant Uwamori reassigned Pollak from administrative duties to the more practical roles of camp air raid warden, fire-fighter-in-chief, construction boss of an air lookout platform on the barracks roof, and manager of trench digging in the camp yard with Lieutenant Finn as chief carpenter — air raid shelters for the prisoners when American bombs began to fall.

Pollak and Dockweiler continued to justify their rations as officers by tending their 65-by-16-foot vegetable garden behind the barracks where they had planted seeds and seedlings bought from the camp interpreters with their officers' allowances. The limited crops — tomatoes and pumpkins — were often raided by the camp guards but produced enough to provide one vegetable ration for one meal for the entire camp at harvest time.

From the men's point of view, the better weather was a welcome addition to an already reduced workload. Ship production remained minimal, thanks to the January fire. The little being produced, Reid heard, was close to useless, as were the local workers:

> They would have a [ship] launching, pieces of hull would fall [through the cradle] and some of them when they hit the water were not seaworthy.... In the early summer of 1944 the Japanese civilians who worked in the shipyards ... quit work and weren't interested anymore. They felt the war was lost, they were getting no food or clothing and didn't care to work anymore.
>
> A number of Koreans [also] worked there and spent most of the time making knives and fighting the Japanese and trying to sabotage some of the parts. In the case of a casting the Koreans would get hold of it and sledge-hammer it....
>
> During the last year [at 3D] there was practically no work done [at Nippon Kokan]. It finally got that the men would take their knitting and sewing and sit out on the deck of the ship and knit and sew all day. It was amusing.[46]

And then, of course, there was the trading:

> A lot of the Japanese [civilian] workers got to be very friendly.... The Japanese would steal all kinds of things from the company — tools and tables and any equipment they could get. If they wanted a table or

something taken out from the company, they would
be searched themselves coming out of the gate, [so]
they would get our boys to carry it out in the middle
of their ranks. Nobody could stop them so our boys
would carry it out and turn it over to the [civilian]
guards. Meanwhile, the civilian guards would bring
or carry the stuff we wanted in the camp and turn it
over to our boys. Several times there was some little
dissatisfaction and our boys would say, "You better
not report it; if you do we'll report all you stole last
week from the company." They all got so involved
with each other no one ... could split on the others
without the whole shebang being involved.[47]

With the better weather came an invitation from Dr. Iino, the
Japanese doctor who visited 3D regularly, suggesting that Reid accompany him as consultant to a nearby civilian hospital. For more
than a year, Iino's sympathetic and respectful manner toward Reid
had been manifested in the form of small personal gifts and by the
Japanese doctor's delight in conversing with Reid on topics of an
elevated nature — befitting, as Iino intimated to him, their status
as professional colleagues. But this invitation to be a medical consultant was an extraordinary favour — Iino making up an excuse
to give Reid something he had not had for more than two and
a half years: a few hours' complete freedom "outside the fence."
Until now not known as a religious man, his two outings with Dr.
Iino led to Reid's strangest experience of the war, and the source of
whatever spiritual belief he harboured after he came home.

Dr. Iino was about fifty years old, short and rotund, with a glistening black moustache under his small olive nose and, in character, a mix of discipline and oriental propaganda on the one hand, and a natural bent for kindliness and wordy philosophy on the other.

He used to visit the camp once a week. After clumping in most formally, almost tripping over his long sword, he would line up the sick for inspection and designate about fifty percent as quite well enough to work. Having accomplished the distasteful part of the job, he would repair to my cubicle at one end of the long hut for some conversation (and I do not doubt for a moment that he knew as well as I that his stern medical decrees would be entirely ignored the following morning when time came to make up the work party).

Then, in our Japanese-English pidgin, he would talk to me at length of Japan and the inherent kindliness of her people, of their appreciation of beauty, their natural ability to paint and arrange flowers, of their understanding of music, and of the ineffable grace of the silhouette of Mount Fuji's twelve-thousand-foot cone.

He often embellished his commentary by waving about the sprig of plum or cherry blossoms he had brought me, for he frequently plucked a tender bough from some far-off hillside, beyond my ken, to mark his understanding that one of our rank did not live by rice alone. I enjoyed his bounce and his confidence in the Nipponese viewpoint — the latter all the more since it obviously contained a number of deep-rooted, though unvoiced, reservations.

When the day came for our first visit to the hospital we set off through the bamboo gate by bicycle, I arrayed in my one uniform — produced in shining splendour by my men who were determined that my appearance should bedazzle all chance beholders, Iino less splendidly attired in dull green fatigues.

Wheeling through the streets was a joy in itself. Children were everywhere and the black-eyed tots curled away from my prow in awe at the tall, blonde foreigner, only to close in behind in an ever-increasing wake as curiosity overcame fear. On both sides the shops hugged the pavement: the apothecary's, whose cure-alls were concocted from the essence of pickled snakes; the bawdy houses — identified in a friendly, winking grin by Iino, and marked, as in all such well-arranged businesses, by their quiet dignity; and the communal baths, where a stream of giggling girls and grinning men traipsed in and out from the huge, steaming, wooden tubs of water where they splashed with childlike gaiety.

Iino patiently explained that we had better go to the hospital in case the commandant checked on our movements and we so we swung into its yard, then strode along its bare corridors, peering at odd intervals into rooms where a wasted shape in a bed was surrounded by the whole family camped on the floor, rice boiling on a charcoal burner. After a few hurried questions here and there on Iino's part, and several questions to me for advice, we emerged again into the brilliant sunlight.

Now the adventure began. Turning our backs to the hospital, we pedalled through the narrow streets to the edge of town and on out into the green countryside. Here, away from the whole, long, ugly horror, nature reasserted itself. The trees were trees — silent and soothing as always, the sky blue, as it had been in the carefree growing-up time: in all, the balm of Gilead.

We wound up through a suburb, past an outlying railway station where we had to dismount to push the bicycles under the safety gates, and then up a hill where the peace and quiet and isolation descended on us like a cloak. We tossed our bicycles into a thicket and took to foot, mounting a winding trail through a park-like area where the trees towered overhead, opening at intervals to wide expanses of sky.

As we climbed, there was suddenly on the right a long, clear space and at its far edge a low, graceful, stone building with pillars at each end and massive double doors in the centre. This, Iino whispered, was a Buddhist temple, representing a power set apart from, but as specific as the Emperor's.

We lingered a moment. Then, urged on by Iino's obvious reluctance to gawk, we turned again up the trail. As the crest of the hill came into view, a little glade opened out before us and here Iino was content to rest. As I flung myself down on the soft turf I noticed a statue at the edge of the trees to my left. Twenty feet high, moulded from some smooth, green stone, it blended almost perfectly into the background. So inconspicuous it was, despite its size, that it seemed banished, as though expressing some idea a little unconventional, a little too disturbing to be in the full light of day.

I had seen scores of traditional Buddhist statues: a male figure with placid, thick-set face, topped by a peculiar, tight, scrolled turban, and, below, heavy shoulders and arms sliding into a fat, round belly which bulged over the almost unnoticed crossed legs on which it sat. Ugly, these replicas had always seemed to me, yet encompassing a feeling of inevitable, quiet strength: God-like power above human fallibility.

But as my gaze roved over this huge, green Buddha, I realized that whoever moulded it had moved quite beyond the conventional treatment of his subject. Not for this forgotten craftsman the ritual figure alone, but instead a combination of Buddha, life as the craftsman saw it with an eye for beauty, and inspiration from a woman he loved. All these had crept into his creation. The face was lacking the usual heaviness, the shoulders were beautiful and full rather than thick, the belly was not obese but fecund and, below the waist, still held hints of a thin, virgin beauty, fulfilled, but still tense with fulfillment.

For a long time I stood, bemused by the flood of conjecture and emotion my thoughts aroused. My eyes passed on. I stared at the azure sky, I heard the murmur of the leaves in the branches, I felt the heat of the sun creep through my skin.

Iino called out that it was time to go. At this point in my existence I had learned to flip myself into any escape that was offered, asking no more than the moment. Now I accepted the return to captivity as readily as I had thrown myself down for a touch of freedom. Back we went, coasting along

the dusking streets and at last through the flimsy
but inevitable bamboo gate.[48]

Unlike the men, Reid was never out of camp, except on the
rare occasions when he was shepherded by Uwamori or an interpreter to a local pharmacy to buy drugs. Day in, day out, his only
freedom beyond the fence was in looking up, to gaze at the sky and
clouds, and at night, the stars, with nothing to hold him back. The
day of freedom with Iino, his discovery in the little glade, left him
craving for more:

> The next week when Iino came I was anxious for
> his coming. I even smiled at his pompous diagnoses
> and grinned when he stroked through half my sick
> to mark them for work. I was as restless as a housefly
> as he mumbo-jumboed in my room, waiting only
> for the moment when at last he rose, stretched, and
> suggested that there were several cases in the civil-
> ian hospital he would like my opinion on.
>
> Leaving the hospital after our brief visit, I did
> not ask, I only hoped. But, sure enough, he took
> the turn that led to the Buddhist park. Once again
> we walked our bicycles across the railway track and
> headed up the green, still slope.
>
> Up to this point I had not analyzed my inter-
> est. Nevertheless, I pushed ahead of Iino, up to the
> glade, leaving the little man panting behind. On this
> occasion I did not loll on the grass. I headed straight
> for the Buddha, walked around it, printed its every
> curve on my mind and gradually felt contentment
> sweeping through me. A sense of peace. But there
> stirred in me, too, something long repressed, deep

and powerful as a hibernating bear, incessant as all the dark forces we have within us.

Iino was most complacent that afternoon. Probably he had been full of sake the night before and for a while he droned away about the superiority of Germanic science compared to the Anglo-American variety, until he fell asleep.

For an hour I was completely free. Lying on my back in the soft, green grass, idly noting the drifting passage of cloud wisps in the blue above, the swaying tracery of the leafy boughs, I had only to turn my eyes a little to see the shadow of the Buddha, lying as though prostrate in worship at the feet of the towering idol. At such times one does not wish for the soft touch of a happy past, nor feel the tiny shocks of fear for a future probably ending in a blood-stained shambles. One is just grateful for the oasis of the moment, the simple warmth and smells of nature that remain unchanged forever.

When Iino suddenly grunted and sat up, I felt no regret. It was only an interlude. All the way back to camp, foot up, foot down, I scarcely saw the turns, my mind slumbering at ease in memory of the still afternoon.

We arrived back in time for me to bolt my bowl of maize just as the work party tramped through the gate and drew up between the huts to roll off their staccato numbering in the strange tongue grown so familiar to my ears. I wound down the dirt path to the evening sick parade and was swallowed up by the camp routine once more.

A few nights later I headed up to my cubicle later than usual. Two of my men were desperately ill and I had been working on them after lights out in the small camp hospital, then sat in the gloom to smoke a treasured cigarette butt before turning in. I lay down on my pallet, tucked in my mosquito net, which also provided the rats with enough amusement as a slide to keep them away from me, and stretched out to blot away a few more imprisoned hours.

Through the cracks between the boards of the wall the moon laid fine slivers of light across my bed and, drowsy, I stared at them, seeing odd patterns flicker to and fro. I slept and dreamed of fitful, un-remembered scenes and once half-awakened at my own murmuring. I slept once more.

Sometime later in the night I began to stir in that strange half-light where personality exists, but is lashed with thongs, helpless. Gradually, I began to sweat and shiver like a prisoner on the rack awaiting the terror. Above me, the shadows began to take shape and come alive — blurred, then sliding into focus, swaying like jelly, and, at last, settling: the Buddha emerged, looking down with a sure, fulfilling, god-like smile. Almost imperceptibly it inclined towards me till all the tenseness of the breasts and belly filled my body and stretched it tight as a violin string.

How long I lay transfixed, transfigured, I do not know. Life came back after all the barren years, the deep core of being flared up again, and my Buddha, without a motion, passed an invisible hand across my face and smoothed away all doubts, all fears.

Again, I slept.

In the morning I woke refreshed. As I went about the tasks of the day, piece by piece the whole experience came back, till the jigsaw was complete. With it came awareness that life still ran through pulsing, subterranean channels, awaiting the moment to flow again to the surface.

All my cultivated insensibility had vanished. Up to this point I had put my nose to the grindstone of oblivion and refused to lift it for a glance left or right. Ever afterwards, through the moments of terror, under all the rain of bombs, a golden thread shone fine and indivisible for me: so much left undone, and so much — be it good or evil — that I must, yes, must do.

I knew I would come home again.[49]

The Association of Relatives of Men at Hong Kong: The Home Front II

I n Toronto, 6,431 miles east of Camp 3D, Jean Reid could only hope. But she wasn't alone. Beyond family and friends, her husband's capture and imprisonment had been of special concern to the doctors who had trained him at Toronto General Hospital (TGH), and in 1939, saw his outstanding promise rewarded with a senior internship under Duncan Graham, the professor of medicine. Moved by Reid's plight, members of the senior medical staff considered how they might be of help to his wife, whose miscarriage had been treated by one of their own in the winter of 1942.

That fall, Dr. Ray Farquharson, assistant professor of medicine at the University of Toronto and TGH, offered Jean a part-time secretarial job in his office. His wish was to provide her with occupational therapy in supportive surroundings, a posting, as it turned out, legitimized by the extra work Farquharson took on as consultant to the Royal Canadian Air Force, and later in the war, as physician-in-chief of Christie Street Veterans Hospital. Under Farquharson's protective wing, Jean began working at the university three days a week as assistant to his secretary, Stella Clutton, who became a lifelong friend.

A brilliant teacher as well as idealistic and kind-hearted, Farquharson set the pace as TGH's head of the Department of Therapeutics in teaching his interns, residents, and medical fellows the fundamental importance of patient observation and the need to realize and evaluate the psychological effects of any serious organic disease. Farquharson had been a favourite teacher of Reid's. Learning of Jean's job in the first letter he received from her in June 1943, Reid used precious space on the small, one-sided card he wrote back to respond to the news: "Beloved, a secretary! My deep thanks to Farquharson; no better to take care of you."[1]

Another friend and colleague doing all he could on Reid's behalf was Dr. Lyall Hodgins of The Clinic in Vancouver. Now in his early fifties, Hodgins's affection for Reid bordered on the fatherly. His natural concern for "Jack" and rumours of difficult prison camp conditions galvanized him to find a way to alleviate Reid's personal situation. Although the *Melbourne Argus* reported that Reid was alive in a Hong Kong internment camp in March 1942 (news, as previously related, that reached Canada in early May), it was hearsay, based on recollections of refugees. Hodgins could make no headway until the International Red Cross confirmed the status of a partial list of "C" Force personnel in October 1942 and Reid was officially listed among the living.

With confirmation that Reid was alive, Hodgins wrote to Ernest Maag, the Canadian delegate of the International Red Cross Committee, who was based in Montreal:

January 28, 1943

Dear Mr. Maag,

> My junior partner and great friend, Doctor Jack
> Reid, was captured at Hong Kong. I am wonder-
> ing if it is possible for myself and medical partners
> here to do something to aid Doctor Reid in the way
> of supplies, personal things, and especially medical
> supplies. Any expenses will be gladly refunded by
> his friends.[2]

More than an official contact, Maag was a recent ally of
Hodgins. The sudden, forced resettlement of 23,000 Japanese
Canadians away from British Columbia's coastal areas — ordered
as a security measure by Prime Minister Mackenzie King's government in January 1942 following Japan's attacks in the Pacific —
attracted the concern of the International Red Cross Committee
in Geneva. Maag, based in Montreal, was asked to report to Swiss
headquarters on the manner and effects of the Canadian government's draconian relocation program.

Coincidently, Hodgins had been invited to act as medical ad-
viser to the British Columbia Security Commission, the new provincial organization set up to implement King's edict. Appalled
by the resettlement order, which was tearing families from their
homes, their businesses, and one another, Hodgins spent the first
six months of 1942 doing all he could to mitigate its impact, first by
setting up and overseeing hospital facilities in Vancouver's Hastings
Park, the cramped, squalid compound where thousands of Japanese
Canadians were concentrated prior to shipment inland, then by lobbying the government to rescind the order that was breaking up
families by forcibly sending all males between the ages of 18 and 45
to work as labourers on road gangs in the B.C. interior.

In June 1942, Hodgins journeyed to Ottawa with RCMP
Deputy Commissioner Frederick Mead to plead the case for family
reunification. Several weeks earlier, Hodgins had visited sites in the

B.C. interior where Japanese Canadians were being settled and found little or no opposition from local residents to Japanese-Canadian males rejoining their families: "The white populations of the interior towns," Hodgins told government officials, "almost without exception are pleased with the advent of the Japanese, are kindly, and have but one criticism which was expressed often and definitely — that the Commission was not treating these people well enough."[3]

During his own investigation, Maag had been impressed by Hodgins's efforts on behalf of Japanese Canadians, and now, with respect to Reid, was eager to help. In his reply to Hodgins's letter, Maag said he would contact Lieutenant-Colonel F.W. Clarke, the DND officer in charge of care of Canadian prisoners on the Chinese coast. He would also write the International Red Cross in Geneva, which had representatives in Hong Kong and Tokyo. Maag concluded his letter to Hodgins on an upbeat note: "When I tell Geneva how much you have been doing for the Japanese population in B.C., I am sure they will fall over themselves in Tokyo to do all that is possible in order to help your friend."[4]

Maag's official letters to Clarke at DND and to the International Red Cross Committee in Geneva emphasize the point:

> Personally, I feel sure that if the Japanese authorities knew how much Dr. Hodgins has been doing for the Japanese population in Canada, and if they had any knowledge of the admiration which the Japanese of Vancouver have for him, they would do everything in their power in order to make life as pleasant as possible for Dr. Reid, and give him all the assistance that his friend would like him to get. It cannot be stressed too much that the activities of Dr. Hodgins have been a great blessing for the Japanese population on the Pacific Coast.[5]

Maag also contacted Dr. Fritz Paravicini, a personal friend and a delegate to the Red Cross in Tokyo. A Swiss national, Dr. Paravicini had been a resident and practising doctor in Japan for many years and had built up a personal network of connections at high levels in both diplomatic circles and the Japanese government.

All this seemed promising, and Hodgins kept Jean up to date on developments by sending her copies of the Hodgins-Maag-Clarke correspondence. His note to her in February 1943 was encouraging: "I would judge from what I know of Mr. Maag and his connection with the International Red Cross, especially in view of the fact that his great friend, the medical man who has practised for many years in Tokyo, is the International Red Cross representative in Japan, that we may be able to make life more pleasant for Jack."[6]

That didn't happen.

To begin with, the Canadian government and the International Red Cross didn't know where Reid was in early 1943. They only learned that he and a large group of Canadians had been transferred from Hong Kong to Japan after the first Radio Tokyo broadcast by Tokyo No. 5 prisoners was picked up by American ham operators in July 1943, six months after the move.

Even with this information, DND's Lieutenant-Colonel Clarke couldn't respond in a practical way since his role as "caretaker" of "C" Force prisoners was in name alone. Until a route for mail and Red Cross parcels was set up via Siberia later in the war, the only way the Allies could send aid to Far East prisoners was in conjunction with the internee exchange and repatriation program arranged between the Allied and Japanese governments in 1942 and overseen by the International Red Cross.

To say the least, this exchange program didn't accommodate special deliveries to particular prisoners. Throughout 1942 and 1943, civilian and diplomatic internees from both sides were freed and picked up by ship at various points, then exchanged at a neutral port, usually Lourenço Marques (present-day Maputo) in Portuguese East Africa (today's Mozambique). About a dozen such swaps were made over two years. Along with Japanese nationals being repatriated to the Home Islands, tons of Red Cross supplies were transferred from MS *Gripsholm*, the Allied ship chartered for the exchanges, to its Japanese opposite number for shipment to Hong Kong and Japan and eventual distribution to prisoner of war camps. But this last step was far from guaranteed. Typically, supplies were held up for months once they reached Japanese or Japanese-held ports and were often confiscated by the Japanese for their own use as the supplies moved down the distribution line. Sometimes there was little or nothing left for the camps.

Unaware of the spotty outcomes of these aid shipments, Canada's Lieutenant-Colonel Clarke, whose main function, in effect, was domestic public relations, updated the relatives of "C" Force prisoners whenever he had something positive to report (reports with personal implications: his son, William, a captain in the Royal Rifles, was a POW held at Sham Shui Po). Lance Corporal William Bell of the Grenadiers, whose family preserved these government missives, later pointed out the gullibility of Clarke and other Canadian and Red Cross officials in their belief that the Japanese would do as expected in distributing Allied aid, and otherwise treat prisoners decently:

> July 7th, 1942, the Canadian Red Cross sent a load of supplies overseas aboard the ship *Gripsholm*. I don't recall ever seeing any of this shipload of 150 tons of cigarettes, food and medical supplies. It was reported to my family in a letter from Lt. Colonel F.W. Clarke ... that "Treatment of the prisoners is

good and food supply is much better." This could not have been further from the truth....

Another letter my family received from Colonel Clarke stated that "magazines, books, games and other comforts were to be sent on a second sailing of the *Gripsholm* from New York on October 29th, 1942." They were hoping to send "winter and summer uniforms, warm clothing, boots and blankets before the cold winter set in. This shipment was to proceed to Russia and continue to the Orient when a steamer was available." I can safely say that I don't recall seeing any of these supplies.[7]

On the international stage, Ernest Maag's optimism about arranging help for Reid through his Red Cross connections — the expectation of Japanese goodwill due to Dr. Hodgins's efforts on behalf of Japanese Canadians — was likewise unfounded. Embroiled in the vast war to establish the Greater East Asia Co-Prosperity Sphere, the Japanese warlords had no particular interest in Canadian citizens of Japanese descent, more than two-thirds of whom were Canadian-born, nor in Dr. Hodgins's efforts to remedy their situation in Canada.

In Tokyo, Dr. Fritz Paravicini's assumption that his Japanese hosts would act humanely to prisoners of war — a belief instilled, presumably, by his civilian experience of Japanese behaviour as a long-time Tokyo resident — seems to have blinded him to the possibility of the Japanese acting otherwise in wartime. It isn't known what effort Paravicini made to further Hodgins's initiative to help Reid. But naivety clearly had the upper hand in the official report he submitted to the International Red Cross Committee in 1943 after visiting several prison camps that the Japanese had "staged" to generate precisely the sunny assessment Paravicini accorded them. Australia's *Sydney Morning Herald* carried the story on June 15, 1943:

PRISON CAMPS IN JAPAN

Favourable Red Cross Report
"Prisoner of War News," Aberdeen, publishing further reports from the Far East on war prisoners' camps, states that Dr. F. Paravicini, of the International Red Cross Committee, visited the main camp at Keijo (Korea) and the Jinsen division camp at Keijo.

Dr. Paravicini reports there are several hundred Australian and British prisoners in both camps, which are efficiently administered, and at which there is good, nourishing food in sufficient quantity.

Dr. Paravicini also visited Tokyo camps designated Section 1 and Section 2. Section 1 is occupied by British, American, and other Allied prisoners who are well housed in 10 wooden huts. A good many prisoners arrived at this camp in a poor state of health, but as a result of the care they have received their condition has notably improved.

Section 2 includes a camp situated in Central Park, Yokohama. Here the huts are constructed of concrete. Playing fields in the park are used by the prisoners for five hours daily. Prisoners are also permitted to walk outside the camp for an hour a day. Discipline and morale are excellent.

The designation Tokyo Sections 1 and 2 also includes another camp at Yokohama, two at Kawasaki [3D was one], and one at Horokka.

Dr. Paravicini adds that the Japanese received him with great courtesy, and he praises the generous help of the Japanese Red Cross.[8]

Misleading reports such as this would have comforted the relatives of Canadian prisoners, Jean among them, and reassured Canadian officials. But on the other side of the Pacific, Reid and his men knew too well how Japanese shams were put on for the benefit of Red Cross observers, and what happened if prisoners didn't play along.

A few months before prisoners were shipped to Japan, Sham Shui Po had been window-dressed in just this way, with truckloads of sports equipment, sports clothes, and copious amounts of food for the prisoners. After a one-of-a-kind feast that noon, the men were ordered outside to play baseball and volleyball with the new equipment while a Red Cross inspection party toured the prison camp (its misery-filled hospital had been hastily fenced off to appear unconnected to the camp). Japanese orders to prisoners: no talking to visitors!

Tantalized beyond endurance by the chance to expose the deception to the outside world, Captain John Norris of the Winnipeg Grenadiers recklessly disobeyed, shouting at the Red Cross party as the tour was coming to an end: "This is all fake! The prisoners are dying of disease and starvation. There's the hospital — behind those barbed wires. See for yourself!"[9]

The Swiss officials insisted on being shown the "Agony Ward," were appalled by what they found — including the bodies of several dead prisoners — and declared that these shocking conditions would be reported to the International Commission and that a formal complaint would be sent to the Japanese government.

Such threats didn't faze the Japanese. The next day, all the "props" were removed, camp life returned to normal, and during prisoner roll call Captain Norris was called out, screamed at, then knocked to the ground by Sergeant Kanao Inouye, the vicious Japanese-Canadian prison camp guard the POWs called the "Kamloops Kid."[10]

William Allister was one of the horrified onlookers:

> The beating began: kicking, pounding the silent figure on the ground, shrieking with each blow. We stood at attention, lined up, silently, helplessly watching as it continued, on and on. He would not stop. Norris must be unconscious by now. Would he kill him? We felt the blows as though they were our own bodies. Red Barlow couldn't stand it any longer — cheery, clowning, happy-go-lucky Barlow suddenly yelled: "You goddamn murderer!"
>
> We jumped on him and shut him up, wanting no new victims.
>
> We were dismissed at last, with the limp body left lying on the parade ground. Later he was carried to the hospital and revived. Norris didn't die but was never the same ... a quiet, slow-moving figure limping along with a cane for the rest of the time.[11]

In the cruel underworld of Japanese prison camps, Dr. Hodgins's wish to personally intercede and "make life more pleasant for Jack" never stood a chance. With no progress reported by Clarke or Maag, Hodgins's encouraging letters to Jean petered out. He stayed in touch. But like her other "war correspondents" — the people Jean was in contact with because they, too, had a loved one captured at Hong Kong — Hodgins could only offer sympathy, an exchange of news, shared hope.

From the time of the surrender on Christmas Day 1941, the over-riding state of mind for the family members of Hong Kong prisoners was a sense of helplessness. So little was known, news was so long in coming, and the end of the war — now a world war — had become impossible to foresee, a bleakness reinforced by Winston Churchill nearly a year after the Canadians were captured. In a speech after the first major Allied victory of the war — the British defeat of German forces at El Alamein in November 1942 — Churchill cautioned his listeners at the Lord Mayor of London's Luncheon at Mansion House: "Now this is not the end. It is not even the beginning of the end. But it is, perhaps, the end of the beginning."[12]

With hope of seeing their loved ones receding into a future unknown, the families of the Hong Kong prisoners turned to each other. Four associations, formed by wives, parents, and siblings of the prisoners, sprang up in Quebec, Ontario, Manitoba, and Saskatchewan to keep up spirits, share news, communicate with government officials, and — the main activity of their meetings — assemble Red Cross parcels for prisoners of war.

The Ontario group (Jean a prime organizer) was formalized in Toronto in the spring of 1942 by 36 "Hong Kong" relatives who held their inaugural meeting at Maurice Cody Hall, St. Paul's Church, Bloor Street, where Jean's family had long attended Sunday services. The group named themselves The Association of Relatives of Men at Hong Kong and agreed to meet at the church the first Thursday evening of each month to do their work. Elizabeth Renison, the wife of St. Paul's rector, was named the association's honorary president. Willa Glassco, sister of Major Jack Price, second-in-command of the Royal Rifles, was elected president. Other officers of the new association were committee conveners Jean Reid and Marguerite Gray, Gordon Gray's wife.

Strong and lasting friendships grew quickly between association members — Jean Reid and Willa Glassco would remain fond friends for the rest of their lives — and such personal connections soon extended to members of the other Hong Kong associations. In June 1942, Jean wrote to Maude Crawford, one of the founders of the Manitoba Hong Kong Association and wife of Major John Crawford, "C" Force's senior medical officer and Reid's direct superior in the Grenadiers.

Like Jean, Maude had received unofficial word in May 1942 that her husband was alive. At the end of August 1942, the first POW mail from North Point Camp reached Canada. Among the lucky ones, Jean and Maude both received letters from their respective "Jacks." At Jean's suggestion, her father-in-law, Harry Reid, paid a visit to Maude's home when he was in Winnipeg on business several weeks later. Maude responded:

> September 16, 1942
> 203 Oak Street, Winnipeg
>
> Dear Jean,
>
> Your very welcome, very lovely, and very friendly letter called for an immediate reply.
>
> It was so nice of you to ask Mr. Reid to call. I enjoyed so very much meeting him — and hearing of your news. He is very devoted to his boy, and it was grand to hear about "your Jack" — to get to know him better — and to find that in so many ways he is similar to mine!
>
> The thrill of hearing that your letter came through just added to my own joy in my own wee note. When I saw [my] Jack's handwriting on the

envelope I could just scarcely believe my luck. I seem to have been so fortunate — Jack's name being on every list — when so many have had no word. This letter seemed almost too much.

He was very cautious, much more so than many of the [Grenadier] boys [whose letters home also arrived] — but I think in his anxiety to get something through, he just didn't take any chances. It was just a sweet little letter to the three of us — and the children's excitement was boundless when the letter arrived. My small girl cried herself to sleep, and my nine-year-old boy just looked bewildered that it had come. He just could not believe it. Kept reading it over and over again. It's pitiful that children have to go through what our children have had in the last year. With radios and newspapers screaming the awfulness of it — it's impossible to keep children away from the news. And it's bound to affect them.

Did Mrs. [Gordon] Gray get a letter? How many of your group there were fortunate?

There were a great many disappointed people here. The letters must have been severely censored or else the Japanese just weren't bothering to read them all — and just sent a few through. Our letters did, though, seem uniformly cheerful — and I don't believe they would have all stressed that if conditions were not "fou" [crazy] — do you?

Have you stopped writing — or are you continuing to do so? I have been sending two [letters] a week and will go on sending one a week until further word comes.

Is your small group there still active — and
still meeting? I think it is wonderful that you have
become friends. You deserve a great deal of credit
for organizing the group. I have just written the
Saskatchewan Prisoners of War Relatives Association
to see if we cannot enlist their aid in getting some
official recognition.[13]

Nothing came of her efforts. A year later, Maude, now in regular touch with Jean, registers the frustrations many association
members were feeling:

July 9, 1943

Dear Jean,

I get so het up, really I feel as though I'll explode if
something is not done soon. I cannot help but feel
that in the government's scheme of things our men
are more or less forgotten for the time being. They
are such a small part of the whole that they have
ceased to figure very largely in government headaches — and not much is being done for their relief.

Colonel Clarke, while very soothing, does not
seem to accomplish very much and the whole situation just seems to have been shelved.

If you feel as I do, Jean — and can do anything
there to enlist the support of the whole group — I
do wish you would do so.[14]

Lobbying efforts made by the associations went nowhere. The most
the "Maudes" and "Jeans" could do was continue to pack Red Cross

parcels and share any news they received. No detail was too slight: when Reid's letter of March 1943 reached Jean 10 months later, report of its arrival was mentioned in the Toronto newspapers simply because it was "the most recent letter to arrive from any prisoner of the Japanese."[15]

The strain of the years of uncertainty for "Hong Kong" relatives is hard to fathom. For Jean, brought up in a Christian household by a devout mother and a practical-minded father who believed strongly in the importance of Christian guidelines, it was, ironically, religion that provoked her one breakdown of the war years. During a visit to 5 Scholfield to offer spiritual guidance, a churchman dwelt too persistently on the need to accept the mystery of God's purpose as a source of comfort for Jean's suffering, a line of thought she'd had enough of in patriotic Sunday sermons. That night, Jean erupted in a fit of anger at such bleak piety, an outburst her parents sternly reproved: God's ways *were* mysterious; difficulty must be borne through belief, and with a stiff upper lip. She retreated to her room in tears.

Jean forgave her parents. But the strength to endure her situation was, as before, of her own making — the same toughness that pulled her through the peritonitis and septicemia that nearly killed her at the age of 12. By September 1944, when out of the blue she received a letter by "Air Mail Special Delivery" from someone named Marianne Pollak in New York City, she had been waiting for Jack for nearly three years:

> 895 West End Ave.
> New York, 25, NY
> August 31, 1944
>
> My Dear Mrs. Reid,
>
> Enclosed you will find the copy of a short wave broadcast from my son, which I received this

morning. The message was telephoned to me on Tuesday evening, shortly after the broadcast, by some people who had heard it. Several other people sent me letters telling me of the radio message and giving me the text as correctly as they could understand it. I wanted to deliver the news to you myself and thought it best to send you the copy of the government telegram.

My son is a Naval Architect who was stationed at the Navy Yard in Cavite, Ph.I. He was taken prisoner in Cebu in June [*sic*] 1942 and was taken to Japan several months later along with Lt. Cmdr. Dockweiler and Lt. Finn.[16]

I trust that you will get some comfort and relief out of this message — brief as it is.

Wishing the best of luck to you and your husband.

Yours sincerely,
Marianne S. Pollak
(Mrs. Alfred Pollak)[17]

Enclosed was the carbon copy transcription of the voice message from George Pollak — his portion of a Radio Tokyo broadcast recorded at 3D in July 1944 and picked up by American ham operators on August 29. After thanking his mother for two letters he'd received from her and giving reassurance about his health, Pollak's transcription went on: "[I am] ... here with my friends Lieutenant Commander E.V ... [Dockweiler] and Lt. Charles R. Finch [Finn] of 1439 Myrtle Avenue, San Jose, California, and Captain John A.D. [*sic*] Reid, Royal Canadian Army Medical Corps from 5 Schoolfield (?) Avenue, Toronto. Communicate with their wives please."[18]

All Jean needed to know: Jack was still alive.

Allied Bombing Begins:
The End of POW Camp Tokyo 3D

During the summer of 1944, American reconnaissance missions over Japan gave way to bombing missions. Taking off from bases in China and later from the Mariana Islands, recaptured by the Americans that August, waves of B-29 Superfortresses began hitting the Home Islands. Factories in 3D's Tsurumi neighbourhood of Yokohama were early targets of the raids.

Sergeant Tom Marsh and his comrades were both heartened and appalled by what they witnessed:

> One night in July a large-scale attack with firebombs was made in our district. The ack-ack was terrific. The whole world seemed aflame. In spite of the efforts of the guards to keep us from witnessing the sight we stood and gazed at the conflagration. Only a river running nearby and the fact that our huts had tiled roofs saved our quarters from the fire. Smoke

and sparks were all around. I saw a terrible sight that night. I watched a string of American bombers, in line astern formation, following their leader. The lead aircraft made for the very centre of the ack-ack fire and at this point burst into flames. Plane after plane followed to the same point and were shot down. Altogether I counted five. I felt sick. We all prayed for those gallant lads.

One of the Jap guards, like quite a few of the Japanese who prided themselves on their esthetic qualities, got quite a kick out of seeing his home town destroyed. He stood gazing on the burning city in rapt ecstasy and then, raising his arms to the sky, he turned to us and said in English, "Drama! Drama!" He was convinced he had a front seat at a good show, all for nothing. He appeared quite mad and if he had a fiddle like Nero I'm sure he would have played us a tune.

For several days following the bombing we saw long files of civilian refugees filing past our camp trekking into the hills. The Japanese Officials had cleared the whole district of its inhabitants. The remaining hovels and dwellings that had survived the firebombing were pulled down to prevent the further spread of the fire, but little was left to save.[1]

Another sign of the war's changing picture was noted by Lance Corporal "Blacky" Verreault of the Corps of Signals in his 3D diary entry for September 10, 1944: "Well! The army just arrived to take over guarding of the camp. I think that things are getting difficult for the Japanese and that these thirteen soldiers taking over from the civilians are to prevent reprisals by the civilian population against the prisoners. The end is getting near, evidently."[2]

The "end" — an Allied invasion of Japan — was more perilous for prisoners than anything local civilians might attempt in revenge for American bombing. That summer, Lieutenant-General Kyoji Tominaga, the Japanese vice-minister of war, issued a standing order to all POW camp commandants in the Home Islands and Occupied Territories to be followed in the event of an American land invasion in their area: the prisoner of war "kill-all order."

> Japanese War Ministry — August 1, 1944
> At such a time as the situation became urgent ... the POWs will be concentrated and confined in their present location and kept under heavy guard until preparations for the final solution will be made. The time and method of this disposition are as follows:
> 1. The Time.
> Although the basic aim is to act under superior orders, individual disposition may be made in the following circumstances:
> a. When an uprising of large numbers cannot be suppressed without the use of firearms.
> b. When escapees from the camp may turn into a hostile Fighting force.
> 2. The Methods.
> a. Whether they are destroyed individually or in groups, or however it is done, with mass bombing, poisonous smoke, poisons, drowning, decapitation, or what, dispose of them as the situation dictates.
> b. In any case it is the aim not to allow the escape of a single one, to annihilate them all, and not to leave any traces.[3]

By the fall of 1944, Commandant Uwamori was doing all he could to protect the prisoners at 3D. He was now treating Reid as a sort of partner whose suggestions for health betterment of the camp he chose to follow as best he could, in spite of pressure from headquarters. Reid's mix of warnings and diplomacy was paying off:

> [There were] several inspections by the Tokyo headquarters staff, several times of which they took great umbrage at the medical setup [at 3D] as they said we had far too many sick men entirely the fault of the doctors.... We took the screaming ... [which] didn't come to very much because the Commandant after they would go said he was responsible for the health of the camp and that was the thing that interested him most and not the work they were doing.[4]

A new double-decker hut, built to accommodate the entire camp, was finally finished in November 1944, more than a year behind schedule. It was still crowded but better outfitted and warmer than the old huts. Food rationing increased somewhat.

That month, Japanese doctors from Shinagawa Hospital came to 3D and asked to see the most seriously ill prisoners. Of the 150 men that Reid presented, the Japanese ordered 23 to the convalescent hospital in Omori Camp for rest and another 73 to Shinagawa Hospital for treatment.

All this activity, said Reid, was a definite effort on the part of some Japanese to improve the health of the men as they saw the Americans closing in.

What never improved were the dangerous conditions at the Nippon Kokan Shipyard in the little work still being done there. On November 5, 1944, company Sergeant Major Earl Todd, a well-liked and respected career soldier who had trained the "C" Force recruits at Valcartier Camp in 1941, was killed when a frayed rope attached to a crane suddenly parted and dropped a load of wood, crushing him. As Reid noted in his diary, Todd's was a death due not so much to negligence as to the shoddy equipment the men had to work with — machinery and materials that would have been condemned in Canada.

Christmas 1944 brought a few days off. Like the previous year, the men worked their magic creating decorations out of scraps. A church service and carol singing were held on Christmas Eve and a concert on Christmas day. Red Cross parcels were distributed, the first of four disbursements over the next several months — far more than the Canadians had received during their first three years of imprisonment. Like Uwamori, other Japanese higher-ups were evidently showing increased concern for the prisoners' health as the American bombing raids escalated and the war tilted further in the Allies' favour. To everyone, the evidence of American capability was stark — not just the destruction but the instruments of destruction. George Pollak remembered the words of a Japanese guard who went out to inspect the wreckage of a downed B-29. The guard came back in the afternoon, shaking his head: "We can't win this war," he said. "We haven't got anything like that."[5]

At the end of December, the Christmas cheer was marred by news from Shinagawa Hospital. On Christmas Eve, Fred Wyrwas of the Royal Rifles died of liver failure. On December 27, Victor Smith of the Winnipeg Grenadiers died of a gastric haemorrhage and hepatitis. Rifleman Wyrwas and Private Smith were the 22nd and 23rd men in Reid's group of Canadians to die while prisoners in Japan. They were the last to be lost.

Thanks to better weather and additional Red Cross medicines, the winter of 1945 saw improvement in the men's health. It was still cold, but instead of being changeable and wet, there was almost no rain and the temperature was steady.

During this period, air raids continued to increase in intensity. As Reid says, despite the danger, the raids had some salutary effects:

> Frequent general alarms and rather frequent local alarms. The Japanese civilians got very excited, but to my surprise the Japanese staff in the camp remained remarkably unexcited compared to what I expected. The men — whenever an air raid warning was blown — the men were all brought into camp quickly, into a shelter which had been constructed under Lt. Finn's supervision with roofs which were six inches of timber and dirt. The men were usually run into the camp from the company and put into these pits....
>
> All through these raids the men showed extremely good morale and discipline, no trouble at all. That was part of the reason why the Japanese in the camp were so cool: our men were getting so confident and were showing such confidence that that had a lot of bearing with the Japanese getting much less excited than we would have expected them to get under these conditions.[6]

Always a standout at six foot three, Sergeant Major George MacDonell exemplified that confidence. Whether it was his height, rank, poise, or a combination of all three, he had caught the commandant's attention, leading to a strange encounter.

One cold night in January 1945, two guards woke MacDonell in the wee hours of the morning and escorted him without explanation to Uwamori's office in the camp administration building. After ushering him into the office, the guards withdrew, sliding closed the rice paper door behind them.

Understandably, MacDonell was apprehensive. But, chilled as always in winter, his first sensation on entering the office was the pleasurable feeling of the enveloping, almost stifling heat coming from its pot-bellied stove. He came to attention and saluted Commandant Uwamori, who sat behind his desk, sake cup in hand. They were alone. Uwamori motioned to a cushion on the floor in front of his desk (there were no chairs), and MacDonell sat down cross-legged. The commandant, he sensed, was a little drunk:

Uwamori: (Gesturing to the bottle of sake warming on the stove) "Would you like some?"

MacDonell: "No, thank you, sir."

Uwamori: "That's a shame."

The Commandant gave MacDonell a long stare, then spoke again.

Uwamori: "Is Japan going to win the war?"

MacDonell: (Pause) "No, sir. It is not."

Uwamori leaned forward and looked at MacDonell intently: "Why is that?"

MacDonell: "Sir, no matter how brave your soldiers are, no matter how great the spirit of the Japanese people, you have no chance against the combined forces of Great Britain and the United States of America, the most powerful nation in the world."

There was a long silence.

Uwamori: "Are you sure that is correct?"

MacDonell: "Yes, sir."[7]

MacDonell had the impression that the commandant expected these answers. He knew Reid had been telling Uwamori what he told his own men: Japanese defeat was inevitable; it was just a matter of time. But after a night of lonely drinking, Uwamori apparently wanted a second opinion. For reasons unknown, he selected the towering 22-year-old Royal Rifles sergeant major as his oracle. Answers given, a mystified MacDonell was dismissed and returned to the hut by the waiting guards.

Throughout January and February 1945, the American air raids made work of any kind almost impossible, allowing continuing gains in the prisoners' health. The wailing of air raid sirens was music to the men's ears — the harbingers of approaching freedom. As bombs burst in the vicinity and the camp was occasionally sprinkled with pieces of shrapnel and machine-gun bullets, they resorted to grim humour in their flimsy funk holes — useless protection against a direct hit.

The shrapnel came from bombs, but the bullets were the calling card of a new American presence: carrier-based fighter planes. Their arrival on the scene meant two things: the U.S. Navy was close enough to the Home Islands for short-range fighters and fighter-bombers to fly sorties over Japan, and the Japanese navy was helpless to stop their encroachment. Seeing the American fighters gave a special lift to the prisoners' spirits. George Pollak remembered how marvellous it was to watch these nimble invaders — F6F Hellcats and F4U Corsairs, their pilots clearly visible through their cockpit canopies — strafing the dock areas, buzzing low down the main streets of Kawasaki on bombing runs, then weaving up and away through the smokestacks of the industrial area after hitting their targets.[8]

The war was going in the right direction, but at the end of February came an unexpected blow to Reid's carefully constructed balance of power: change at the top. Uwamori's leniency with the prisoners finally provoked headquarters to remove him as camp commandant. Faced with this loss, Reid then met its depressing corollary, Uwamori's replacement:

> At the end of February Uwamori was shifted to Omori Camp.... I was very sorry to see the old commandant go. He had tried during a long period to better our conditions....
>
> The camp was taken over by Lieut. Nakamura. This man impressed me as a simple type of psychopathic case. He had definite ideas of grandeur, and made such remarks as, "He couldn't understand why it was every camp he came into always became the best in the district, immediately."
>
> He couldn't understand it, but there it was.[9]

Sergeant Tom Marsh retained vivid memories of Takso Nakamura. Nicknamed "Charlie" by the Canadians because of his Chaplinesque moustache, Lieutenant Nakamura let it be known that he once owned a chain of hotels in Japan, but one after the other, they had been destroyed in the bombing — hence his residence in camp, along with two young female companions. Nakamura regularly helped himself to the prisoners' Red Cross parcels, now and then turning over small portions of them to the camp cooks to be added to the prisoners' rice rations as a show of his personal magnanimity. He would lecture the men:

> You must all be prepared if this camp is struck. Look! I am always prepared. My hotels are burned down. What do I care! I have plenty of money. Do not be scared of what people may do to you. The Japanese Imperial Army will protect you. I am the Army! One Japanese soldier can protect you from everybody. The people respect the Army! Many great men in Japan are soldiers. I am soldier![10]

Two weeks after Nakamura took charge, the Americans hit Tokyo again. On the night of March 9–10, 1945, 279 B-29s dropped nearly 1,700 tons of incendiary bombs throughout the night hours, burning out 16 square miles of the city (the raid, code-named "Operation Meetinghouse," remains the single most destructive bombing attack in history). For the prisoners of 3D, 12 miles south of Tokyo, the rolling thunder of the planes and the growing glow of the fires lasted all night.

Signalman Gerry Gerrard was in "the hole" with the others while the raid took place:

> The night they did the big bombing they took a mile-wide strip right through Yokohama and Tokyo, they were just coming in one after another.... We had a shelter that ... was no good. It was a hole in the ground with some planks on top and some sod thrown on it. The other thing was, the guard standing out there, he made us all go in the hole and when that bomb landed he ended up in the hole with

us. We just lay there all night with the flashes, the guns and the bombs exploding, and loudspeakers all over — you could hear the Jap telling them what's happening. And you could tell when the bombers were coming in; he'd get excited as hell and the next thing, you'd hear them roar through and the bombs go off. There were a lot of firebombs too.[11]

This raid provoked a Japanese policy change. The strategy of relying on the presence of prisoner of war camps in the Tokyo-Yokohama district as a deterrent to American bombing clearly wasn't working (in fact, the Americans had no idea where 90 percent of the prison camps on the Home Islands were). Three weeks after Operation Meetinghouse, the Japanese began moving prisoners to more isolated camps in northern and southern Japan.

In choosing the first batch of 3D prisoners for transfer, Commandant Nakamura's method to improve his camp "immediately" was to get rid of the sickest men first. On March 30, 1945, 200 of the weakest were shipped north to Ohashi, an iron mining camp whose gruelling work these men were the least fit to do.

Reid was to go to Ohashi. But the evening before the transfer, orders came through from headquarters that he was to remain at 3D, after all. Instead, Lieutenant Commander Dockweiler was placed in charge of the Ohashi group, with Ensign Pollak second-in-command. Reid said his goodbyes and wished them well: "The group left camp about 4:30 a.m. on March 30. They took one Red Cross parcel for every five men and one-third of our medical supplies without Japanese authority. Although they always promise you wonderful things at the other end, it was never so and always worse, so we sent the extra medical supplies."[12]

Later that day, another 3D group consisting of 50 prisoners was sent to a camp on the outskirts of Tokyo to work in a brickyard. No officer was assigned to this group by the Japanese, so Reid placed Staff Sergeant Clark, the clever fire saboteur, in command and sent them on their way:

> After these men left we settled down to a very rest-less time in the camp. Little work was being done at the company and air raids were constant and very close to our camp and there were constant rumours that the remainder of the camp would move out of this area soon. The air raids had gained in frequency and intensity and proximity.
>
> On the night of the 9th of April the whole area in a half moon around the camp was completely burned out.... They came in very low that night, about seven or eight thousand feet....[13] The raid lasted through all the hours of darkness with the trail of planes passing directly overhead.... Eleven B-29's were shot down immediately above us in the glare of searchlights, with a wing disappearing on this one so that it spun on its long axis like a giant pin-wheel, another becoming a Roman-candle-like ball of flame which sailed about the sky for fully five minutes under the guidance of the automatic pilot before dipping somewhere in Yokohama. And the constant din of the anti-aircraft guns perched beside the camp fence mixed with the whistle and crump of bombs while the whole panorama about us, as far as one could see to the horizon, became a literal dancing red sea of flames. The fierce joy at the realization that the ring of rescue was closing in, combined with the niggling dread that one might not, at long last, survive the assault.[14]

A month after the April 9 firebombing of Tokyo — a city now five-eighths destroyed — Camp 3D was emptied and closed. The morning of May 12, 1945, a group under Major Kagy, comprising the remaining tuberculosis patients from Shinagawa Hospital and 17 cooks and shoemakers from 3D, was sent to Suwa Camp, 93 miles south of Tokyo. At six o'clock that evening, Reid, Lieutenant Finn, and the remaining 198 Canadians were shuttled to Yokohama where they were to board a train for the 60-mile trip north to Sendai Branch Camp No. 1 (Sendai Camp 1B) near Hitachi, half-way between Tokyo and the northern coastal city of Sendai.

Several hours before leaving camp, Reid's group was called out to the parade ground for a departure speech by the Japanese admiral in charge of Nippon Kokan Shipyard. In his brief exhortation, the admiral made no mention of the world news: five days earlier, on May 7, 1945, Germany had signed an unconditional surrender at Allied headquarters in Reims, France. The war in Europe was over.

– *12* –

Sendai Camp 1B: Dignity and Disarmament

Sendai Camp 1B was opened in April 1943 to provide slave labour for the Yumoto mine site of the Joban Coal Mining Company, operator of the largest coalfield on the island of Honshu and the main coal supplier for the Tokyo-Yokohama region.

The first POWs brought in to work with the local Japanese miners were 145 members of the Royal Netherlands East Indies Army, most of them of Dutch-Javanese descent, who had been captured after the surrender of Java in March 1942 and suffered a year in Batavia's (today's Jakarta) Glodok Convict Prison before being transported to Japan in the spring of 1943. In August 1944, the Dutch group was supplemented by 252 British POWs who had survived the fall of Singapore in February 1942 and then spent two years working under dreadful conditions on the Thailand-Burma "Death Railway."

In contrast, the Canadians set off for Sendai 1B with lighter hearts. Rumours of Germany's surrender had filtered into 3D and given the men a huge boost. In a last gesture of grandiosity, perhaps prompted by Japan's rapidly falling fortunes, Commandant

Nakamura released to the departing prisoners a number of Red Cross food parcels, underwear and other clothing, as well as quantities of soap, cigarettes, and various small items long held back.

Sergeant Tom Marsh was part of Reid's contingent:

> By Japanese standards, we were well equipped when we left 3D. Each man had a uniform, overcoat, shirt, underwear, and new boots. Most of this was from our own British Army stores. The boots were from a shipment of Red Cross supplies. In comparison to what had happened to us in the last three years, we now considered ourselves well off. Most of us now felt that the war could not last much longer and that we stood a fair chance of survival. We had also been issued a little extra food from Red Cross stores on our departure. This bucked us up a lot.[1]

During the train change at the Yokohama Railway Station, Reid was met by Lieutenant Uwamori who, for old time's sake, had come from Omori Camp to see the Canadians off. Uwamori told Reid that the new commandant at Sendai 1B, Lieutenant Takeichi Chisuwa, was a friend of his and that Reid and his men could expect fair treatment from him.

Detraining on the morning of May 13 at a coal-loading siding in the port of Onahama, the Canadians were dealt the usual cuffs and slaps by surly guards as they were packed aboard trucks. But the nine-mile drive over a winding and hilly dirt road to the prison camp showed the men something they hadn't seen in years: peaceful countryside untouched by war.

Here and there were quaint, thatched farmhouses surrounded by small, well-cultivated fields, some already showing the fresh green growth of early spring crops. Fruit trees were in blossom.

Sendai Camp 1B, spring/summer 1945.

The road the trucks followed rose and fell through quiet land-scape, then descended into a deeper valley and ran alongside a river. Across the water, tranquil vistas glided by.

Too soon these glimpses of serenity were behind them. Sendai 1B came into view at the base of a steep hill. Just down the road was the mine pit where the men would be working. The camp had the usual low-roofed huts for the prisoners, a nine-foot perimeter fence enclosing them, and a sentry box at the entrance. The trucks stopped outside the main gate to unload. Through the wire, the men could see a cluster of strange figures — British prisoners, they later learned. Optimistic at the start of the trip, Tom Marsh's heart soon sank:

We filed through the gate to the curious inspection of the rest of the guards. We soon found out how out of place the word "home" was when applied to Camp Sendai. It was just another form of hell.

Our first inkling of the conditions at Sendai was the group of human scarecrows standing near the gate. They were half-naked, emaciated to the point that it was difficult to imagine how life could possibly remain in such a pathetic form. Their faces were pale, gaunt, and haggard with hollow, unseeing eyes which stared at nothing. Their almost lifeless bodies were crippled and covered with scabs and sores. They were supposed to be brushing mats, but each movement was one of utter exhaustion, as if in slow motion.[2]

Inside the compound, the Canadians were lined up to await the arrival of the camp's senior non-commissioned officer. Pulling on white gloves as he did so, Sergeant Koju Tsuda strutted onto the parade ground in polished jackboots, barked out the usual greeting to prisoners — "You work, or else!" — then ordered the Canadians to empty their pockets and make a pile of their personal belongings on the ground in front of them. Next, he told them to strip off their clothes, underwear included, don the G-strings the guards provided, and stand back from their belongings. Tom Marsh explains what followed:

Now Frog Face [Tsuda], the quartermaster, and his minions had their innings. They began carting off our clothes and piling them on the sidelines. They took practically everything. They also rummaged through our personal possessions, taking what they fancied and treading over and kicking the rest in every direction.

These little piles constituted the whole of our belongings. A few letters, a snapshot of loved ones, a package of Red Cross cigarettes, a handmade comb, a carefully whittled spoon, razor blades — all were kicked around or stolen. The men stood and watched anxiously, hoping their own pile would not be disturbed. Naked and shivering with cold for two hours they constantly edged towards their clothes only to be beaten back when they did so.

At last we were allowed to march back to where we had left our possessions. All was confusion and disorder. Some found that all was gone while others were more fortunate.... We were each given a small cotton work shirt and a suit of overalls or work clothes which were made of sacking. The pants fastened around the waist with string and the bottom of the leg reached to my knees. A jacket with sleeves that came to my elbows completed the outfit. These clothes were obviously intended for Japanese workmen and were much too small. We made ludicrous figures and the whole scene would have been laughable if it were not for the tragic circumstances. We were dismissed and allowed to find our allotted place in the sheds.[3]

Marsh's group talked over the situation in their cramped, dirty quarters, beginning with curses for Tsuda and his pilferers. A few men sat in quiet despair, but the majority thought they could see it through. Summer was coming, and the war must soon end. After more than three years in captivity, they knew the foibles of the

Japanese, how to string them along. Committed to doing this as often as they could, they felt a little better. Then, says Marsh, came an inkling of what they were in for:

> That evening, we saw the other prisoners come out of the pit, returning from the day's work in the mines. There were two hundred British and two hundred Malayan-Dutch prisoners. It was an unbelievable vivid scene of tortured humanity. Half-naked emaciated bodies, black with coal dust. Barefoot and adorned in rags. Hardly able to walk with backs bowed. It was like view[ing] a procession of the living dead. These living skeletons paid no attention to us as they shuffled into camp, dispersing to their huts, the ultimate in human misery somehow maintaining the power to live....
>
> Later, we learned that the Dutch miners were in much better shape than the British. This was explained that the British were survivors of Singapore and had been sent to help build that infamous railroad along the peninsula through Indochina. They were riddled with malaria and other tropical diseases as well as severe malnutrition. The Japanese hated the British for their defiant stubbornness and unwillingness to cooperate. The Japanese had reduced them to dumb driven beasts, sick both in mind and body. Later, when we spoke to them, they told us it was only a matter of time until we would all die. They had seen thousands of their comrades die. They had heard no news from anywhere for years, no letters, no Red Cross parcels, nothing. We told them that Germany had surrendered and

that Japan, too, would soon fall. They refused to believe us. They hated the Jap and lived to thwart him. Perhaps it was only hate that kept them alive.[4]

For three days after arriving in the camp, the Canadians were put through a series of physical tests to classify them for work: in the coal mine or at its rock face for most of them, for the less able building a railway spur, carrying coal, farming, or digging air raid shelters in the mountainside. Thanks to Reid, Tom Marsh, whose arm had been badly broken by shellfire during the Battle of Hong Kong and healed crookedly, ended up repairing shoes:

> The day following our arrival we had a visit from a Jap doctor who was to decide which of us were most fit to do the hard work in the mines. We all assembled in the compound where the doctor, with spectacles and buckteeth, sat on a box attended by Captain Reid and several others. Through the ... interpreter ... we were told: "This great man he say give you big prize if you are strong. Run quick." The doctor gave a grin with his buckteeth.... I was determined not to go into the mine and decided to fall right away.... The Frog was right on the spot to beat me for malingering when I pointed to my arm saying, "Hong Kong." Captain Reid explained to the Jap doctor and I was excused from further tests.[5]

Reid's assessment of Sendai 1B while his men were being tested proved his dictum: when the Japanese promised wonderful things at the other end, it was never so, always worse. Conditions were always atrocious in this camp, and had apparently been atrocious ever since its inception:[6]

This camp was a coal mine camp and they were the filthiest huts I have ever seen. They were very old, rickety, papery — the walls were all simply paper, most of it torn off. The [sleeping] mats were filthy with all kinds of vermin and dirt....

The Japanese staff was a mixture of army personnel and veteran personnel. They used these veterans, that is people who had been wounded or otherwise incapacitated from tuberculosis or something ... in the staffs of the camps. One of the veteran personnel called Tsuda [had] a long record of barbarous qualities.... A very bad camp indeed and we were extremely lucky we didn't have to stay this winter. We would have lost a lot of men....

The English group had lost twenty-four men in eight months.[7]

The Canadians began work on May 16. There were generally two work parties in the mine at a time, one at the coal face about a half mile below the surface, and one at the rock face at a higher level. The calibre of work was the same, but the temperature at the coal face was hotter — often hovering at 122 degrees Fahrenheit compared to 86 degrees at the rock face. None of the mine shafts had proper timber supports, and rock falls were common (an English prisoner had died of a fractured skull two weeks before the Canadians arrived). Nor was there proper ventilation: the air was stale, toxic, and at the lower level thick with coal dust. The men sloshed through water up to their knees, sometimes their bellies. For light, they wore caps holding miners' lamps powered by wet cell batteries attached to the rubber belts at their waists. Because of the heat, the men wore nothing but loincloths, and the batteries sometimes slipped off their flimsy belts and burned their backs and buttocks. Men often collapsed from exhaustion and lack of oxygen. Three work shifts ran in the mine 24 hours per day: 06:00 to 14:00, 14:00 to 22:00, 22:00 to 06:00.

As terrible as the conditions, Reid discovered, were the mine bosses:

> The Japanese who worked down there were the lowest type I've run into. Little above animals. These were "Sensei," or professors, supposed to be the bosses and teachers of men. Very many were extremely brutal and cruel and when they themselves got down under these atrocious conditions, many of them seemed to go almost insane and it was a regular thing for the men to be very badly beaten. The Japanese in camp would not let a man stay in when he was sick, then he was beaten by the Sensei [for not being able to work in the mine], and when he came back into camp he was beaten again because he'd been beaten by the Sensei.[8]

Despite Uwamori's assurances of Commandant Chisuwa's fair treatment of prisoners, he was unable to rein in the savagery of his staff. A youngish man, new on the job (the Canadian POWs called him "The Child"), Chisuwa was dominated by Sergeant Tsuda. As at 3D, Reid began exerting pressure and persuasion. Like Uwamori, Chisuwa began to respond:

> When we began to work in this situation, the Canadian group particularly, we rapidly got this stuff cut down and finally almost completely cut out. We complained to the commandant and every single case of a beating we took to the commandant with all

the details. He was a better type and got the [Joban Mining] company officials in and got the Sensei in and warned them again and again. The company wasn't too particular. However, by persistent effort over the time we were there — and we were there about three months — after the first six weeks there were no more beatings in the Canadian group. They still beat the Dutch and the English. They had been in the camp so long some of them had given up hope.[9]

Further complicating things was the in-camp feuding Reid had to deal with — rancour that had built up between the British and Dutch prior to the Canadians' arrival:

The British and Dutch groups did not get on in this camp well at all. They had been at each other's throats for some time. The kitchen was the most contentious point — very bitter. It was almost completely controlled by the Dutch and there was always a great argument over how the rations had been distributed — the British always felt the Dutch got more than they had coming.

Our group coming in, being Canadian, sort of leaned half[way] between the two and acted as a sort of catalyst between the two. The English came and complained about the Dutch and the Dutch came and complained about the English and we managed to smooth things out and got things working in a fairly orderly fashion in camp.[10]

Leeway for Reid to intercede where he saw fit came about when the Japanese reorganized medical arrangements soon after the

Canadians arrived. There were already two Allied doctors in camp: Captain James Bartlet of the Argyll and Sutherland Highlanders and Captain A.A. DeWolffe of the Royal Netherlands East Indies Army. Under the new setup, Bartlet was assigned the minor surgical procedures for all camp nationalities, while DeWolffe handled the medical cases. Reid was to supervise the camp hospital, and as sanitation officer, to revamp latrine and washing arrangements and modify the controversial cookhouse practices.

Putting in place the rigidly operated mess system he had set up in 3D, Reid solved the camp's biggest internal problem by ensuring equal food portions for everyone. With Canadians working in the cookhouse, hostility between the Dutch and British lessened. As supervisor of the camp hospital, Reid instituted a first-aid system in the mine and gradually took over many of DeWolffe's medical duties:

> I insisted on sending a medical orderly with each shift to the mine to immediately treat minor injuries in the mine and that itself cut down a tremendous amount of infection ... because they were immediately scrubbed up and cleaned and rubbed up [and] when they got into the camp it wasn't long before they got treatment.... It took a lot of argument, but by going back to see [the Japanese staff] it was just a matter of keeping at them and keeping at them and keeping at them all the time.
>
> Also during that time [after reorganizing the latrine and washing facilities], I looked after all the medical cases in the hospital, since medicine had been the thing I was particularly interested in.... I looked after all nationalities of medical cases in the hospital from that time on.[11]

Deprived of practically all medicine and facilities, this was more a matter of basic care, comfort, and keeping up spirits than of active treatment. But it worked. Lance Corporal Robert Warren, the member of the Provost Corps who sang under the street light with his pal William Allister at the Nagasaki train station in January 1943, was one of those now toiling at the coal face:

> We used air drills to bore holes in which we planted dynamite to blow down the coal. We would leave the drift while the charges detonated, then we were hustled back into the drift to shovel the coal, which was usually under a foot or two of hot water. The air was always heavy with coal dust from the air drills and the explosions. Our naked, sweating bodies were always coated with rock and coal dusts.... We were covered in pimples, boils, and various skin eruptions. The embedded coal dust gave our faces a dark gray nightmarish appearance. We were starving, emaciated, exhausted, despondent, and frightened.
>
> I set down these details in order to give a glimpse of Captain Reid's predicament. He was not only a fine, sensitive human being, he was also a conscientious doctor. And we were his patients. And he had no medicine for us. But he did have a way with him. When you were ill, he always gave the feeling that you were being treated, medicine or not.[12]

But as time dragged on, the impulse to survive led some to extreme behaviour. In July, an Imperial Army soldier was caught by the Japanese stealing food from a pig trough. For the Canadians, the incident prompted a timely reminder of who they were. Sergeant Tom Marsh writes:

> The Japanese Commandant decided to humiliate him, and indirectly all of us, by having the trough brought out on the square. Filling it with swill they drew a line and made the culprit crawl on his hands and knees from the line to the trough and eat. Many of the prisoners, myself included, were ashamed to see one of their own people so humiliated, but the victim did not seem to mind. Grinning broadly he scrambled up to the trough, put his face in the swill and ate.[13]

Robert Warren never forgot that night:

> Word [of the incident] got to Captain Reid. It genuinely saddened him. It caused him to make the one speech I ever heard from him.
>
> To properly understand the feelings we experienced when he spoke that night, you would have to have seen us: those skeleton frames in tattered clothing that was much too small for us, those grotesque, skull-like faces. And, you see, we only had each other to look at. All our waking hours we were faced with these pitifully ugly reflections of ourselves.
>
> The situation must have laid heavily on Captain Reid's mind because it was late that night when he decided to call us from our huts. That he was dismayed was beyond doubt. I cannot recall his words as clearly as I can recall my feelings of that night. It seemed to me that in some sense he wanted to

scold the individuals seen at the garbage cans, but his message came across as more of a plea.

He told us how proud he was of us. How he admired us for the way we had withstood our miseries for so long. But, above all, how we had retained our dignity through it all.

"Don't let down now," he said. "Don't let down now."

There is no doubt that his words affected all of us. They were well chosen words. "Dignity" came across with considerable impact. No one was in a hurry to go to sleep that night. For the first time in months the huts buzzed with conversation. Perhaps we were desperate to enjoy that "dignity" before it slipped away. For those few short hours we were much more aware of the way we felt than how we looked. No one was ever more loved than was Captain Reid during those few hours.[14]

At Sendai 1B, as at Tokyo 3D, Reid's main escape was music. There, he listened to Beethoven on an old gramophone powered by elastic bands. Here, he composed songs. This wasn't out of the blue. In their conversations at 3D, George Pollak had heard about Reid's musical aspirations: "I discovered that Jack was quite frustrated about his music. From what he told me, he would have liked to become a professional pianist. I think he feared that he was not quite good enough to reach the top ranks. And I also suspect there may have been some family pressures. At any rate, he went to medical school instead. Not that he regretted that. I think he merely would have preferred the other."[15]

The catalyst to songwriting in such unlikely circumstances was Captain Adelbert "Ab" Franken, the commander of the Dutch contingent. Eight years older than Reid, a professional soldier of Dutch-Javanese background, Franken's natural talents were exceptional: music (he composed and was a self-taught player of the piano, guitar, ukulele, trumpet, and accordion); languages (he spoke Dutch, Indonesian, French, English, German, and some Japanese); fine art (superb drawings of fellow prisoners); magic tricks that he invented and performed; and — the most unusual of his gifts — Ab Franken's powers to alleviate pain and sometimes heal through hypnotism and the "laying on" of hands.

Franken's men weren't his only "patients." His healing hands and way with magic had given him considerable leverage with the Japanese camp staff who came to him with their toothaches, headaches, and other discomforts, and along with the prisoners, enjoyed being astonished by his tricks and sleights of hand.

Sergeant Tom Marsh was impressed by Franken, if a little bemused:

> The Dutch Captain was quite a performer of stage magic and once in a while he would put on a performance. He would mesmerize the Jap Commandant's chickens, and sew two prisoners together by passing a needle and thread through their throats without pain. Many of the prisoners swore by his magic powers, so I asked them: "Well, if he has so much mystic power, why can't he get himself out of here?"[16]

Powerless in that respect, Franken also had worries about the safety of his family. Back in Java, his wife and three children were

Sendai Camp 1B, late August 1945. Reid (front row, second from right), Captain Adelbert "Ab" Franken (front row, second from left).

living under the Japanese occupation. Fortunately, his wife was half-Swiss, qualifying her as a foreign national. This saved Beatrix Franken and their children — Willem, now seven, six-year-old José, and three-year-old Renée (a newborn when Franken was captured in 1942) — from forced internment in a crowded civilian concentration camp. As far as Franken knew, his wife and children were still in Batavia. But since coming to Japan, he had no news of them.

Thrown together by circumstances, Reid and Franken hit it off, not only as fellow officers sharing camp responsibilities but in the way they cared for their men and for their shared love of music. Franken, like Reid, had been doing what he could to keep up his men's spirits. Along with his magic performances, he organized soccer matches, taught English and Japanese, and put on musical shows, including some of his own compositions — spritely creations such as "Where Coconuts Grow," "Clavesles Blancos" ("White Carnations"), "Charming," and "A Nice Young Lady with a Car."

It is unlikely that Reid consulted Franken for mystical help on medical cases. But once they established their musical collaboration, their songwriting — music by Franken, lyrics by Reid — melded the daydreams of the two long-imprisoned men. Like the show tunes of the 1920s and 1930s both grew up with, the songs they co-wrote were sentimental, lighthearted, and slyly funny, with titles to match: "Sweet Jailer of Mine," "I Still Remember," "Springtime in My Heart," "Tell Me a Bedtime Story," "Dry All Those Tears," "You Drive Me to Distraction," "The Jail House Blues."

Incongruously, it was here at 1B, in the last months of the war, that Reid devoted himself to music more than he ever would again. Eight other songs are preserved from this time for which he wrote both music and lyrics — a private medley expressing a yearning for his life before the war, paeans to nature, thoughts of Jean: "Don't Mention My Name," "The Petals of a Rose," "Darling I Can't Believe It," "When the Pale Moon Beams," "Dawn," "The Swan Song of Love," "Moonlight on the Poppies," and "Mr. Breeze":

> If your name passes by,
> On the wings of a sigh,
> You will know what I send to you.
>
> On the wings of a breeze,
> In the sigh of the trees,
> You will know that I still am true.
>
> I must tell you today,
> Tho' I'm so far away,
> Of the longing within my heart,
>
> So give ear to the breeze,
> When he carries my pleas,
> For the breeze was a friend from the start.[17]

The end of it all — the waiting and the war — wasn't far off. On July 17, 1945, two months after the Canadians arrived at Sendai 1B, U.S. President Harry Truman, British Prime Minister Winston Churchill, and Premier Joseph Stalin of the Soviet Union met in Potsdam, Germany, for the final "Big Three" conference of the war. They were meeting to decide how Germany, whose Nazi regime had surrendered unconditionally nine weeks earlier, was to be administered in the postwar era.

On the opening day of the conference, Truman, who had been president for only two months following the death in office of President Franklin Roosevelt on April 12, learned that the first test detonation of the Manhattan Project's secret atomic bomb had been carried out successfully in the New Mexico desert, 24 hours earlier. This changed the war. Rather than the savage and protracted bloodbath certain to be suffered on both sides from Operation Downfall, the Allies' two-part land invasion of Japan set to begin in November 1945 and continue into the spring of 1946, the United States now had the weapon to end the war in the Pacific quickly and decisively.

In Tokyo, Emperor Hirohito had already concluded that Japan couldn't win the war. On June 9, Marquis Koichi Kido, Lord Keeper of the Privy Seal of Japan and the emperor's closest confidant, had presented a brief entitled "Draft Plan for Controlling the Crisis Situation." By the end of 1945, said Kido, Japan would no longer be able to wage modern warfare and civil unrest would become uncontainable.

Most of Japan's navy was at the bottom of the sea. Its air force was practically impotent. Its occupied territories were shrinking. And in the battle now raging on the island of Okinawa — an assault by unprecedented numbers of American naval, air, and amphibious forces launched on April 1 with the support of the British Pacific Fleet, Japanese resistance was crumbling. Once the Allies conquered Okinawa, in what had become the biggest and bloodiest battle of the Pacific war, this strategic island just south of mainland Japan would be the springboard for the invasion of the Home Islands.

On June 22, Okinawa fell to the Americans after 82 days of terrible fighting. That day, Emperor Hirohito summoned Japan's Supreme Council for the Direction of the War — the "Big Six" decision-makers of the 11-member government Cabinet — to tell them his wishes: "I desire," said the emperor before anyone else spoke, "that concrete plans to end the war, unhampered by existing policy, be speedily studied, and that efforts be made to implement them."[18]

Most of the military-dominated Big Six members — Prime Minister Kantaro Suzuki, Foreign Minister Shigenori Togo, General Korechika Anami and Admiral Mitsumasa Yonai (ministers of the army and navy), and General Yoshijiro Umezu and Admiral Soemu Toyoda (chiefs of the army and navy General Staffs) — were still in favour of continuing the war. But if peace was to be contemplated as the emperor decreed, it must come about as the Supreme Council members had always foreseen when first going to war with the United States and Britain: a negotiated peace with conditions favourable to Japan, including a final settlement in which at least a portion of the new territories it had absorbed would be retained. Since Japan and the Soviet Union had a 1941 Neutrality Agreement (though soon to expire), Stalin was seen as Japan's logical go-between to find terms with the Allies for an acceptable conditional surrender. Emperor Hirohito acceded to this approach.

Diplomacy was set in motion, and throughout July, Naotake Sato, Japanese ambassador to the Soviet Union, pursued this objective in Moscow in discussions with Vyacheslav Molotov, the

Soviet foreign minister, and other officials. But the Soviets were engaging in talks with Sato simply as a delaying tactic. More than a dead end, the true Soviet position was an impending disaster for the Japanese.

At the previous Big Three Conference, in Yalta in February 1945, Stalin had secretly pledged to Roosevelt and Churchill that three months after Nazi Germany surrendered, the Soviet Union would abrogate the Neutrality Agreement, declare war on Japan, and launch immediate invasions of Japanese-held Manchuria and Korea — occupied territories more lightly defended by the Japanese because of the Neutrality Agreement. The date set for the Soviet invasion was August 9.

By mid-July, after several weeks of meetings with the Soviets, Sato's report to Foreign Minister Togo was largely negative. A demand for "unconditional surrender or terms closely equivalent thereto"[19] was all that Japan could expect from the Allies, said Sato, clarifying a few days later: "I made an exception of the question of preserving our national structure [i.e., the Imperial system]."[20]

On July 21, speaking in the name of the Supreme Council for the Direction of the War, Foreign Minister Togo, with no reason to suspect that the Soviets had a secret change of plan, replied to Ambassador Sato: "With regard to unconditional surrender we are unable to consent to it under any circumstances whatever.... It is in order to avoid such a state of affairs that we are seeking a peace ... through the good offices of Russia."[21]

At Potsdam, Truman revealed to Churchill that the atomic bomb was ready. On the strength of it, Truman, Churchill, and President Chiang Kai-shek of China issued jointly the Potsdam Declaration to Japan on July 26: "These are our terms. We will not deviate from them. There are no alternatives. We shall brook no delay.... We call upon the government of Japan to proclaim now the unconditional surrender of all Japanese armed forces, and to provide proper and adequate assurances of their good faith in such action. The alternative for Japan is prompt and utter destruction."[22]

On July 28, Japanese newspapers reported that the declaration, which the Allies broadcast in Japanese and dropped by leaflet to millions of Japanese civilians, had been rejected by the Supreme Council. Now worried about civil unrest, Prime Minister Suzuki attempted to guide Japanese public perception in a statement to the press on July 29:

> I consider the Joint Declaration a rehash of the Declaration of the Cairo Conference [held in November 1943 when the Allies first called for Japan's unconditional surrender and the return of all conquered territories].
>
> As for the Government, it does not attach any important value to it at all. The only thing to do is kill it with silence. We will do nothing but press on to the bitter end to bring about a successful completion of the war.[23]

The Potsdam Conference ended on August 2. With no official reply from Japan to the Allies' July 26 declaration, President Truman ordered the first atomic bomb to be dropped. Bad weather on August 3 forced the mission to be scrubbed, but on August 5 the weather was forecast to clear. On the morning of Monday, August 6 (coincidently, Jean Reid's 31st birthday), an atomic bomb was dropped from an American B-29 Superfortress over the city of Hiroshima in southwest Honshu.

Later that day, President Truman broadcast America's resolve:

> We are now prepared to obliterate rapidly and completely every productive enterprise the Japanese have

above ground in any city. We shall destroy their docks, their factories, and their communications. Let there be no mistake; we shall completely destroy Japan's power to make war.

It was to spare the Japanese people from utter destruction that the ultimatum of July 26 was issued at Potsdam. Their leaders promptly rejected that ultimatum. If they do not now accept our terms they may expect a rain of ruin from the air, the like of which has never been seen on this earth.[24]

For two days following the bombing of Hiroshima, Japanese leadership was paralyzed. Initially, authorities were uncertain about the nature of the device. Once the atomic bomb was confirmed, the Supreme Council remained divided over whether to fight on or to admit defeat and accept the Potsdam Declaration terms. Privately, Emperor Hirohito expressed his continuing wish to end the war. Yet by the night of August 8, the Japanese government still hadn't formally convened to reassess the war situation in light of the new weapon.

With silence the answer, the Allies proceeded as planned. Just before midnight on August 8, Ambassador Sato was officially informed in Moscow that the Soviet Union had declared war on Japan. In the early hours of Thursday, August 9, the Soviets launched a mammoth, two-pronged invasion of Japanese-occupied Manchuria. Roused in the middle of the night to be told of the attack, Japanese leaders in Tokyo were incredulous. A little after eleven o'clock that morning, while this stunning turn of events was being absorbed at a hastily called meeting of the Supreme Council, news arrived that the Americans had just dropped a second atomic bomb on the city of Nagasaki on the southern island of Kyushu.

The message was clear. Hiroshima wasn't an anomaly. The Americans had multiple atomic bombs, and Truman would use them until Japan accepted the terms of the Potsdam Declaration.

Over the next six days, Japan staggered toward surrender. The twin shocks of the Soviet attack and the second atomic bomb forced members of the Supreme Council and the rest of the Japanese Cabinet to accept that the war must somehow be terminated. But in meetings of the Big Six throughout the morning and afternoon of August 9, two factions, evenly split, vied for the way in which Japan would offer to surrender.

Led by Foreign Minister Togo, half of the Supreme Council favoured accepting the Potsdam Declaration, with one condition: that the emperor's position as head of state be guaranteed. The second, more militant faction, led by General Anami, insisted on four conditions: retention of the emperor as head of state, Japanese self-disarmament, Japanese control of any war crime trials, and above all, no occupation of Japan by the Allies.

In the early hours of August 10, Emperor Hirohito entered the hot, humid air raid shelter 60 feet below the Imperial Palace's library to receive the opinions of the Big Six and resolve how to proceed. Wearing a badly fitting field marshal's uniform because tailors, like other mortals, weren't allowed to touch this man venerated as a god, Hirohito took his place on a straight-backed chair to learn his advisers' views. After hearing each minister speak, the emperor, barely containing his emotions, rose to his feet and gave his decision, his words in these special circumstances becoming a divine edict called the "Voice of the Crane" because, like the emperor's own invisibility to his people, the sacred crane could be heard even when flying and calling unseen:

> I have given serious thought to the situation prevailing at home and abroad and have concluded

that continuing the war can only mean destruction
for the nation and prolongation of bloodshed and
cruelty in the world. I cannot bear to see my innocent people suffer any longer. Ending the war
is the only way to restore world peace and relieve
the nation from the terrible distress with which it is
burdened....

It goes without saying that it is unbearable for
me to see the brave and loyal fighting men of Japan
disarmed. It is equally unbearable that others who
have rendered me devoted service should now be
punished as instigators of the war. Nevertheless, the
time has come when we must bear the unbearable....

I swallow my own tears and give my sanction to
the proposal to accept the Allied proclamation on
the basis outlined by the Foreign Minister.[25]

The emperor had chosen Foreign Minister Togo's "one condition" offer of surrender. An hour later, the entire Japanese Cabinet
assembled and officially adopted the Imperial decision. At dawn
on August 10, the Japanese Foreign Ministry dispatched cables to
the Allies saying that Japan would accept the Potsdam Declaration
"with the understanding that the said declaration does not comprise any demand which prejudices the prerogatives of His Majesty
as Sovereign Ruler."[26]

The emperor and Japanese government had made the fateful
decision to end the war. But dangers for the regime remained.
Would the Japanese military refuse to obey the surrender order?
Would martial law, which the government imposed on August 9 after the Soviet attack and the bombing of Nagasaki, fail to hold civil
unrest in check? Would army fanatics in Tokyo, thinking the emperor's advisers traitorous, resort to "government by assassination,"

liquidate the executive powers that be, then ask the emperor to renew his support for the Japanese war effort? All seemed possible.

The Allies' response to Japan's "conditional" acceptance of the declaration came two days later. It had been deeply considered and carefully crafted. While wishing to shepherd the surrender to a swift conclusion, the Americans were adamant that the Allies hold absolute power in postwar Japan. Japan's surrender must be unconditional. But in constructing the official response to ensure this point was clearly understood, American secretary of state James Byrnes left the "Imperial condition" a possibility by suggesting that the institution might continue if the Japanese people themselves later made that choice:

> From the moment of surrender the authority of the Emperor and the Japanese Government to rule the state shall be subject to the Supreme Commander of the Allied Powers who will take such steps as he sees proper to effectuate the surrender terms....
>
> The ultimate form of government of Japan shall, in accordance with the Potsdam Declaration, be established by the freely expressed will of the Japanese people.
>
> The armed forces of the Allied Powers will remain in Japan until the purposes set forth in the Potsdam Declaration are achieved.[27]

Receipt of the Byrnes Note in Tokyo on the morning of August 12 caused outrage among the most militant factions of the Imperial Japanese Army and Navy, provoking another two days of turmoil and uncertainty.

Emperor Hirohito and Kido, Lord Keeper of the Privy Seal, were in favour of accepting the Byrnes Note's terms. But according to normal procedure, a supporting vote by the Big Six had to be unanimous. Two of them — General Anami and General Umezu — remained diehards, as Anami's statement, addressed to the army and published in the newspapers on August 11, made clear: "Even though we may have to eat grass, swallow dirt, and lie in the fields, we shall fight on to the bitter end, ever firm in our faith that we shall find life in death."[28]

Ultranationalist sentiments like those of General Anami were widespread. On the evening of August 13, as the Big Six were meeting yet again to try to end the stalemate over the terms of surrender, Admiral Takijiro Onishi, vice chief of the navy's General Staff and "father" of the Kamikaze Special Attack Units, burst into the conference room and reported the last-ditch, suicidal tactic that many army and navy officers wanted the entire country to embrace, right down to civilians attacking the American invaders with sticks and stones: "Let us formulate a plan for certain victory, obtain the Emperor's sanction, and throw ourselves into bringing the plan to realization. If we are prepared to sacrifice 20,000,000 Japanese lives in a special attack [kamikaze] effort, victory will be ours!"[29]

Onishi was ignored. On August 14, the deadlock was broken. That morning, Kido learned that the Americans had dropped millions of leaflets containing the full text of the Japanese offer of surrender as well as Secretary Byrnes's response. Fearing the news of Japan's secret dealings with the Allies would convulse the public, throw the country into chaos, and provoke a military coup supported by many of the million Japanese soldiers stationed on the Home Islands, a frantic Kido met with Hirohito and said that another Imperial conference should be called immediately and the emperor must again invoke his sacred power — the Voice of the Crane — to break the executive deadlock and command the Cabinet to accept the Byrnes Note as the basis for surrender.

The emergency conference began at 11:00 a.m. Once again, General Anami, Admiral Umezu, and Admiral Toyoda spoke in favour of the "four-conditions" surrender. But undercutting their position was the brief but weighty statement given by Field Marshal Shunroku Hata, commander of the island of Kyushu (Japan's first line of defence against any Allied invasion), who had just arrived in Tokyo from an inspection of Hiroshima. General Anami thought Hata would downplay the impact of the atomic bomb on the city and support the militants. He didn't. With tears in his eyes, Hata said he didn't think an Allied invasion could be repelled and that he agreed with the emperor's choice to accept the Potsdam Declaration. Foreign Minister Togo's peace faction on the Supreme Council strongly concurred.

After hearing all opinions, the emperor rose to give his Imperial command. His thoughts were unchanged, he began. Continuation of the war promised nothing but additional destruction:

> I have studied the terms of the Allied reply and have concluded that they constitute a virtually complete acknowledgement of the position we maintained in the note dispatched several days ago. In short, I consider the [Byrnes] reply to be acceptable....
>
> In order that the people may know of my decision, I request you prepare at once an Imperial rescript so that I may broadcast to the nation. Finally, I call upon each and every one of you to exert himself to the utmost so that we may meet the trying days which lie ahead.[30]

The emperor's divine will was respected. The Cabinet convened and unanimously ratified his decision. Transmission to the Allies of Japan's official acceptance of the Byrnes Note's terms of surrender was sent within hours. Late in the afternoon of August 14, after numerous additions and deletions, Hirohito's advisers finalized the text for his speech announcing the end of the war.

That evening, radio listeners across Japan were told during the regular nine o'clock newscast that a special broadcast to the nation would be made at noon on August 15. Two hours after the nine o'clock announcement, a team of radio technicians from the Japanese Broadcasting Corporation (NHK), led by its chairman, recorded two copies of Hirohito's speech at the Imperial Palace, the emperor reading the "Imperial Rescript on the Termination of the War" twice because in the first recording, said one of the technicians, some words were indistinct.

In case renegade elements of the army tried to obtain the recordings and thwart the peace broadcast, the disks were hidden in the palace, to be couriered in the morning (by different routes for safety reasons) to NHK headquarters for the noon transmission.

These precautions proved necessary. At 2:00 a.m. on August 15, three hours after the recordings were made, army conspirators led by Major Kenji Hatanaka murdered the commander of the 1st Imperial Guards Division, the special unit that protected the emperor and his family, and forged an order directing the Guards to occupy the Imperial Palace. The conspirators' goal was to separate the emperor from his peace-mongering advisers, install a new government, and fight on to victory or until the Japanese people were annihilated — recklessness inspired by the belief that national extinction rather than ignominious defeat was the wish, if not of the weakling Hirohito, most certainly of Hirohito's implacable Imperial ancestors.

In taking over the palace, the conspirators' first objective was to find and destroy the emperor's recorded speech before it could be sent for broadcast. In this, Hatanaka and his followers were frustrated by a court chamberlain's wiliness — the recordings were too well hidden to be found — and while the search was on, General Shizuichi Tanaka, the loyal commander of the Japanese Eastern District Army, arrived at the palace, restored order among the Guards Division, quashed the insurrection, and within hours rounded up most of the rebels. By 8:00 a.m., August 15, General Tanaka could assure the emperor, who was kept safe in his fortified personal quarters during the rampage, that the palace was secure and there was no further cause for concern.

At noon on August 15, the recording of Hirohito reading the "Imperial Rescript on the Termination of the War" was broadcast over Japanese radio. This was the first time the Japanese people had heard the voice of their emperor. For that reason, people everywhere stood to attention as the divine voice — high, shaky, unfamiliar — began to speak. But as Hirohito's words sank in, silence gave way to sobbing, to outbursts of anger, to cries of disbelief. As the editor of the *Nippon Times* later wrote, "It was a sudden mass hysteria on a national scale."

Emperor Hirohito's words to the nation:

> To our good and loyal subjects: After pondering deeply the general trends of the world and the actual conditions obtaining in our empire today, we have decided to accept a settlement of the situation by resorting to an extraordinary measure. We have ordered our Government to communicate to the Governments of the United States, Great Britain, China, and the Soviet Union that our Empire accepts the provisions of their Joint Declaration....
>
> Despite the best that has been done by everyone — the gallant fighting of military and naval forces, the diligence and assiduity of Our servants of the State and the devoted service of Our one hundred

million people, the war situation has developed not
necessarily to Japan's advantage, while the general
trends of the world have turned against her interest. Moreover, the enemy has begun to employ a
new and most cruel bomb, the power of which to
do damage is indeed incalculable, taking the toll of
many innocent lives. Should we continue to fight,
not only would it result in an ultimate collapse and
obliteration of the Japanese nation, but also lead to
the total extinction of human civilization....

It is according to the dictate of time and fate
that We have resolved to pave the way for a grand
peace for all generations to come by enduring the
unendurable and suffering what is insufferable.[31]

As though to deny the undeniable, nowhere during the four-
and-a-half-minute speech did the emperor use the words *defeat* or
surrender.

It was now that orders from Washington, the events in Tokyo, and
the very last American bombing of Japan converged for Reid and
his men at Sendai Camp 1B. On August 10, five days before the
emperor's speech of surrender, President Truman ordered a halt to
all bombing while awaiting the Japanese response to the Byrnes
Note. With no answer by August 13, and Japanese radio traffic
showing that an "all-out banzai attack" was possibly in preparation, American air and naval commanders in the Pacific were
ordered to resume shelling and conventional bombing "so as to

impress Japanese officials," said Truman, "that we mean business and are serious in getting them to accept our peace proposals without delay."[32] The orders to recommence the attack echoed Truman's folksy, straightforward style: "The President directs that we go ahead with everything we've got."[33]

On August 14, just as the decision to surrender was being formalized in Tokyo, the Americans launched one of the largest bombing raids of the Pacific war — more than 1,000 aircraft on sorties across Japan over a 24-hour period. One of the night missions — a round trip of 3,852 miles (making it the longest bombing mission of the war) — was carried out by 315 Bombardment Wing, whose flock of B-29s flew from Guam in the Marianas to the northern tip of Honshu to destroy the Nippon Oil Refinery at Tsuchizaki. Sendai Camp 1B was directly beneath 315's flight path. That night, as wave after wave of B-29s rumbled north over the camp, then south again after dropping their bombs, Reid and his men had no way of knowing that the end of the war was only hours away. When the news of Japan's surrender came the next day, says Reid, it seemed almost anticlimactic, surreal:

> During the time we were here planes went over us very many times.... The planes were flying up the coast and our camp was apparently on their line of travel.
>
> The biggest raid of all, for about six hours there was a continual heavy drone of large numbers of planes going over us, was on the night of August 14th, 15th. We had seen numbers of fighter planes around this camp, fighter planes all around this camp and we had seen B-29s going over in the daytime.
>
> On the 15th the men were told by the civilians that the war was over. Everything was very placid.

There was no work done that day and the men on shift were told as they came up [from the mine]. On the 16th we began to bring some pressure on the Japanese, but there was no official word from Tokyo, but on the 17th Tokyo informed them and the commandant told us the war was over.

He said that in the last war both sides had said poisoned gas was outlawed in war, but in this war the Americans had used a very much worse thing — an atomic bomb, that was the first time we heard of it. The Japanese had been forced to surrender to preserve their race, because of this brutal weapon. We thought at the time this was just another example of Japanese exaggeration, but when we got magazines dropped on us by the planes we realized it was something new and different.[34]

After his curt announcement of the surrender, Commandant Chisuwa made a personal speech to the men. It was a far cry from Colonel Suzuki's laughable tirade when the Canadians arrived at Tokyo No. 5 Branch Camp (3D) in January 1943. This time, there was no need for an interpreter. As Reid describes, Chisuwa addressed the assembled prisoners in his best, polite English:

The war [he said] of course had been a terrible mistake. Everybody had realized that it was no good for people to be fighting each other this way, that they had enjoyed having us with them during the time we had been there and they always would preserve the kindest thoughts toward our men, that they hoped our men would also preserve very kind thoughts about them and they were very anxious that when [we] went home — which [we] were sure to do soon — that [we] would go home and forget any incidents, while prisoners, due to some bad Japanese, and remember only the beautiful spirit of Japan and be ambassadors of good will to explain Japanese ideals....

It was of a different tone from any official speech we had heard before. [He said] we had been honourable men who had fought in a hopeless situation and that they honoured us, and there was no stigma to being a prisoner under such conditions, and saluted us when he got through his speech.

The men thought that was really something. They felt the war must really be over now.... The thing had been going on for so long you refused to let yourself think it was possible. It came gradually — the civilians telling us, and then the official word, and then ... there was a feeling of intense relief.... There was no moment of great celebration, but everybody was very happy. It went on for about a week.[35]

Yet, during that first week of "liberation," they lived in a vacuum. The prison gate was open, the military guards had disappeared, the remaining Japanese had been disarmed by the prisoners. But communications between Tokyo and the northern areas of Honshu were broken down. No one knew how or when the evacuation of prisoners would proceed.

In the meantime, Reid and Franken demanded that rations be increased immediately, that money be issued to the men, and warned Commandant Chisuwa that hated staff — Tsuda and others — should be removed from the camp or they couldn't be responsible for what the prisoners might do to them. The offenders were gone within 24 hours.

The men knew nothing of the official "kill-all order" of August 1944 (never activated because no land invasion of Japan took place). But in recent months, with the Allied victory seeming inevitable, all prisoners had become uneasy about what reaction against POWs the Japanese defeat would provoke among disgruntled elements of the army and civilian population. Some guards even hinted at planned reprisals. Despite these worries and finally free, some of the men began to think they were the "suckers" of the war and now wanted to go "whole hog" in the neighbourhood and "liberate" whatever food and anything else they fancied from the Japanese living nearby. Reid didn't want anything to go wrong at this late stage:

> I dissuaded them. We had come this far, and we knew there had been an attempt at a revolt by a certain portion of the [Japanese] Army who tried to get the Emperor in Tokyo, and there was an Army barracks a short distance away from us, supposed to be in turmoil, and the civilians were doubtful. I was most anxious that there be no disturbance under these conditions, and perhaps give rise to real difficulties, and I told the men time and again — "Let's proceed with caution. There's just a few more days to go" [before the Americans arrive] and I didn't want anything to go wrong at the last minute.[36]

Nevertheless, the men started to embrace life outside the wire. Nearby was Yumoto. They began leaving the camp during the day and venturing into town to shake off the dust of prison. Reid went along to see how things were going:

They [now] had lots of money, no place to spend it during the whole time in this camp and I remember the day following the general exodus from the camp into town. I went down on bicycle. Every [Japanese] male I saw scowled at me, and every female grinned. The girls were happy, being paid well and treated well and they were very happy. The men got on very well with the civilians. They were able to buy small things and bought chickens and vegetables and there were fires all over camp, everybody cooking up something and there were no incidences. Japanese soldiers were being demobilized in the towns and, generally speaking, everybody was friendly.[37]

After a week with no outside news, messages began to trickle in from Tokyo. On August 23, Reid and Franken were told by Commandant Chisuwa that the International Red Cross wanted the two of them to attend a conference in the city of Sendai, 93 miles up the coast, to prepare for the evacuation of 1B and other prison camps in the vicinity. They were to travel north by train in a special car on August 25.

This led to some personal business. The day they were told of the conference, Ab Franken wrote and signed a typed declaration regarding the 13 songs he and Reid had written together. As a career officer in the Royal Netherlands Army, Franken would be returning to duty in war-torn Java, far from the entertainment centres of New York and Los Angeles, where new songs might find a musical life. Reid would at least be back in North America. Whether or not Franken and Reid thought they would meet after the war, Franken obviously wanted the best for his compositions as well as for his friend and collaborator. In the declaration, he states:

Franken, A.L., hereby fully empowers John Anthony Gibson Reid to copyright and/or sell said musical compositions or to alter these compositions and after altering them to copyright, sell, and otherwise deal with them as he (J.A.G. Reid) pleases.

This declaration is made in duplo and by free will of the undersigned, on the twenty-third (23rd) of August in the year nineteen hundred and forty-five (1945) A.D.

(Signed) A.L. Franken

Onahama, Japan, Prisoner of War Camp No. 1 of Sendai POW Camps.[38]

The next day, August 24, came a bolt from the blue — an American search plane. After a week in limbo, the surreal became real. Sergeant Tom Marsh, like many others, was overcome:

It was a fighter, and as it circled high above our camp we all ran into the compound. It made a long loop over the hills then dived on the camp. Six hundred men went wild. We could plainly make out the red, white, and blue and the white American star. A little figure leaned out of the cockpit making the "V" sign. Overcome with joy, naked figures dressed only in G-strings jumped and sprang around like a bunch of savages. Men slapped each other, shook hands, and cried. It was true. It was really over. Our liberators were here. Now we would be free.

The little fighter disappeared and returned shortly with a whole squadron. They dove all around us, did stunts, and were as wildly excited in the sky as we were on the ground. We danced, waved blankets, shirts, or any rag we could find. Men climbed onto the roofs of the sheds signaling and waving their arms....

With the sun shining on their silver wings, each plane would dive, skimming the roofs of the huts. The pilot would slide back his canopy and lean out waving and making the sign for victory. They were so close and powerful I was certain one of the pilots would fall out. We marveled at the cohesion and control the pilots had of those splendid little planes, the gallant figures waving so cheerfully. They were God's own angels sent to liberate his people. They meant freedom and happiness. It was a beautiful day — the best day of my life!

I was overwhelmed by the sudden release of emotions that had been suppressed for four long years. I could not control my feelings and a wave of tears flowed down my face. I returned to my hut and cried like a baby without any shame. Others were so hysterical they had to be hospitalized, while others sat motionless, too dazed with happiness to be able to speak.[39]

Soon, supplies of all kinds were raining down, although, as Reid says, not always safely:

Japanese came in and said American planes were coming over to drop food, clothing, and medical supplies to us. The men made very large P.W. signs, about twenty feet high, and placed them on the hills around the camp so they could be seen from the air. The first day that planes came over, they were American Naval planes from the *Lexington*. This was the day, and I believe it was true of all the prison camps, of the first real celebration, the first day some of our people flew over us. They came stunting over the camp, you could almost touch them.... The back blister was open and you could see the newsreel cameras. Some of the men broke down and cried. There was a terrific emotional re-action that day, we felt we were really out of the woods. Navy planes dropped things on us all day, things out of their own canteen — shaving soap, magazines, candy, cigarettes, chewing gum, fresh bread, meat, coffee — small articles, actually, and morale builders.

On numbers of occasions the B-29s came over, loaded from Saipan. They dropped the main amount of their stuff in 45-gallon gasoline drums, a tremen-dous amount each time, dropped all over the camps and all over the country side, and if they hit a wall, they tore the wall all to pieces, went right through. Rather a dangerous business because about twenty percent of the parachutes didn't open and the thing came hurtling down.[40]

To avoid casualties from this uncontrolled cascade (a number of prisoners and Japanese were killed by falling drums in other camps), Reid and Franken broke the men into groups and sent them outside the camp. Injuries were avoided and it made spotting the landed drums easier. Soon the men were gorging themselves on the contents — Hershey bars, canned fruit, canned meat-and-vegetable stew, bread, cheeses, butter, milk, cookies, rice pudding with raisins — a medley consumed in any order, sometimes to the point of vomiting. Among the medical supplies, Reid found penicillin, a medicine he had only heard of. The miraculous results after he injected 30 serious infection cases among his men showed what a wonder drug this new antibiotic was.

Leaving Lieutenant Finn in charge of the Canadians, Reid and Franken boarded a private train car on August 25 and journeyed up to Sendai. They were treated like princes on the trip, put up at a luxurious hotel with fellow Allied officers from other prison camps in the neighbourhood, and next morning welcomed by Lieutenant-Colonel Kitajima, evidently a camp commandant himself, who in his opening remarks to the conference stated that he had made every effort in the past to see that prisoners were as well treated as possible and (now unwittingly echoing Commandant Chisuwa) that he hoped any individual breaches of proper POW treatment by bad Japanese would be forgiven. He, his staff, and two interpreters were present to fulfill every request of the Red Cross delegates and Allied officers.

Over the four-day conference, the delegation, consisting of an official from the Swiss International Red Cross, another from the Swiss embassy, and a third from the Swedish embassy, worked with the POW officers to tabulate prisoners, their prison camp locations, the number of sick who would need special travel arrangements, and transportation options as well as coastal departure points if the Americans opted to extract the POWs by sea. Reid and Franken learned that neither the Red Cross nor the Americans had been aware of the 4,000 Allied prisoners in camps in the Sendai area — indeed, that the whereabouts of 90 percent of the 32,000 Allied prisoners in Japan had been unknown to the Allies until Japanese authorities began releasing the information.

During the conference, communication with Tokyo continued to be patchy. Tentative travel schedules were drawn up for the various camps, and Lieutenant-Colonel Kitajima was given directives to send to all northern area camp commandants. The instructions said commandants were to disregard any previous Japanese orders and to comply with all requests from prisoner officers for food, clothing, and whatever evacuation preparations and facilities they asked for. All communications between the Red Cross and the prison camps were to be shared with the prisoner officers, and if Red Cross delegates called the camps by telephone, the prisoner officers were to speak to them directly without any Japanese interference.

As for Sendai 1B, Reid and Franken were promised that the camp would be evacuated by train via the spur line running through the camp soon after the official signing of the Japanese surrender on September 2. The signing had been scheduled to take place aboard the USS *Missouri* in Tokyo Bay on August 31, but due to a typhoon in the Tokyo area, Reid learned, the ceremony had been postponed for 48 hours: "We returned to camp at six in the evening on August 29, attended at the train by Lieutenant-Colonel Kitajima and his staff, who arranged for a European meal before we left the hotel. We were supplied with meat and bread for our journey. Again, utmost politeness and courtesy were shown at all times, and this treatment continued during the remainder of the journey. Arrived at camp 6 a.m. August 30, 1945."[41]

Back in camp, Reid found that all was going well:

> The average weight gain, 10 days after the surrender, was 15 pounds per man ... it was just incredible — they ballooned before your eyes. They ate all kinds of food and there was very little gastrointestinal upset. They arranged great feasts, and there were poker games going on all over camp....[42] They roamed over the countryside, caught trains and so on and ... would phone me occasionally from

where they were and say they'd missed the train and were coming back in the morning....[43] They were just having the time of their lives after four years.[44]

Reid was also happy to hear of the special honour bestowed on Lieutenant Finn during his absence. A week earlier, when the first naval planes from the aircraft carrier *Lexington* stunted over the camp, the British and the Dutch had waved their national flags in reply — patchwork replicas cobbled together earlier from scraps of cloth scrounged in camp. Inspired by the sight, the Canadians felt they should make a flag of their own. Reid approved the plan before departing for Sendai. Sergeant Tom Marsh was one of the chief instigators:

> I spoke to Captain Reid about this. He reminded us that American planes were dropping our supplies and that our own Lieutenant Finn was an American naval officer: "I'm sure he would like to see an American flag." It was a great idea and with the Captain's blessing a few others and I formed a flag committee and got busy.
>
> We began by collecting all the red and blue materials we could find in the camp. These colours were very scarce and hard to find. We were almost stumped for blue when we heard that one of the prisoners had received a blue shirt in the supplies that had been parachuted into camp. The flag committee searched out the individual and only after great patriotic pressure was put on him was the shirt surrendered. We used a six by four cotton sheet for backing and, vowing everyone to secrecy, set up a workshop in a vacant room in one of the huts.

Private N. Zytaruk of the Grenadiers, [who] had worked as the prisoners' tailor, brought over the sewing machine and we went to work. For a guide we used a card with a picture of the American flag provided by one of the prisoners. All forty-eight stars were carefully measured and cut out and the bars spaced correctly. Within two hours the project was completed. We only had enough material to finish one side of the flag so someone suggested having the Canadians sign the back. Over two hundred men left their signatures on the flag. A bamboo pole was provided and the flag was ready.

It was suggested that we form a colour party so the flag could be presented with full military honours to Lieut. Finn. At this time we had recovered our old uniforms and the American planes had dropped other supplies. We were therefore able to turn out a fairly smart guard dressed in khaki shirts, shorts, socks, and boots, and even our old Grenadier wedge caps with badges. I was the sergeant in charge of the colour party. When all was ready it was decided to draw Lieut. Finn over by subterfuge. Sgt.-Major "Pop" Corrigan of the Rifles was detailed to go over to Finn's quarters and tell him there was trouble among the men and to come immediately.

Soon, Lieut. Finn could be seen hurrying across the compound.... Most of the other Canadians were gathered around our small group and as Lieut. Finn approached I called the colour party to attention. The flag was unfurled, and our impromptu bugler, a bandsman who had recovered a cornet somewhere, blew the general salute. Every man within the camp stood to attention with hand raised.

Lieutenant Finn looked perplexed, as if he were still ready to deal with some dispute. When he saw the flag and the colour party he stopped, stared, and slowly raised his hand, giving a salute with tears welling up in his eyes. I presented it to him, and asked that he accept it on behalf of all the Canadian [prisoners]. The flag was a tribute to the United States of America, its armed services that had liberated us and to Lieut. Finn who, at all times, under the most adverse circumstances, had conducted himself towards the prisoners and towards the enemy as an American Officer and a man. As I presented the flag to him I could see his lips quivering with emotion. He accepted it and said, "It's just what I wanted."

Clutching the flag close to his chest, he hurried away to his quarters while the boys gave him a great cheer as he went....

Say what you will, a little piece of bunting can mean a great deal to those who had lost what it stands for — Liberty, the rights of man, tolerance, fair play and freedom. Long may it wave![45]

For Reid, victory was captured in another symbolic moment:

Walking down a country road outside the camp one morning, and seeing three disarmed, tattered Japanese soldiers straggling thro' the dust towards me. And suddenly three American Navy Corsairs roaring along the road above them. I thought a camera recording of that scene would have paid a lot on the front cover of *Time*. It was a fitting picture for the end of hostilities.[46]

Then, in the midst of victory, a tragedy. On September 4, a B-29 code-named "T-21" of the U.S. Air Force's 874th Bombardment Squadron lifted off from Isley Air Field in Saipan on "Prisoner of War Mission No. 8" to Japan. Piloted by Captain Harry Sompayac of Shreveport, Louisiana, "T-21," with its crew of eleven and three passengers, began its relief mission by overflying the Nagoya and Tokyo areas in an effort to locate a POW camp sufficiently in the clear to drop supplies. To no avail: the weather over both sites was socked in.

Previously briefed on the general location of Sendai 1B, Captain Sompayac then proceeded up the coast to Onahama where he was joined by two other B-29s — "T-3" and "T-7" of 873rd Squadron. Interplane contact was established, and Captain Sompayac advised the other two aircraft to remain out over the water and circle in a holding pattern until he contacted them. He further advised that he was going to try to get below the undercast and locate the POW camp known to be in the vicinity.

B-29 "T-7" was piloted by Captain Andrew Black:

> The ceiling over the bay was estimated at 600 feet, and over the land at 300 feet. Peaks on the mainland could be clearly seen over the undercast. In the last radio message received from Captain Sompayac he stated he was following a railroad track which according to his maps would lead them to the POW camp. He also stated that maneuvering space was extremely limited. I estimated that "T-21" was approximately ten miles inland at the time of the reception of this message.[47]

Clouds covered the valley where Sendai 1B lay. It had grown foggy that morning, and a light rain was falling. Invisible, but suddenly audible and growing rapidly louder, plane engines could be heard roaring in very low. Running out of a hut, Sergeant Robert "Flash" Clayton of the Royal Rifles looked up to see a B-29, gigantic in its closeness, screaming out of the fog: "This plane came down and it was too low. And everybody was saying, 'Get up! Get up! — Jesus!'"[48]

Then, in an instant, the huge plane vanished into the fog and its roar died away. Sergeant Clayton reports:

> About three hours later, Captain Reid came to me and said, "Flash, I need half a dozen men in the best shape you can find. You're one of them. That plane crashed into a hill. The Japanese are bringing a truck to take us out there."
>
> We drove for a couple of hours and came to the bottom of this hill and we started up and we met these Japanese coming down with stretchers — nobody on the stretchers.
>
> They said, "Everybody dead. Everybody dead."[49]

Sergeant Léo Bérard of the Grenadiers was one of the men on the rescue mission:

> When we started climbing the hill, we realized then it was a long way up. It had been raining and the mud was so slippery that we seemed to take one step forward and slide two back. But [Dr. Reid] was in better condition than any of us and he kept going. I was the next one behind him. When we arrived there, the doctor sat on a stump. He was really beat

and so was I. Then he asked me to try to locate the remains of the crew.

This was horrible work. The bodies were all cut up and burnt. He said you had to look at their fingers for rings, their necks where their numbers [identification tags] would be, their arms for wrist-watches, and anything else that could identify them. So, we started with one body; we would try to fit one person together and eventually we found and put together thirteen bodies; we could not find fourteen.

The B-29 had ... crashed and exploded. You could put the remains of the wreckage inside a sixteen-by-sixteen-foot room. All the bodies were burnt; when you pulled the ring off a finger, you'd pull the skin off, too. Oh, I don't know how I could have done this!

After we finished doing what had to be done, the doctor took us back to camp and made his report.[50]

It was an incident Reid never discussed again. That night, he made a decision about his men most in need of medical attention. It would mean the real end of the war for him:

Communication between any place in this north-ern area and Tokyo were completely broken down. The Red Cross were unable to get through by tele-phone, telegraphs never got there, and messengers who went never got back. The Japanese couldn't get through any better. Around September the 4th ... I decided I would take the seriously sick patients down to Yokohama ... but that night we got the warning of evacuation by ship from Onahama and two other [POW] camps came out of the hills and camped on the [Onahama] beach and there was another camp nearby, that made four camps.

On September 5th we had been told by the Japanese we were going to be evacuated by sea. On the 5th nothing happened. On the 6th nothing happened. We heard at noon on these two days a broadcast by the Americans from Yokohama, saying there was a shortage of ships there and things were pretty disorganized and to stay in your camps until they got to them.

However ... I decided the night of the 6th because it was very uncertain when we were going to be evacuated [that] I wasn't going to wait with the sick, and I took the seriously ill from the four camps and told the Japanese I wanted a special car on the train and left the next morning. I had four seriously sick and I took a medical orderly and some carriers....

Between Tokyo and Yokohama we ran into an American officer and he jumped into the breach with us and got an ambulance in Tokyo, and we went down to [U.S.] 42nd Hospital which was in a godown [warehouse] on the dock with hospital ships docked right on this dock actually. They received us with wide open arms and took over the sick immediately and the other boys that I brought with me. I considered I would go back to the camp and go with the camp. The boys who came as carriers didn't have to go back and I signed their dismissal and let them go....

I saw the Americans and told them the situation in our camps at Onahama and they said they would arrange to bring out all four camps the following day. So it was no use going back, and I couldn't get a train anyway. There were three doctors there and Finn to look after the boys so I breathed a big sigh and said, "I guess I'm finished."[51]

The irony of Reid's decision to bring out the seriously sick ahead of the others was that after nearly four years together — all his shepherding, fighting for, and treating of them, he lost the chance to see his "boys" safe and heading home, to say to them: goodbye, good luck, well done.

One farewell Reid attended to before leaving Sendai 1B was his letter to Commandant Uwamori — last seen in May waving them off at the Yokohama train station — testifying to Uwamori's humane treatment of the POWs held at Camp 3D. With war crime trials certain to be commenced by the Allied Powers occupying Japan, Reid wanted to clear Uwamori's name. As things turned out, it wouldn't be enough:

27 August 1945
Lieutenant Uwamori
Imperial Japanese Army

Dear Sir:

We have learned from Lieutenant Chisuwa that you are well. He has kindly offered to have this letter delivered to you.

We both hope to see you before we leave Japan but in case we do not, we wish to thank you for your efforts to treat us and our men both kindly and fairly.

If we can, please send our regards to Mr. Koyanagi and thank him for us for his good work as interpreter at Tsurumi.

J.A.G. Reid, Captain
Royal Canadian Army Medical Corps
Charles R. Finn, Lieut.
United States Naval Reserve[52]

– 13 –

Safe in Allied Hands – A Time Outside of Time: The Home Front III

Reid spent his first night in Allied hands talking late with a fascinated group of American and Canadian officers, the latter just arrived in Tokyo to prepare for Canadian POWs coming out of the camps. After a short sleep on the American hospital ship *Marigold*, he was given the choice of flying out to Manila or having a sea trip to Guam on the USS *Ozark*. This was the day the U.S. Navy decided to take over care and transport of all Canadian POWs and foreign civilian detainees as well as American POWs in Japan. The *Ozark* was loaded with 250 just-released Canadians from other prison camps. Given the choice of air or sea, Reid's new American friends recommended the latter: "They said there is only one way to go home and that is by ship. You get food and rest and reoriented and so on. By flying you arrive looking a wreck. So I got out to the *Ozark* and fifteen minutes after I got aboard we sailed."[1]

The *Ozark* departed Tokyo the morning of September 8 and arrived in Guam on September 12. Here, the men were put into hospital for a battery of tests — chest, blood, electrocardiogram, stool examination, urine examination, hemoglobin, blood smear examination, dentists for the teeth, a special examination of the eyes. Food-wise, they were treated to whatever their hearts desired. A week later, the men well enough to travel, Reid among them, re-boarded the *Ozark* and sailed on to Pearl Harbor, moving along the enormous pipeline put in place by the Americans to get the sick and rescued safely home. "A very thorough going over, with the seriously ill kept in hospital [in Guam], but any particularly ill ones were flown out by priority from Guam," says Reid. "There was just a sort of leapfrog going on across the Pacific all the time. Coming in by plane, out by boat, in by boat, out by plane and so on — just as fast as possible."[2]

To while away the time on board, Reid wrote letters. Almost 40 years later, Doug Dadson, his old school friend, recalled the one to him, filled with Reid's plans of all the things he was going to do when he got home. Clearest in Dadson's memory was Reid's closing declaration: "And, I shall sire a son!"[3]

The *Ozark* arrived in Pearl Harbor at noon on September 25 for a 24-hour stopover before continuing to San Francisco. That evening, Reid called home. Hawaii was six hours behind Toronto, so it was the middle of the night when the telephone rang at 5 Scholfield and the overseas operator identified the caller as Captain Jack Reid, on the line from Honolulu. The pandemonium of emotions overwhelming Jean as she took the phone can be imagined. Yet this dreamed-of moment, coming without warning, was the prey of its circumstances: two disembodied voices, separated by four years and 4,700 miles, trying to reconnect over a telephone line suffering transmission delays, sound dropouts, and the hissing and buzzing of static interference. Reid's low-key, almost cross-sounding murmurs were hard to understand, and what Jean could make out wasn't what she was longing to hear. His voice was clipped, giving the basics of where he was, how he was coming home, handling this surreal reunion, hindered by technical difficulties, the best he could.

"Say something nice to me," Jean finally blurted.

Reid's questioning garble was lost on her, so she said again, "Please, say something nice to me."

He mustn't have understood because he paused. Now the overseas operator, still on the line, piped up: "She says, 'Say something nice to her!'"[4]

In recent months, Jean had been on a roller coaster of hope, fear, and guarded exultation. After hearing nothing since George Pollak's radio message of July 1944, good news had reached her in early June 1945. Several weeks earlier, a Radio Tokyo broadcast was picked up by ham operators in Corvallis, Oregon, Sacramento, California, and by a serviceman aboard the aircraft carrier USS *Tripoli* in the South Pacific. It was a recording of Reid speaking. The civilian reports came later, but the broadcast transcript and an accompanying note from the serviceman on the *Tripoli* were forwarded to Jean by the U.S. War and Navy Departments V-Mail Service on June 5:

> Dear Mrs. Reid,
>
> I am a radioman serving aboard a carrier attached to the Pacific Fleet. While listening in on a shortwave radio broadcast from Radio Tokyo, I intercepted quite a few messages from boys who are interned in the Japanese homeland as prisoners of war. Not

knowing whether or not the government notifies the people back home about these messages I have taken the liberty to do so in the hopes that it will throw a little light as to the whereabouts of your loved one. These messages are copied as accurately as possible. I sincerely hope this letter reaches you and with it brings a little ray of sunshine you so rightly deserve.

This message was intercepted on May 27, 1945, and came from the War Prisoners Camp at Tokyo.

Yours sincerely,

Julio Gonzalez, United States Navy[5]

Reid's message had been recorded at 3D in March 1945, shortly before the camp was closed. It runs as follows:

From: Captain J.A.G. Reid

To: Mrs. J.A. Reid

Text: Dearest One

I take this opportunity of sending to my wife, parents, and friends best wishes that will embrace your hearts' desires. On my account, I am well and busy and find little change from day to day. I have received letters from you telling me of your well-being. I hope that all is still so with you. The other officers here are: Lieutenant Commander C.D. Dockweiler, United States Navy; Lieutenant C.R. Finn, United States Naval Reserve; Ensign E.G. Pollak, United States Naval Reserve; and Major E.S. Kagy, United States Medical Corps. All are well. The men are in relatively good health and spirits and their jobs pass the time. You dwell constantly in my memory and have my love always.[6]

Jean was elated. But the topsy-turvy reports of the war situation in the daily papers throughout June, July, and the first half of August gave no clear picture of what was going to happen next. Headlines from Toronto's *Globe and Mail* show the uncertainty of the outcome, right up to the end:

- June 11: "Worst Weekend of the War for Japan — Jap Homeland Battered for the Fourth Day by Every Type of American Warplane."
- June 15: "Hints Japs Might Surrender Within the Next Ninety Days."
- June 16: "Japanese Peace Feelers Rejected."
- July 9: "Think Japanese Will Be Beaten by End of 1946."
- July 16: "Japan Invasion Could Be Soon."
- July 27: "Total Destruction Coming, Allies Warn Japan."
- August 7: "Atomic Bomb Rocks Japan."
- August 8: "New Ultimatum to Follow Bomb."
- August 9: "Russia Fighting Japan."
- August 9: "Second Atomic Bomb Dropped on Nagasaki."
- August 10: "Japs Hint Surrender."
- August 11: "Conditional Surrender Offer Made Officially by Japanese."
- August 11: "Peace Bid Made Unanimously by Jap Cabinet."
- August 13: "Allied Patience Running Out: May Loose Destruction upon Japan."
- August 13: "Must Await Command of Emperor, Says Tokyo."

In the late afternoon of Tuesday, August 14, Jean left work at Dr. Farquharson's office and boarded the Bloor streetcar at St. George Street, heading east to Sherbourne Street and its northbound bus into Rosedale. It was the sixth day of a heat wave in Toronto — the temperature was 86 degrees Fahrenheit — and the car was not only hot but slow-moving. At Queen's Park, Bay Street, then at Yonge Street, there was growing clamour at the intersections, rowdy noise, then headlines being shouted by the paper boys: "Japanese Quit!" and "Peace at Last!"

Dumbfounded, Jean stumbled off the streetcar at Yonge Street and waded through the jostling maelstrom of revellers. Around her, as though at a great distance, swirled sounds of laughter, whistling, shouts, honking horns. She stared at the newspapers, trying to absorb the sudden, stunning truth: it was over, the war was over!

How she got home that summer evening remained a blur forever after, a time outside of time, a glorious walk on air: Jack was coming home!

On August 17, Jean received a telegram from Bill Bigelow, still posted to a military hospital in Britain with the Royal Canadian Army Medical Corps: "I join you in thanksgiving today," wrote Reid's old friend. And though these *were* euphoric days for Jean, they were shadowed by the need to know Reid was safe. Word finally came three weeks later, the day after Reid reached Tokyo. At 10:15, the evening of September 10, the phone rang at 5 Scholfield and an operator at the Canadian Pacific Telegrams office in Ottawa read the longed-for message to Jean: "An Unconfirmed Report Has Been Received That Captain John Anthony Gibson Reid Is Safe in Allied Hands" — Stop — "No Further Information Presently Available."

It was enough.

The USS *Ozark* docked in San Francisco on October 2. For 24 hours the several hundred Canadian troops who disembarked were billeted at Fort McDowell on Angel Island in San Francisco Bay, prior to travelling north. This gave Reid time to call his father in Toronto, to phone Lyall Hodgins in Vancouver for help with travel arrangements home, and to buy a ring.

Charles Finn had given Reid the name of a San Francisco jeweller who would give him special treatment as an ex-POW. When Reid walked out of the jewellery store that afternoon, he had in his pocket the emerald-and-diamond ring that became the keepsake Jean would wear for the rest of her life. With this and little else, he boarded a train to Seattle with the other Canadians the next day, where they embarked on a boat to Victoria.

In Toronto, Jean booked a suite at the Royal York Hotel and moved in to await Reid's arrival — exact time unknown. It was a homecoming of sorts. The Royal York, completed in 1929 and the tallest building in the British Empire when it opened, was the site of the annual medical school parties Jean and Jack had attended throughout the 1930s as well as their destination on personal evenings out when they went dancing to live bands in the Royal York's grand Imperial Room. Just walking into the elegant, balconied lobby of the hotel recalled those happy, innocent times. Royal York staff, knowing the reason for her stay, coddled her like a queen. But once in her suite, with no idea when Jack would arrive, all Jean could think of to pass the time was to take bath after bath. On the other side of the country, Reid reached Canada:

> On the morning of October 5th we got into Victoria, at noon on the 5th actually…. They were prepared to do medicals on all the prisoners coming back and I went to Gordon Head [Military Base] about 2 o'clock — I had had my medical in Guam, but I

was to have waited for the other records — the only one who had to because the others came through Hong Kong and Manila. I argued my way for three hours — a number of officers ... saw no necessity for my being held there for an extra two days and as far as uniforms and pay went, I wasn't interested. Meanwhile my [medical] friends in Vancouver were working on a plane for me. I was through [the administrative hoops] by five [o'clock] and by six I was on the plane flying home and got into Toronto the next day with my [medical] records as the only baggage.[7]

Early in the morning of October 6, 1945, four years to the day since he went away to war, Reid landed at Toronto's Malton Airport. During the flight, somewhere over the Prairies, he had turned 32 years old. His father was at the airport to meet him. After a stop at 9 Grenadier Heights in High Park for a reunion with Eva, Harry Reid drove his son to the Royal York. Except for outgoing calls, the telephone in the Reids' suite was off the hook for the next 10 days.

Part III:
1945–1994

– 14 –

Picking Up the Pieces: A Bunch of Canes

Medical doctor, professor, and author Charles G. Roland interviewed Jean Reid about her husband in 1993 for his book *Long Night's Journey into Day: Prisoners of War in Hong Kong and Japan, 1941–1945*. Roland asked her: "And how was he then, that first week or so?"

Jean answered:

> The first week or so. I think he was so — it was so unbelievable to him, that he was back in his own city, and there we were, together.... He was sort of quiet and subdued. He hoped no one would ask any questions about what it was like.... It took some time before Jack began to — well, they're never the same. There was just no way that someone can endure these things without some changes. I knew that. I recognized that. That is just human, it doesn't matter what terrible event ... it's going to

make a difference to your personality, the way you think....

Because this is the truth — there was a lost sequence of years to be made up, to return to our society after what they'd been through.... You're making up for over four years. It was almost more than they could contend with....

Of course, everybody wants to have you for dinner, or the evening, and look at this person that's returned after that. And Jack would say, "I can't do it anymore."[1]

Two weeks after his return, Reid was sent for medical follow-up at Chorley Park, the temporary military hospital occupying what had been the lieutenant governor of Ontario's palatial residence in North Rosedale. Here, a short walk from 5 Scholfield, he underwent 10 days of observation, tests, and treatment for symptoms of dysentery and beriberi. Dr. Hoyle Campbell, who had known Reid in medical school, was consulted about the latter condition:

I examined him for some neurological problems he had — numbness. I thought it was beriberi — vitamin B1 deficiency, that was causing these symptoms. He was very emaciated when I saw him. Vitamin B1 deficiency over a long time can cause a lot of damage to the neurological system. I thought it was beriberi, and unless the vitamin B1 administrations they were giving him would help, I hadn't anything to offer. I

can see him still in my mind's eye. I was shocked at
how thin he was.[2]

At the end of October, Reid travelled to Ottawa to be de-
briefed on his experiences as an interned medical officer and prison
camp commander. While there, Reid reconnected with Major John
Crawford, his former commanding officer, who on return from
Hong Kong had been promoted to assistant director of medical
services at Ottawa Army Headquarters.

Reid's debriefing, conducted by Lieutenant-Colonel C.A.R.
Gordon, the Department of National Defence official medical

Captain Reid, Ottawa debriefing, October/November 1945.

historian, took several days to complete and ran to nearly 200 pages once it was transcribed. The case histories of Reid's prison camp patients and other medical records he had kept secret from the Japanese helped guide the narrative.

Back in Toronto, Jack and Jean remained temporarily at 5 Scholfield. Reid was finding his feet, seeing old friends, considering the future. But throughout these early days, the person he kept talking about, says Jean, was George Pollak. Repatriated in October from the prison camp at Ohashi and now living at his mother's apartment in New York City, Pollak was in the same frame of mind:

> Shortly after I got back I managed to get in touch with Jack and heard that he was well. Officially, I was attached to the Brooklyn Naval Hospital for three months as an outpatient and I was free to do pretty much as I pleased. Somehow Jack and I agreed on his and Jean's visit to New York, and in December they appeared for a week. It was a truly marvellous week for me, and I think they enjoyed it also.
>
> They were a strikingly handsome couple. Usually we would meet in the afternoon and cram as much as possible into the short time available. It was a rather euphoric time anyway, and the gay atmosphere of the city enhanced everyone's spirits. I recall that on several occasions we ended up in their hotel room in the wee hours, reviewing the day and planning for the next over glasses of milk and sandwiches. Jack seemed relaxed and happy, and I suppose it was a process of recourting Jean all over again.[3]

Jean remembered this week in New York as a perfect dream come true. Here she was, the agony of the war years behind her, gadding about the city where she and Jack had spent their

Jean Reid soon after Jack's return.

honeymoon, a handsome officer in uniform on each arm, getting
to know George, Jack's comrade-in-arms, and meeting Marianne
Pollak, George's mother, whose unexpected letter a year and half
earlier had reassured Jean that Jack was still alive.

Alfred Pollak, George's father, the clever Austrian chemist
who made good in America with his patents and food consulting,
had died in the summer of 1943, still wondering if his son was
alive. After his death, Marianne continued to reside in the family's
four-bedroom apartment (plus maid's quarters) at 895 West End
Avenue in Manhattan's Upper West Side. It was a grand establishment entered via a gracious wood-panelled and book-lined foyer
leading to a spacious salon and a separate dining room that easily
accommodated the baby grand piano that Marianne played beau-
tifully. Jean found her utterly charming and described Marianne

Jack, Jean, and George Pollak, Copacabana nightclub, New York City,
December 1945.

as "transfixed with happiness that everything was 'right' again against all odds," now that George was safely home.[4]

Forty years later, Pollak recalled this time with Jack and Jean in the festive, postwar New York of December 1945 as one of the best weeks of his life:

> The week ended all too soon. We were both return-
> ing into our own little worlds and an era was ending.
> Concern and affection from afar can remain, but one
> ceases to be a direct and daily influence on the other
> person, and vice versa. Accepting that, I still found
> great satisfaction in seeing Jack in gay and buoyant
> spirits and apparent excellent health. Moreover, after
> meeting and observing the lovely Jean during that
> week, I felt most reassured and confident that they
> would work out something good. Up to that time,
> to me Jack was a singular individual, with Jean's face
> as an unknown hazy apparition in the background.
> After that visit, I found that I thought of Jack and
> Jean as an indivisible unit. Inasmuch as she seemed
> to be part of Jack, she entered into our friendship as
> a most delightful partner.[5]

Early in 1946, the Reids moved into a duplex apartment at 25 Rose Park Drive in Moore Park. Welcomed back into the Toronto medical fold by admiring mentors and colleagues, Reid accepted a position as consultant in medicine at the Toronto Military Hospital on Christie Street and set to work on his fellowship in cardiology, which in keeping with his brilliant medical school performance, he would receive in record time later that year. He also began a medical study with John Crawford, funded by the National Research Council, examining the effects of prolonged nutritional deprivation on the Canadians held in Hong Kong and Japan.

Personal developments were proceeding in tandem. When George Pollak visited Toronto in July 1946, Jean was expecting a baby, and Reid, still officially on active service, had been promoted to the rank of major as well as learning he was to become a Member of the Most Excellent Order of the British Empire (MBE) for his service in the Far East. Five years younger, still single, Pollak had now decided on a professional career in the U.S. Navy.

Member of the Most Excellent Order of the British Empire (MBE) awarded to Major John Reid, 1948.

I made a brief visit to Toronto in the summer of 1946. We had a fine few days, very relaxed. I remember that liquor rationing was still in effect and the first morning Jack took me down to the alcohol Board or whatever it was called and talked them into giving me an honorary temporary card so that we wouldn't deplete the liquor locker too far. Jack seemed to be entering the mainstream of normal affairs, and although I don't recall any specific plans, he seemed to be feeling his way with interest. It was a good and satisfactory visit.[6]

Reid's postwar life seemed to be jelling. Tony, the son so resoundingly foretold in Reid's shipboard letter to Doug Dadson the year before, was born in November 1946, with Pollak named as godfather. The household on Rose Park now revolved around the baby, with Jean in her glory and Reid the proud and smitten father. Early in 1947, he was offered a staff appointment as resident physician at the Wellesley Division of Toronto General Hospital. On the research side, "Nutritional Disease Affecting Canadian Troops Held Prisoner of War by the Japanese," the scientific study co-authored with John Crawford, was published in the *Canadian Journal of Research* that April.

Yet the war continued to intrude. Reid's letter of commendation, sent to Masao Uwamori from Sendai 1B in August 1945, hadn't prevented the ex-commandant of Camp 3D from being arrested by the Allies as a possible war criminal in November 1945 — one of nearly 6,000 Japanese who would be tried in the War Crime Trials conducted in Japan by the Allies' International Military Tribunal between May 1946 and November 1948.

Reid had been alerted to Uwamori's arrest in June 1946 by a friend in the War Crimes Section of Canada's Department of

National Defence. Wanting justice done, he wrote letters in Uwamori's favour and travelled to Ottawa to be interviewed and file an affidavit in Uwamori's defence. Reid's main argument was that, over time, Uwamori had responded to Reid's persuasions and within the constraints of Japanese military hierarchy had done the best he could for the Canadian prisoners — so much so that in 1945 Uwamori had been relieved of his command for being too soft on POWs. Despite this testimony and unbeknownst to Reid, Uwamori was formally charged in December 1946 for mistreatment of Canadian prisoners, for permitting atrocities, and failing to provide prisoners with adequate food and shelter.

In April 1947, with Uwamori's trial soon to begin before the U.S. Military Commission, Ira Kaye, his court-appointed American defence counsel, made a last-ditch effort to mitigate the charges. Having reviewed Reid's letters and affidavit supporting Uwamori, Kaye contacted the Canadian War Crimes Section in Ottawa, hoping to solicit further testimony from Reid in favour of his client. When Reid heard that Uwamori was, indeed, standing trial as a war criminal, he was furious. He wrote a second affidavit in Uwamori's defence and had it transmitted to the Military Commission in Yokohama where it arrived midtrial. In this second affidavit, Reid hammered home detail after detail of Uwamori's positive behaviour before concluding:

> I could go on recalling incidents for some time, but I feel that these will give you a skeleton picture of the man. Such a state of cooperation was of course not obtained overnight. It took several months of constant effort, largely on my part, to establish such a frame of mind in Lieutenant Uwamori. But several decades of such efforts would not have established it in other Japanese Commandants I have known.

One must also consider that Lieutenant Uwamori was a Japanese propagandized to feel that we were the bitter and treacherous enemies of Japan; that he had never been in a western civilization; that he was an officer in the Japanese Army, acting under orders that were certainly not favourable to us as prisoners, and that physical punishment, drumhead justice, semi-starvation, the inadequate care of the sick, and the lack of dignity and the value of the individual were not only part and parcel of his army's organization and philosophy, but of the life of his whole country, in order to understand that he required personal qualities of fairness and consideration to be so far won over by any means.

To sum up, I did not observe any actions under the circumstances for which I would feel Lieutenant Uwamori should be punished as a war criminal.[7]

The trial ended on April 28, but final determination of the sentence was postponed until September 8, 1947, when Ira Kaye presented the "Defense Motion for Modification of Sentence in the Case of United States of America vs. Masao Uwamori" to the Reviewing Authority of the U.S. War Crimes Defense Division. In his summation, Kaye gave Reid the last word: "The opinion of Major Reid is so superlative and lengthy that no quotation from his affidavits and letters is necessary. To him, Uwamori was an outstanding exponent of humanitarianism."[8]

A year later, in a carefully handwritten letter, Uwamori describes the outcome in his own words:

1st December 1948
Major Reid

Dear Sir,

I have learned through your affidavit which was written by you at the City of Toronto on the 21st of April 1947 that you are well and are still very sympathetic and warm-hearted toward me. My lawyer Mr. Kaye has kindly offered to have this letter sent to you.

Right after the termination of the war, you were kind enough to send me a letter of bidding farewell, but I was very sorry that I could not see you before you left Japan. Neither could I write you until now. Therefore I think I had better write down the events in detail which happened to me so far.

On the 17th of November that year I was arrested and since then was being incarcerated in Sugamo prison as a war crime suspect. Around about the middle of December 1946, I was charged with violation of the Laws and Customs of War. The charges and specifications were the biggest ones which the defence section ever handled; the latter were more than eighty. At that time I was quite at a loss without knowing what to do.

However my lawyer did his utmost to defend me and also to obtain favourable evidences from the ex-prisoners of war. My serious concern then was how they felt toward me and how they knew my efforts during my service as camp commandant. The lawyer pried into all affidavits and concluded that you would be the life saver for me, because you were deemed the fairest and most humane person he ever came into contact with through all the documents gathered up at the Yokohama trials. Indeed I was in a firm belief that you would be the only one who would do me a great favour.

On 16th of April 1947, I was able to face the trial with a light spirit and an excellent health expecting your favoured statement. To my great joy, as was expected, you sent a wonderful disposition on my behalf just in due time during the trial. One thing that delighted me most was that you stated so many concrete evidences without any prejudice and with stepping over the colour line to enable the Commission to appreciate the estimate of me. One thing that impressed me very much was that you did mention them [in a] different way from the affidavits of other prisoners of war, for instance, analysing not only the Japanese Army's organization and philosophy but also the life of my whole country.

Thus, to sum up you praised me by saying I had most un-Japanese personal qualities of fairness. It seemed to be overestimation of me indeed. As a matter of fact, during my duty I did my best to treat you and your men fairly and kindly. However, because of lack of my ability and intelligence I could not satisfy you to the full extent. And if there was anything entitled to receive your hearty appreciation, I believe it had been done only through your sincere co-operation and wise suggestion to me. Your letter and affidavits were introduced at the final argument by my lawyer and they put the court into a surprising move.

On April 28th, I was sentenced three years hard labour, but after having weighed the mitigating factors — my humane treatment of Allied prisoners of war through your and other personnel's letters, the Commission made the recommendation for clemency to the Convening Authority. And at last, I was released from the prison and could be a free man under suspended sentence.

How I can express the greatest joy I ever felt in my life. Arrived home in the evening of the big day. I was welcomed by my family and could not help hugging each other and shedding tears. I think I could imagine your deep emotion which you might have felt when you came home after the war.

It was entirely of your favour to enable me to get rid of such a very hard case. I hereby explain my sincerest gratitude for your fairness and kindness to me during and after the war.

Now I am trying to find [a] new job without taking a rest, because during my absence my family has been making a from-hand-to-mouth living and been almost on the verge of starvation. However, the last two years' imprisonment never let me feel any hard feeling to the Allies, because I could not have treated you and your men as I had expected and felt the utmost regret and remorse in this respect also because I have learned that a great many of the personnel in my camp still feel warmest friendship and sympathy toward me.

My eager hope now is that I could use my person and capabilities for the benefit of the Allies and Japan during the formative years that lie immediately ahead as the Military Commission recommended, and I believe it might be the best compensation for the hardships from which you and your men had suffered in my camp and also might be a small gift to you which would please you to a certain extent.

If you allow me, I wish to write you often and see you anytime after normal relationship revived between your country and Japan.

Never would I forget your efforts, kindness and fairness as long as I live.

May I extend a happy new year to you and your wife.

Yours respectfully,
Masao Uwamori
No. 481 Zaimokuza,
Kamakura City, Japan[9]

Months later, a long, battered parcel arrived on Reid's doorstep in Toronto marked "Bunch of Canes" — the gift Uwamori had cobbled together as an offering of thanks. Inside was an assortment of second-hand canes in different coloured woods — malacca, bamboo, rosewood — and of different designs, uses, and states of repair. Some were slender, polished, and delicately carved, others were simple, utilitarian, somewhat battered walking sticks.

One stood out as belonging to a Westerner — an officer's swagger stick. This octagon-shaped cane had been personalized by its owner. Into the top of the pommel, a rudimentary British crown and laurel wreath in brass had been pressed. Affixed in one of the pommel's eight facings was a tiny Hong Kong five-cent piece. Encircling the pommel's crown and wreath, roughly carved, was the owner's name: "CSM E.C. Todd R.R.C." In assembling his "bunch of canes," Uwamori had found in some little shop or street vendor's cart in postwar Yokohama the swagger stick of one of Reid's own men — Sergeant Major Earl Todd, the popular Royal Rifles NCO who was crushed to death under a load of falling wood at Nippon Kokan Shipyard in November 1944.

Whether or not Uwamori tried to contact Reid again is moot. Reid's postwar aversion to anything that brought back memories of his experience meant he avoided or cut off any contact from that time, including involvement in the Hong Kong Veterans Association, founded in 1947, many of whose members had been the men in his camps.

Receiving Uwamori's "bunch of canes" is the last known connection that Reid had with his former commandant.

In the summer of 1947, George Pollak returned to Toronto to see Jack and Jean and to meet Tony, his infant godson. Pollak's career was progressing. He was now a lieutenant commander stationed in Washington, D.C., soon to be posted to the U.S. naval base in San Diego. He wanted to see Reid before distance became an impediment:

> Another short visit in 1947 was not quite the same. It may be at that time that Jack first mentioned the possibility of the [medical] practice in Vancouver. There was nothing obvious or specific, but I felt somewhat of a restlessness or dissatisfaction in Jack. Jean was as gracious and friendly as ever. Since it wasn't any of my business I didn't try to delve into the situation any further. Jack seemed to be sorting things out quite methodically and I didn't think much more about it.[10]

Some of Reid's Toronto friends met Pollak during his summer visits in 1946 and 1947. Doug Dadson said the gatherings were often full of fun, with Reid and Pollak recalling the ludicrous absurdities of prison camp life under the Japanese — the time, for instance, a guard delivered a ration bag to the prisoners' cookhouse containing nothing but four horses' hooves, or the time Reid was called into the camp office to help the Japanese puzzle over an order from Tokyo Area Headquarters: "Take one shirt and give it to each prisoner and take one shirt from each prisoner." What to do? Gales of laughter at 25 Rose Park Drive followed as these and other lunacies were recounted.

But, like Pollak, Reid's Toronto friends sensed his discontent. Some sort of disaffection with the Toronto scene had set in, increasing the lure of returning to Vancouver, where he had been happy in 1940–41. Since the end of the war, Lyall Hodgins and other Vancouver colleagues had been badgering him to return to The Clinic on Seymour Street where his name was still on the letterhead. In the spring of 1948, after vacillating about the staff appointment at Wellesley Hospital, Reid decided to go. Life in the west would provide the fresh start his restlessness craved.

Reid's long-time friend Frank Woods recounts:

> I didn't think he should go to Vancouver. But Jack said he didn't want to stay in the medical rat race. While other doctors [back from the war] were diving into practice and moving up fast, Jack was more spread out in his interests, not interested in money particularly. He liked his comforts, but they weren't all-important.[11]

According to Woods, Reid said he wanted — in symbolic terms — to get as far away as he could from the Medical Arts Building in Toronto, the Georgian-style palace at the corner of Bloor and St.

313

George Streets that since 1929 had housed the offices of much of Toronto's medical establishment. For someone whose career before and during the war seemed to have destined him to have an office there himself, this rejection of the beaten path was characteristic of Reid's eccentric postwar persona.

Jean was now expecting their second child, so plans were laid to make the move to Vancouver in the fall of 1948 after the baby's arrival. At the beginning of October, two weeks after Jon was born, Reid set off alone to drive to the coast. Jean was to follow six weeks later by train, with a nurse to help with two-year-old Tony and the baby. But before she left Toronto, something she'd been missing — a clearer picture of her husband's war experience — came by roundabout means.

Until now, Jean's glimpses of what Reid had gone through overseas had been limited to anecdotes and isolated details he mentioned if the mood struck him. Most of the time he was silent on the subject. Jean didn't ask for more than he was willing to reveal: the cries in the night caused by nightmarish dreams of being back in prison camp were warning enough not to probe too deeply. Thus, it was a kind of serendipity that his war decoration — the MBE — arrived by registered mail a week before Jean departed for Vancouver. The MBE citation, which encapsulated the 44 months of Reid's experience in Hong Kong and Japan, was an objective account based on military records and the testimony of the men he had served with or commanded. In the heartbreaking times to come, it was something Jean would later read and reread, trying to understand what had happened to the man she once knew so intimately, trying to fathom how the war had changed his way of being:

Award of Member of the Order of the British Empire
to Major John Anthony Gibson Reid
The Royal Canadian Army Medical Corps

Major Reid was medical officer to the Winnipeg Grenadiers when he was taken prisoner of war at Hong Kong in December 1941. The problems that arose following the capitulation were mainly those of care for the sick and wounded and the large task of ensuring a high standard of sanitation and hygiene in the prisoner of war camps.

Being an area in which tropical diseases and diseases of filth thrived, a very real problem confronted the medical officers, and, judging by the universal acclaim granted to these self-sacrificing men, they rose fully to the occasion regardless of the consequences to themselves. The fact that the conditions were made worse through inadequate rations and disinterest and interference from the Japanese authorities seemed only to spur the medical officers to greater efforts.

Major Reid threw himself whole-heartedly into the difficult task ahead of him and shortly was confronted by epidemics of diphtheria, dysentery and malaria which had to be treated without medicines and at the gravest risk of personal infection. In the early stages, anti-toxin was not available and the possibility of getting diphtheria was great and carried with it the strong likelihood of death.

As time went on, due to a shortage of rations, lack of vitamins caused diseases such as beriberi, pellagra, etc., which continued to ravage the prisoners of war throughout the period of captivity.

In January 1943 a draft of six hundred and sixty-three Canadian prisoners of war was sent to Japan as labourers, and Major Reid was the only

Canadian officer to accompany them. Here he was met with the most discouraging conditions; no medicine, short rations, an ever-present doubt as to what the unpredictable Japanese might do, and besides his medical duties, many responsibilities that devolved naturally on him which would ordinarily have been handled by a combatant officer.

Such was the character of the man that he not only overcame the difficulties as they arose, but eventually won the respect, confidence and admiration of the Japanese themselves. Throughout the entire period of his captivity Major Reid spent almost all his money on medical supplies for the benefit of his patients. In Japan, he arranged through black market sources a small supply of medicines. He took an active hand in controlling the prisoners of war, and on many occasions interceded for them with the Japanese, ensuring as fair treatment as was possible, particularly in regard to punishments which might have been visited on them by the camp authorities and in excluding the sicker men from working parties.

On one occasion when two Canadians were being beaten by Japanese guards, Major Reid elbowed them aside, picked one of the men off the ground and carried him to hospital where he found him to be injured severely.

Major Reid was able to maintain case histories of his patients, contrary to the orders of the Japanese authorities, and his records are now proving of considerable value to Canadian medical authorities both from the standpoint of the welfare of the individuals concerned and for their value in research in a field heretofore unexplored in this country where similar conditions and diseases do not obtain.

Possibly because of his continually firm stand with the Japanese, but undoubtedly because of his qualities as a man and a medical doctor, the Japanese themselves came to look on him with an attitude almost of worship. A Japanese doctor named Iino thought so much of him that he made a practice of bringing him gifts. Major Reid also won the complete confidence of the camp staff, and by doing so, was able to help the lot of his men immeasurably.

Despite the fact that his health suffered from the excesses of work and consideration for his men, Major Reid continued to display the highest qualities of humanity, skill and devotion to duty throughout his entire period as a prisoner of war.

The opinions of his men under his care are the final test in this case, and, although there were many outstanding deeds performed by many of the men who had the misfortune to become prisoners of war of the Japanese, there is no individual to whom so much gratitude has been expressed. In no single instance has anything but the highest praise been heard of this officer, and considering the unusual difficulties, depression, near starvation and disease experienced continuously for such a long period, there is no doubt that he deserved the highest possible recognition.[12]

Jean and her children departed for the West in mid-November 1948. When she stepped off the train at Pacific Central Station in

Vancouver three days later, the husband waiting on the platform —
in good spirits when he departed six weeks before — was strangely
subdued, matter-of-fact, distant. The reason would take time to
come out, but its effect Reid couldn't hide: he had met someone,
been thunderstruck, fallen head over heels.

– 15 –

Vancouver and the Double Life: A Confusing Correspondence

> I once asked her how she met Dad, and she said, at a cocktail party, where he was surrounded by women — she not being one of them.
>
> — Mary Reid Ramsey[1]

In the fall of 1948, Catherine Gillies was a bewitching 26-year-old nurse with a tragedy in her past. Born in Oban, Scotland, she had immigrated to Canada with her parents and six siblings at the age of three and grown up in Vancouver, where her father worked as an accountant for the Canadian Pacific Railway (CPR). Home was a rambling CPR-owned property on Angus Drive where the Gillies clan led a boisterous family life dominated by the four girls, of whom Cathy — sunny, sporty, down-to-earth — was the youngest.

The start of the war overshadowed her coming-of-age, and when Cathy graduated from Kitsilano High School in 1940, she entered nursing at St. Paul's Hospital, intent on serving overseas with the Royal Canadian Army Medical Corps. During her years of training, her high school yearbook became a log where she noted all the

Cathy Gillies (Reid) in her early twenties on the roof of St. Paul's Hospital, Vancouver.

boys from her school who had gone to war, their destinations, and if she knew, their fates. Eager to contribute to the war effort, she was crushed to learn on graduation that she was too late to be posted overseas. At war's end, she and several nursing friends found jobs at the Banff Springs Hospital in Alberta. But given her adventurous spirit, it was a more exotic posting that soon caught her fancy.

In January 1946, Cathy set off alone to join the medical team of an American-run mining company in Guayaquil, Ecuador. In these rustic surroundings, she acquired a little dog she called Gunga Din, a horse for local transport, and within a year, a fiancé named Jack Lowry, an American engineer whose love of riding, hiking, and mountain climbing matched her own outdoorsy interests. In April 1947, a party in the engaged couple's honour led to hijinks by the swimming pool, where, in jest, their rowdy friends toppled them in. Somehow in the fall, Lowry hit his head and was knocked unconscious. Seriously injured, he was airlifted to the United States to receive medical care but died during the flight, Cathy by his side. Devastated — a niece living at Angus Drive remembered her returning home from South America "in terrible shape"[2] — Cathy sought the comfort of her family as she mourned her loss, eventually returning to work at Vancouver General Hospital.

A year and a half later — the evening of the cocktail party welcoming Reid to Vancouver — it wasn't Cathy's inclination to join the fawning circle of nurses surrounding the handsome doctor and war hero, newly arrived from Toronto. Perhaps beyond her natural attractiveness, it was this cool reserve that first marked her out for him. For meet they did that night, and Reid was soon obsessed with her, a mad attraction that would not be stopped.

Jean was at a loss. Her expectations of a warm welcome dashed, bewildered by her husband's aloofness, all she could imagine was that something during their six weeks apart had triggered a delayed

reaction to his war experience. In response to whatever was torment-
ing him, the course she chose was to provide love, sympathy, and
patient, undemanding support in the hope he would soon return
to himself. For Reid, a man possessed by his sudden, secret infatu-
ation, Jean's misconstruing the reason for his altered state made his
dissembling and excuses to hide the affair all the easier to assume.
He appeared a troubled man, but not for the reasons Jean believed.

After the family had lived in a rented house for several months,
a measure of domestic normalcy was re-established, at least out-
wardly, when they moved into 5388 Laburnum Street, the two-
storey Dutch Colonial–style house in Shaughnessy, which on and
off would be Reid's home for the rest of his life. From Laburnum's
front portico, which faced west, the blue of the Strait of Georgia
could be seen in the distance, with Vancouver Island a band of
darkness separating the ocean and ever-changing sky. Reid would
never tire of the view with its varying weather and mystic sunsets.

But throughout the tumultuous months of 1949, his emotions
out of control, the house was like a prison to him, his only escape the assignations he began to steal that winter under pretense

In 1949, Jack, Jean, and their young family moved into this house at 5388
Laburnum Street in Vancouver's Shaughnessy neighbourhood.

of work, picking Cathy up at a certain corner at one o'clock on Saturday afternoons to share what time they could.

An aficionado of William Shakespeare, and no doubt sensing the name's aptness to Reid's character and experience overseas, Cathy dubbed her lover "Jamy" after the Scottish captain in *Henry V*: "Captain Jamy is a marvellous falorous gentleman, that is certain; and of great expedition and knowledge in th' aunchient wars."[3] And thus he signed his love letters to her. His public disguise, whenever a signature was required, a reservation made, or a phone message left, was "Mr. Saunders."

For them both, the clash of craving and guilt must at times have been ferocious as the affair progressed. But for Reid, especially when things went wrong between them, or if Cathy was away, nothing could suppress the volcanic passion, desperate need, and endless longing that she generated in him.

Three letters written over a short time in the spring of 1949 chronicle his agonies after some unexplained quarrel caused Cathy to decamp alone to Victoria. His description, in this first letter, of a social occasion he was hosting — presumably endured the evening before at Laburnum, is by a man self-admittedly unbalanced, and for whom no one and nothing seems to exist beyond the woman he is addressing:

Saturday, 1 p.m.

Cathy Dear:

This is again the hour that for so many Saturdays held all the essences of joy. But not today, although the sky is blue as yesterday, the wind as warm, but silent as far as the whispers of love.

And to add woe to woe, no communication this morning, despite a thousand searches in the box outside. All the unhappier as I'd somehow not doubted that there would be such.

So, my love, in lieu of actuality of possession, I write, knowing sadly that you will be there to receive. And all the old sickness is in me, the horrid nausea that builds and builds when things go wrong in my expectations of you. I'd gauged myself till tomorrow night and looked so forward as recompense to the next morning. If, then, I have no rights to ask for such disappointments, I still claim the ability to suffer much from them.

As time went by this day there was even a little rearing of the fantastic insanity that I have had occasion to deplore in myself several times. But that was washed all away by the memories of this hour only a day ago when we were so supremely happy in a happiest of all days....

I shall add little else. Last night was one of the most beautiful and one of the coldest to be had on a mountain top. Due to my complete lack of interest in anything, I'm afraid it fell very flat for everyone, but I was in such a partly warm and partly agonized reverie of you that I was quite unable to raise my responses to anyone the whole evening.

It was so like being on top of the world, or even in another place entirely, and those high places in life will never again have any meaning for me. All is empty, my darling.

Come soon again to fill the aching void.

Let it not be long.

All my love, always,

Jamy[4]

A day or two later, Reid has heard nothing back. Apart from clandestine meetings, their daily interactions normally took place at Vancouver General Hospital, where Cathy was nursing and Reid saw patients. Reid's lovesick barrage in this missive — lamenting the daily thoughts not shared, his medical work turned tedious, his fixation causing near-collisions while driving his car, the pointlessness of life without her — ends with a challenge: does she love him, or has it all been, for her, "a mid-winter madness"? For them both, he twists the knife further by describing his passing by "the corner" [*their* corner] and finding it "bare and lonely, though densely populated" in her absence:

Cathy Dear:

So, my love, I take up pen again to you, not that I have more to relate but because my heart turns so constantly in your direction that even the inadequate and vicarious contact seems so much better than nothing at all.

That I adore you, you know, and the little things in which it is overtly expressed in the last twenty-four hours are such as when picking out a tie for the morning and hesitating for a moment to make a selection, one realizes suddenly that it is of absolutely no consequence what is chosen or if nothing is worn, as you will not be there to see in any case. An episode like that makes my heart weep.

Twice yesterday I missed an accident surely only by your prayers as I drove with my mind completely occupied with you, and all my vision turned inwards to the lovely memories I carry with me.

325

All the fun, too, has gone from medicine when I do not have you to tell the tiny events of the cases.... All the little things of justice and injustice and humour and unhappiness that we always spoke about and saw the same view about.

Our life was always full of sparks and even this quarrel only fire struck from the intensity of our emotions.

Or does all this fade for you, by now? Is three days enough to tell you that you suffered a midwinter madness and were totally bemused? Do I hear you enunciate my name with fury, at the content of the last two sentences? I hope so.

I was called [to the hospital] at noon today but it was just [until] 12:35 and wouldn't have interfered. I drove by the corner but it was bare and lonely, though densely populated, under the brilliant sun.

I miss you so.

My love,

J[5]

In the third letter, written several days later, agony has given way to joyous relief. The evening before writing it, "Mr. Saunders" had stolen upstairs, closed the door of Laburnum's master bedroom, and placed a long-distance call to Victoria. However brief the conversation, the quarrel was smoothed over. Reid's "Que passa?" [sic] suggests a touch of uncertainty — a courtly deference to Cathy's independence. But what follows the question seems to show that "the desire so intense" will soon be requited. The crisis, but not the intensity, has passed:

Cathy Dear:

Another tiny note to you as a vicarious means of contact to get through the day.

It is a beautiful eve here and I sit for a few minutes on the frontispiece [of Laburnum] looking over at the island with the heavy sea-clouds along the horizon, which make islands of themselves for every ocean voyageur. When shall we be afloat with only horizons on every hand? So much there is now to work for.

Always now the beauty of such a day makes the heart ache when it is not shared. Love is a very poignant emotion and is made of nostalgias on separation as it is a bounding ecstasy together.

All the world is so quick with you, as though every nerve ending of the senses and every pathway of the brain were sharpened and made facile to an inexperienced degree.

As the warmth of the sun is more caressing than ever before, so the fragrance and loveliness of you is more omnipresent than the real objects around me.

And what with you, my love? "Que passa?"

Does love pass or is it more intense? Are you restless, and is it for me, or for a future still yours?

Are you speaking my name impatiently after those questions? I hope so. Every tone of your voice is so clear, the tilt of your head and the soft, soft nape where the golden hair sweeps up and away, leaving tendrils to kiss.

How imperative it was to speak to you for a moment last night. I'm sure you thought Mr. Saunders was quite mad to waste your money in such a fashion. I had tried earlier, as I told you, at a time when I could have spoken with you. But at 7 p.m. the desire was so intense that I closed the door, picked up the upstairs phone and reassured myself of your reality and the fact that we became known to each other.

Dear great and good friend, I don't know whether this will get to you Sat. or Mon but whenever, may the time between now and our rejoining be as the life of man in the eyes of God, a wisp of a moment.

To you, my love, all of it, for now and for ever.

Jamy[6]

Although living in the same house with Jean and their children, the author of these letters had become an emotional stranger to his wife. For Jean, at sea with worry as Reid's remoteness persisted, and helpless, it seemed, no matter what she tried, to bring back signs of the man she had known for so long, her only option was to look after her sons, keep up appearances, and hope against hope that the psychological damage Jack was suffering from would somehow begin to recede.

It is unknown what Jean may have planned to celebrate Reid's 36th birthday — October 6, 1949 — the fourth anniversary of his return from the war. But anything she attempted would under the circumstances have seemed pathetic, an annoying distraction for him. That day, Reid had driven back to Vancouver from an overnight tryst with Cathy — a celebration of their first meeting the year before. Taking a professional course near where they spent the night, Cathy had stayed on to complete it, while Reid, reluctantly, had returned to Laburnum. But already missing her "unutterably," he was busy planning another night together the following week before bringing her back to the city. A year since they had met, Reid's effusive prose betrays an obsession stronger than ever:

Thursday Afternoon

Cathy My Dear:

I've just tried to call you for no other reason than to reiterate how sweetly and deeply I love you and to hear your voice. Mr. Saunders was told that you were at the University and can only hope that this type of education agrees with you.

Being three times twelve today I am going to dedicate, very quietly, a few double toasts in Dewar's and can wish at least, and in wishing so intensely, see you sipping the other halves.

My dear, as is evident, I arrived without mishap, unless the gradual fragmentation of a heart be called such as it passed place after place where it had not been alone. At one point I stopped and almost turned about. Only your embarrassment at explaining how your "cold" had suddenly cleared, and the knowledge that this was the way to celebrate a very special anniversary next week, made me reluctantly proceed.

It is not as hopeless as ever, without you. It is much more hopeless than ever.

I am desolated by the Scottish tunes that happened over the radio this morning. As I've painted and painted today [housework at Laburnum] the brush strokes intone your name over and over and instead of the surface before me your grace

329

and loveliness appear so that I become completely bemused.

Darling Kit, I miss you unutterably. Do care for yourself as I would and get well so quickly for me. I must dance with you again and instead of meeting at W.R. [women's residence?] will come back for you so that we may stay over one more evening. That will be Monday or Tuesday and the sooner, God willing.

My love, wait for me and don't regain your senses in the meantime. That is to say, love me, also.

Know how I need you. Know how lost I am without you, and know that you have All my love, always.

Jamy[7]

Two months later, Cathy discovered she was pregnant.

– 16 –

The Domestic Tightrope of a Mentally Disturbed Man

I n the spring of 1951, four years after his last visit to Toronto, George Pollak got in touch with Reid to arrange a visit in Vancouver. Pollak had been teaching for a year at the U.S. Naval College in Newport, Rhode Island, and was now under orders to return to San Diego for active duty in the Korean War. With him was his wife, Anne, a beautiful divorcée and sometime model from Roby, Texas, whom he had married in 1948.

Reid replied, and arrangements were made for an evening at Laburnum. In July 1951, the Pollaks left Newport for San Diego by way of Vancouver:

> I wanted to visit Jack in the new environment. We spent a weekend at Lake Louise and then drove down to Vancouver. The road along the Columbia was incomplete (unpaved, no rails, etc.) but we took it anyway. Anne was just a touch pregnant and not

feeling too well. The corduroy effect of the dirt road didn't help much.

I recall that we stayed somewhere along the Fraser River that night and then drove down to Vancouver the next day and got there in the late afternoon. After getting cleaned up we walked into an unexpected, very tense situation [at Laburnum]. Everyone was very polite to everyone else, but as the evening progressed it got more bewildering.

After dinner, Jack said he wanted to show me something, so we left Anne and Jean and went off. I felt badly about leaving them because essentially they were strangers. Jean was distressed and Anne was not aware of what all had gone before. Anyway, Jack insisted and we rode off.

It was night time and I didn't know Vancouver and had no idea where we were going. Jack was un-communicative. We finally drew up at what turned out to be the Nurses' Residence[1] and Jack went and pounded on the door. I think there was a brief contretemps with the Matron because of the hour, but finally Jack's nurse appeared at the door. Jack introduced us with a very brief explanation of the situation. She was embarrassed, I was embarrassed, and Jack was rather grim. After a few minutes of conversation, we withdrew again.

In the course of the evening the alcohol was flowing, perhaps in self-defence. We got back to the house. I don't think Anne and I stayed very long. I do recall that on the way back to the hotel or motel I was damned drunk and shaken. Apparently Anne thought I looked so bad she was afraid I was dying. I was afraid I wasn't.

As I said goodbye to Jack that evening, he said, "After this is settled, I'll get in touch with you."

I never heard from him again, nor saw him.[2]

In the 18 months between Cathy's becoming pregnant and the Pollaks' Vancouver visit, Reid had moved from carrying on a clandestine affair to juggling two families openly. Cathy's pregnancy had forced his confession to Jean in early 1950, along with a plea on his own behalf. He wasn't in his right mind, he told her. He had turned into a horrible person and the affair was just part of his madness. But the madness would pass, he knew, with her help. After all he'd been through, she must stand by him.

Devastated by the truth behind his year of bizarre behaviour — when he confessed, she fainted dead away — Jean chose to give in to his entreaties. She had nothing more to lose, everything to gain. The war had done this to him — wounded him in unseen ways. She would stay with him to do what she could to support his recovery, help him heal, try to save their marriage.

In August 1950, Jean returned to Toronto for five weeks, taking Tony with her. Jon, not yet two, was left in the care of the Laburnum housekeeper. Perhaps Jean needed to escape Vancouver while Reid and Cathy's baby, due that month, was born. In Toronto, Jean revealed nothing of the domestic mayhem she was living with in Vancouver, yet it followed her east. In his letter to her of August 10, Reid proposed an extraordinary solution to his "problem": to divorce Jean "temporarily," marry Cathy, then divorce Cathy and remarry Jean:

Steve Dear:

It's taken me a long time to get this note started to you, being still so tossed to know what to say to you. I would give all in the world not to hurt you and yet it is impossible to know how to say it without taking the chance of your misunderstanding and being unhappy. I've lain awake almost all the last 3 nights with the problem....

I know, you see, that you are the right and important thing in my life. I have been so stupid in the past two years and in a way it's so odd that I should have been as I've always seemed fairly sensible before. What happened I suppose has an explanation but it just seems so out of character.... My one desire is to get back to you again. This is entirely possible for me; whether for you remains for you to say. But there is only one way that I can see for me to get back and that is to discharge what is *for me* my responsibility and have the whole other thing completely behind me. I cannot seem to find my way except [by] legalizing [the baby by marrying Cathy] in order to exorcize it from my conscience. I have cast around for easy means to accomplish this.... A week ago I found out that a Mexican divorce is obtainable by agreement of the two involved with no personal appearances etc. and could be done absolutely quietly and then [our marriage] redone in a month or so without ever breaking the continuity of our association. I suppose this sounds fantastic to you and I suppose in my twistings and turnings I may reach towards fantastic methods. However, this seemed a way in which the whole thing could be cleared up in a week or two and allow me to get ahead again the way I used to do.

Whatever your ideas, please let me know them back here *at once.*

Please try to find it in your heart to forgive me the grief I have caused you, I who always had the idea of making you very happy and now, with the war and this [affair], have totalled so much more sorrow than joy for you. I would so like to be able to sit quietly down, quietly within us, and talk to you in the way before....

Try to understand my dilemma without bitterness. Try to understand me, darling.

I love you,

Mike

On August 25, the day after Cathy gave birth to their son, Reid responded to Jean's reply to his divorce proposal:

Stephen:

Had your letter today as you will my note tomorrow. The evidence in it of how I have hurt you ... breaks my heart all to pieces. I love you. You are my dear one, no matter how much you may laugh at that. There is something sweet, intangible and indestructible in what I feel for you. I love you deeply, completely and forever no matter what blindness, madness and astonishment of heart beset me. I know you must find it impossible to love me anymore, though you say you do, but deep inside me it has always been the same.

I ... have been sitting in the garden for a while watching the full moon come up and wondering what would make me happy again. Slowly I sorted out every possibility as I watched the dogwood tree grow whiter and whiter in the moonlight and knew as I have always known (obsessed as I may be) that I needed above all you to be happy again, to call into the lighted house to [invite you] to come out and sit beside me. The night was so very beautiful and quiet and to me that means you.

In the end, under the apple trees, I grew cold.... If I could only cut the wildness of my body off and give it to you to keep safely for me. Darling, forgive me. I have never been able to talk to anyone but you.... Forgive me and understand me a little and realize my horrible need for you and for your happiness. Darling, really, it's I who need your compassion.

My love,

Michael[3]

There was no Mexican divorce. After Jean returned from Toronto, a semblance of stability resumed at Laburnum. Cathy had moved back to the Angus Drive house, where there was plenty of family to help with the baby, so Reid was home regularly after work. Yet over the coming months, he quietly persisted in his divorce-marriage-divorce-remarriage proposal. In the past so lovingly protective of Jean, he knew well the calm persuasions and honeyed assurances that would most resemble the old Jack to her, the one she wanted back. And so he wore her down, insisting, insane though it must have sounded, that this was the only way of

Reid family, pre-Christmas photo, 1950, 5388 Laburnum: (from left) Jack, Jon, Tony, Jean.

their being together again. She was demoralized and alone. There finally seemed no other choice.

On June 17, 1951, just days before the Pollaks spent the evening at Laburnum, the Reids' divorce was granted on the grounds of adultery in a Vancouver courtroom, with Jean gaining custody of the children and $400 in monthly support. Soon afterward, Jack and Cathy quietly wed. The evening Jack introduced George Pollak to Cathy in a doorway of Vancouver General's Nurses Residence, she was already pregnant with their second child.

Responsibilities increasing, Reid bought a house for his second family, this one on W 49th Avenue, just a four-minute drive from

Laburnum. With the birth of Cathy's second son, in March 1952, Reid's unusual domestic picture was complete: Jean, his ex-wife, and their two sons living in the Laburnum house; Cathy, his present wife, and their two sons living in the "49th house"; and he, like some mesmerizing Svengali, moving between households at whim.

Having organized life as he wanted it, he now attuned his manner with Jean to mollify her and keep her hope alive that, when things were "settled," theirs would be the happy ending he promised. In fact, juggling two families had become his chosen status quo. His mad illusion was that the game need never end. What Cathy made of this freakish arrangement is unknown.

In the summer of 1952, Jean returned to Ontario for a six-week holiday, taking both her boys with her. She planned to see her parents at Scholfield, spend time at Harry and Eva's cottage in Muskoka (Reid's father and stepmother were still in the dark about his goings-on), and visit her sister, Dede, in Montreal. She continued to hide the truth of her situation from family and friends in the east — praying that, as he kept promising, Reid would finally sort things out so that they would never know of the marriage breakdown or his other relationship.

Worn down by almost four years of misery and betrayal, Jean was still in Reid's power, still believing his pleas that he needed her, that he was getting better, that he would come back to her. The letters he wrote her through the summer of 1952, unfettered time he was enjoying with Cathy and their boys at the "49th house," presented an imaginary picture of bachelorhood at Laburnum — promoting the idea that, other than while at work at The Clinic, he was at loose ends, mooning about an empty house, filling his free time with yard work, or with tennis, golf, and social evenings with neighbours and colleagues who, as Reid presented them, were simply concerned for a fellow family man whose wife and children were away for the summer. The impression was of a lonesome husband and father making the best of it. As for her ongoing state of torment, cheap comfort: "you must stop feeling alone," he urges her, "which you will never be again as long as I'm alive":

Tuesday Noon [July 1952]

Dear Ones:

How happy I was to find a second note from you when I came in at noon....

The weather has broken here, the weekend being very cool and cloudy, yesterday variable and today solid rain and cold.... Sat[urday I] worked all day at the office and was on call that night. After things got settled down went down to the ball game by Kerrisdale and saw a dandy between two men's softball teams that had to go 12 innings.... Next morning played tennis with Archie [Johnson, a medical colleague] tho' it was too cool to be really pleasant....

Yesterday left the office at 5:30 p.m. with Archie who wanted to see the country and went to McQueen's [a mutual friend] again arriving about 7:30 to find a fine steak dinner awaiting us. Then Archie went off on the boat with Ned ... and after [we] sat and talked till 10, getting back about 12. A very nice evening....

I hope you are settled in there now and arranging about Muskoka this weekend. I so deeply want you to have a happy time there and you must stop feeling alone, which you will never be again as long as I am alive. Tell me everything that goes on in and out of you, and know how very necessary it is to me.

Jay [their elderly Laburnum housekeeper] comes tomorrow tho' I'm doing fairly well on shirts so far. *To the boys* — do you know what? *Someone* was playing with your wagon so I put it in the cellar. And the robins have hatched out and the mummy and daddy are flying every which way, hopping, stopping, listening and pouncing on worms and then flying to the nest and jamming the worms into the babies' mouths. When I cut the grass I don't know how I will cut the long weeds because Jug and Teej [Jon and Tony] are not here to help me. I guess I'll have to leave them till they get home. Both be good boys for Mummy and do what she says the very first time and (here fill in any instructions of a pertinent nature!!!). Send me some of the fish you catch and don't swim too fast.

I must to work. Take care of yourself, darling, and enjoy every minute of the holiday. I miss you all very much and read one of Teej's books & play with one of Jug's cars every night so that I won't be too lonely. Write little notes often.

All my love,

M.[4]

Busy as he was at work, putting in strategic appearances at Laburnum, spending the rest of the time with Cathy and their sons at the "49th house," Reid's duty letters, such as the following, were decidedly thin. How depressing it must have been for Jean, showered by his love letters and billets-doux since his medical school days, to receive these hasty scribbles, ending with hackneyed wishes and abbreviated salutations:

Thursday Noon [July 1952]

Dear Steve,

Just a note to catch Toronto by Saturday and say that you have, so far, missed no good weather here. Except for last Friday it has been cold and wet, a miserable week....

The house seems very deserted without you and the meek-mice [Tony and Jon] but I hope you are getting good weather and planning for Muskoka this weekend.... If the weather [here] improves at all I hope to get some golf and/or tennis with Archie who is all enthused about it. Slipped my back at the weeding last night.... I certainly missed the two helpers [Tony and Jon] to load up the wagon and tumble them off....

Take care of yourself, darling; relax and have a good time and come back soon,

Yrs,

M.[5]

Reid's letter of early August 1952 shows the gentle, persuasive psychological manipulation he could employ to nudge things in the direction he wanted them to go. After sending belated wishes for Jean's birthday (she turned 38 on August 6, 1952), Reid touched on his main concern of the moment — his fear that Jean would finally reveal to her parents the truth about their domestic chaos. To fend off disclosure, he blithely, cruelly, promises what she most wished to hear from him while currying her compliance: "I'm sure everything will work out finally." If her parents are never bothered — "so much the better":

Monday.

Steve Dear:

Just another note to catch you in Muskoka. Do hope you got the one today before you left. If you did not, both may reach you too late for your birthday & in case you do miss the Sat. letter I repeat here that all my wishing heart is with you for a happy day and many happier in the future. Take kisses three to you from me.

Had your letter today.... Sounds as though your plans had jelled for the remainder of your stay. Perhaps you feel you'd like to talk things over with your mother and dad, but if your desire to do so is not imperative I think I'd leave it. I'm sure everything will work out finally, and if they are never bothered with it, so much the better....

I miss you and the boys very much. The weather has continued absolutely clear and hot. Late Saturday cut grass.... Yesterday had a swim in the a.m., then got my work done & went over to Archie's where we played tennis.... The office has continued very busy right through the hot weather so that the day's end finds you fatigued a bit. By dint of lengthy watering the grass [at Laburnum] is being kept fairly green despite the hot sun day after day and I've not forgotten the geraniums which are doing fairly well, nor the kitchen ivy. Jay is coming Wed. & the transparent apples are ready for a little sauce....

I'll get this off, darling. Do take care of yourself for me and drop me a line whenever it takes your fancy.

Bush the boys for me.

My love, so much

M.[6]

Jean kept the truth to herself, but by mid-August her spirits were flagging. She wished Reid were with them. Chastising her for feeling low, he maintained there would be other holidays together and professed his continuing love. Meanwhile, the picture of household chores around Laburnum filling his time gets what Jean must by now have perceived as an exasperating touch-up:

Wed. a.m. [Mid-August 1952]

Steve Dear:

Have been holding off a day or two to try to estimate your whereabouts. Had a couple from you which seem to indicate that you will be returning to Toronto ... thus I'll head this to headquarters [5 Scholfield] and hope for the best.

Your time at Muskoka sounded wonderful.... I'm so pleased and only wish that it could have been longer. Dear Steve, your thoughts seem so unhappy and so filled with regret so much of the time. Don't be so. We'll have all the holidays together, in the woods and out of them, so look forward to these rather than regretting the present ones. You are so sweet and adorable and I love the way you are in yourself. I miss you and the children so much....

The days here pass rapidly. The weather has been very hot and sunny constantly. This gives rise to considerable fatigue at work ... and a constant warfare with the burned grass. I've taken the latter as a sort of game and though there were great burned patches I think I'm getting on top of it.... Sunday had a lazy day, cut the grass, had a swim, shifted the hose about and picked a mass of blackberries for Jay's administration. Jay has done the transparent apples & is going to make jelly from the berries....

My first patient is at the door so must dash. I'm happily including a cheque for $100. If that is not enough let me know & let me know when you decide to leave definitely [for Vancouver].

Hug the boys.
My love
Mike[7]

At the end of August, the vacation in Ontario was coming to a close. Plans were laid for the return, and words of happy anticipation were sent east: "Miss you all and look so forward to your return." Reid's double life in Vancouver was about to recommence:

Wed. pm

Steve Dear:

Found your note of Monday.... If something unusual does not come up I suppose this will be the last [letter I send] before you leave.... I do hope you get a comfortable [train] berth on the way back and the kidlets will enjoy it and not cause distress.

Little new here with the same routine.... I'm slowly winning the battle of the parched grass but the weeds remain or one has to leave the grass un-watered for a week while killing them and I felt this hot weather was not the best time for that. Have got a great smash of blackberries for Jay but she's off for a couple of days this week with stomach flu and will do them tomorrow or next day.

Take it easy on the way back, darling, and try to come in a little refreshed. I'll be seeing you at the station the a.m. of the 29th. Miss you all and look so forward to your return.

My best to all.

Slug the sluggers [Tony and Jon].

My love

Mike[8]

On August 24, four days after this last letter was mailed, and five days before Reid met Jean, Tony, and Jon at the Vancouver train station, he and Cathy celebrated Jock Reid's second birthday at the "49th house," six-month-old Tavish in tow.

Somehow, Reid walked this domestic tightrope for another year. There was still no talk of a divorce from Cathy. The following summer he took Jean and her boys to Kelowna for a "family holiday," as he had promised the year before. But he didn't stay the whole time. A letter to Cathy at the "49th house," written in stolen moments and mailed from Kelowna on July 8, 1953, shows that nothing in his passionate attachment to her had changed, or was ever likely to:

Kath, My Dear:

Up to the present I've given you very little news as there isn't any except the constant and wonderful news of loving you always.

Let me jot down some isolated incidents that might amuse you. First, I do feel rested and am getting some sun here and there. Second, I grew a beard for you until yesterday and then as it began to get red and blond mixed [I] thought that on my return you might not discern the lover behind the furze and let me have the skillet over the head as one of those strangers you keep away from. Even if I crawled into bed with you in the middle of the night, when your hand came up to my chest and you found the bushes you would probably scream — or would it intrigue you? In any case, it's gone!!! If you desire it, tell me in your next....

Last night went into town in the evening and watched an aquacade put on to garner $ for K's 47th regatta. I looked about me in the crowd and saw a few young men that I thought how much superior they would be to you than me. (Last sentence pure Ogden Nash!) — only a few, mind you.

Then I carefully observed the female half of the population and thought how actually and no compliments not one of the prettiest would even be 49% of you, my lovely one. I also imagined the terrible, driving joy and excitement there would be if you were beside me, as I think in everything I do. I think of the breathless curve and such of your body and the squeezy, wild feeling it gives in my heart.

Heavens, this has got off being a chronicle all by itself and begun to talk of the things I'm trying to keep controlled in missing you.

It was like a knife of happiness to hear your voice t'other day. I hear it every night in my dreams and see you so clearly and so dearly. Last night was positively sweet and poignant. But it is all the time, daytime, nighttime and sleeping or waking. You are beautiful and the most beautiful of past, present and future, including Christendom, Muslimdom, Buddhadom and Confuciandom.

I also keep dreaming of the time we'll have together when I return. The long slow hours that will, of course, go so fast. What we'll do this time and that time. Whether we'll dissipate and be healthy or healthy and dissipate, or both.

Whether we'll go to Seattle or to the mountains or to the seashore or wherever it may be whether we'll even see the place or be confined to the little niche of our own the whole time.

You must be rested and full of Spring, my darling, for this regular life is beginning to make me feel like a tiger again.

It's really very bad of me to indulge myself with a letter like this. If I keep it terse and only feel the wanting of you but don't begin to express it, it is so much easier, or let us say less difficult, to manage. I miss and want you like Hell and Heaven.

Give those sluggers [Jock and Tavish] my love and a wrastle [*sic*] from me. For yourself a wrastle also but with fierceness just controlled enough that I never really hurt you.

God, God, I love you.

P.S. I'll send this in now and hope there's one from you that makes my heart leap like a flame.

My love, My love,

J.⁹

Clearly, by the summer of 1953, Reid's predicament wasn't his passion for Cathy — indeed, it is impossible to imagine a more all-consuming attachment. His predicament was that through some deep-seated compulsion he wouldn't, or couldn't, do the decent thing: let go of Jean and her sons and fully commit himself to his second wife and family. His judgment awry, he was lost in a world of his own making. Only an act of defiance sparking physical abuse finally took things out of his hands.

In the fall of 1953, Jean finally realized that Reid's protestations of love and need had become mere levers of control to keep her and the children near him. He was never going to return to his old self. The Jack she once knew and loved was gone, never coming back. Yet, beyond belief, he kept trying to soothe her with mirages of future happiness. She snapped. One day in a fit of anger and despair she gathered up all his clothes and personal belongings at Laburnum and piled them on the front portico for his removal. His furious reaction when he next visited the house was something hitherto undreamt of in their relationship — the violence of a stranger.

Fearfully, secretly, Jean made plans to return to Toronto. After nearly five years of hiding the truth, she admitted to family and close friends the domestic chaos she had been living with since coming to Vancouver. Staggered by what she had been going through, they bolstered her resolve to return to Toronto for good. The timing she chose for departure was June 1954, after Tony finished grade two at the local school across the street. Their return to Toronto would be explained as another summer holiday in the east.

When Reid realized what was afoot, he tried unrelentingly to dissuade Jean from going. In his frustration, instances of abusive behaviour increased. When rage and supplication failed, he took a demonic turn. Instead of pleading his own mental imbalance, he accused Jean of being unstable, incapable of looking after the children. He proposed that he and Cathy look after the boys while she received psychiatric care. In her darkest moments, Jean had banished thoughts of suicide because of her children. The threat of Tony and Jon being taken from her now steeled her determination.

Given Reid's rashness and unpredictability, a plan was put in place to ensure that Jean and her boys got safely away. Bill Bigelow, one of the few old friends from Toronto that Reid stayed in touch with, was attending a West Coast surgical meeting that June. On his return, he would arrange to take the same train as Jean and escort her and the boys back to Toronto.

The day of departure, Bigelow found Reid in a disturbingly volatile state: "[Jean] was physically fearful of making such a move.

It had reached the point that her elderly father was threatening to go to Vancouver with a gun.... I realized I was dealing with a mentally disturbed man and that I was exposing myself to a dangerous physical attack. It was a touch and go encounter where ... I expected an explosive showdown at any moment."[10]

An emotional Reid came to the station to see them off, but no last-minute drama took place on the platform. With Bigelow at their side, Jean and her sons boarded the train for Toronto and were soon rolling east, never to return.

– 17 –

A Simpler Daily Round: Peace at Last

Jean returned to Toronto a month before her 40th birthday. Home now for her and her young sons was 5 Scholfield, where she had lived from the age of eight until her marriage in 1939. A sad homecoming, but her parents made them welcome, with lodgings on the third floor and a dining room table now set for five.[1] That September, Tony and Jon were registered at Whitney Public School in grades three and one.

Over the following months, Reid persisted in letters and telephone calls in trying to persuade Jean to return to Vancouver with their sons. For a time, she feared he might turn up in Toronto and try to forcibly take the boys away. Instead, Reid settled down.

By now, home life at the "49th house" was well entrenched. "Jean's house," although bigger and better located, was off limits as far as Cathy was concerned, so Laburnum was rented out until such a time as Reid could convince her otherwise. After six tumultuous years, Reid's life was reduced to a simpler daily round of one wife, two children, and one address, from which he departed each weekday morning for work at The Clinic or the hospital. For Jock and Tavish, the only difference was that Daddy came home every night.

But in the summer of 1955, Reid made a surprise trip to the East. His desire was to see his older sons, and his plan was to take them to Harry and Eva's Muskoka cottage, which they had visited with Jean, three years earlier. Arrangements were delicate. The friendship that had grown between the Reid and the Hodge in-laws since their children had married in 1939 — bridge games at each other's homes, the worry they had shared while Jack was a prisoner — had gone cold since Jean's return to Toronto.

Delegated by his son, Harry contacted Jack Hodge to negotiate travel plans and learned that Jean, Tony, and Jon were holidaying with Bill and Ruth Bigelow at a remote island cottage they were renting for the month at Go Home Bay, Georgian Bay. Like all cottages at Go Home, the Bigelows' rental had water access only — a 15-mile trip by water taxi from Honey Harbour. Reid was undeterred.

Pixie Bigelow, the eldest of the four Bigelow children, knew of Jack Reid, had heard her father speak in glowing terms, and with a little sadness, of the bright, handsome, athletic fellow he had met in medical school, the one who had become his closest friend and was best man at his wedding. Pixie never forgot Reid's unexpected arrival at their cottage to pick up his boys — nor its impact on her mother and father:

> When I was twelve, my "Aunt" Jeannie, a pretty,
> kind, soft-spoken divorcée who was my Mum's dear-
> est friend, was visiting our cottage with her young
> sons. One day a taxi boat approached our dock —
> an unscheduled taxi, which was like a phone call in
> the middle of the night. We all came down to meet
> it and suddenly my father was waving his arms with
> a big smile on his face:

"Jack! It's you! What a surprise. Wonderful to see you!"

Jack Reid, handsome and charismatic, stepped onto the dock, hugged my Dad, and swooped Tony into his arms. There was a lot of hubbub, our fathers laughing, my brothers clamouring around, everyone excited by this special visitor landing out of the blue.

I don't know where Aunt Jeannie went, but my Mum, usually the warmest of hostesses, suddenly turned away and hightailed it back to the cottage. Bewildered, I followed her. She was in the kitchen, lighting a cigarette, obviously upset. When I asked what was wrong, she turned and glowered out the window at the happy scene. She was angry:

"Jack!" she said. "He treated Jeannie horribly, terribly! Go get your brothers and take them swimming. Now!"

Jack Reid stayed overnight in the bunkie, where the boys were sleeping. The next day, another taxi came for the three of them. As the boat pulled away from the dock, my Dad left the rest of us and walked slowly down the shore, watching it go. I followed him. He sat down on the rocks and as I came up I could see he was silently crying. I asked if he was okay. He didn't look at me, just kept watching the boat heading out to the open water. Then he said, quietly:

"He had it all. My best friend. In the war, he was a prisoner in a Japanese concentration camp. It was brutal. He came home a different man. He changed."[2]

For six-year-old Jon, this magical reappearance would become an indelible memory. When the boy reached the boathouse that day, just after the others, the tall visitor with the striped shirt emerged from the cluster of Bigelows and strode up the dock with a beaming smile, leaned down, and lifted him into his arms. In an instant, time slowed, voices faded, and the boy suddenly knew that this wonderfully familiar face, missing for so long, now inches from his own, was Dad. Jon tried to say something, struggled to breathe, tried again. He couldn't make a sound.

For 10 summers, Reid and his sons spent two weeks at the Muskoka cottage getting annually reacquainted and sharing a routine of lakeside activities: sawing and chopping firewood in the mornings, cookouts and other adventures by canoe in the afternoons, and in the evenings paddling to "The Hub" for ice-cream cones before pitching horseshoes or playing cribbage in the ongoing and highly competitive double tournaments among the three of them that lasted the length of the holiday. Harry and Eva were always in residence, adding a homey comfort to the proceedings — Eva fussing over the meals, of which she was habitually self-critical, and Harry driving back and forth to Bracebridge to ensure that the supply of corn on the cob and fresh peaches for the boys didn't run out.

There was nostalgia in these Muskoka visits. "Uncle Tom" Dadson had died in 1950, but his cottage was still in the family. In 1958, Reid took his sons on an overnight canoe trip to Foot's Bay, the scene of his golden university summers, where they stayed in "Peter's Finger," one of the fairy-tale, whimsically named guest cottages built on the Cranbrook property by Bill Dadson, the professor's younger brother.[3]

The trip itself left a special memory. Hit by headwinds and rain in suddenly worsening weather the first morning, forced to bail the canoe as they paddled and to eat raw hot dogs on board because it was too wet to land and build a fire, Reid and his sons had to fight their way both days through tough conditions — similar to the weather Frank Woods and Reid had faced on a stormy Muskoka night a quarter of a century earlier. The three made it home late on the second afternoon — exhausted but elated from winning their battle against the elements. After stepping out of the swaying canoe into the sandy shallows as the rollers crashed around them on the cottage beach, Reid grinned his great grin and shook his sons' hands, congratulating them on their stoic accomplishment. That Christmas, a long cardboard box arrived at 5 Scholfield from Vancouver, much like the one marked "bunch of canes" that Reid had received from Masao Uwamori in 1949. This carton contained two new paddles, each personalized with the boy's initials burned into the paddle blade above identical black-branded inscriptions: "D.C.M. '58" — not the military's Distinguished Conduct Medal but, said Reid's letter, a father's commendation for his sons' determination, courage, and merit. This was as close as they ever got to him.

For a number of summers, starting in the late 1950s, Reid brought his Vancouver family to the Muskoka cottage for a holiday visit with Harry and Eva, before or after Tony and Jon were there.[4] A letter to Cathy after she returned home from Muskoka in August 1958 shows Reid's obvious contentment with his new life, four years after fighting Jean's decision to withdraw:

Tuesday Night

Faithfully, darling, it seems like forever since you left me. I seem stunned by the enormity of the time

355

of separation, stunned at how long it has been, and stunned at how much longer it will be.

Your wish that the time go slowly for me is certainly answered. Please wish another. Life just drags without you and it always has hawk's wings when I'm with you....

Tony and Jon have sprung up this year in height. [They] seem well settled [in Toronto] tho T still stammers a lot. Both doing well at school & at sports. Jon has turned into a goal-scoring rt.-winger in hockey. Tony's team has won the championship 3 years running, playing the final at Varsity Arena. Both seem very happy here, eating like horses, getting brown, putting on weight, wildly excited about the canoe trip [to Foot's Bay]. Both state they mean to come out to B.C. to work as soon as they are grown up!

And so I ramble on my dear one. You know I've never been away from you but I see you and our relationship more clearly and dearly. I think you are wonderful, I think you are the most beautiful, and I know I need you completely. I always make intent to be sweeter to you as I really feel, to try to make things easier for you, to make more special effort to keep your love for me alive and fresh. I know also that I slip in these resolves in the daily routine but I feel them, and this year perhaps the resolves will stick better.

In any case, I love you and I love the boys. Sandy [their third son, born that February] is growing up so rapidly that if you are well I think it's about time he had a playmate [Mary, their last child, would be

Muskoka cottage, mid-1950s. From left: Jon, Jack, Tony.

born in January 1960]. I love to join my body to yours. I love to look at you while we are one body and at such a time, besides the awful passion, there is the sweet sure serene knowledge of love, and tenderness and dearness and fulfilment and love, again.

We have been some time together now, my love, and yet I cannot feel a time in my life that I was without you. You comprise all my living and I have always been sure, in full awareness, that it is you for me....

I pray I live to a good, ripe ninety-six with you beside me. I shall try my best to keep slim and attractive to you all the while so that when I look at your loveliness with that gleam in my eye you will never find it odious to take me once more in your arms. You are a very great lady, my Kit, and I respect you as well as wanting you.

And so goodnight. Sleep tight and dream of me if you will, if such a dream is best for you. It's always a little startling to me to try to realize (as you say I am) that I am the one you truly love.

In any case, All my love, Always,

J.[5]

But Reid's feelings were never as simple as that. The previous Christmas, three and a half years after Jean returned to 5 Scholfield, she had written him to ask if he could help with the down payment on a Toronto house for her and the boys. He agreed, but when the plan fell through, he wrote her: "I don't suppose you'd consider coming back to Laburnum? It is for you."[6] One wonders what Cathy, still on 49th Avenue and soon to be the mother of three, would have made of that suggestion.

The childhood memories of Jock, Tavish, Sandy, and Mary are of loving parents for whom family came first. Reid once said to his daughter that Cathy was the centre of the wheel and he and the four children the spokes:

> I knew Dad had an important job, but I grew up believing his family was the most important thing to him. I always felt he loved us all fiercely and that he and Mum had a special deep love. Dad delighted in the here and now, loved leaving bits of doggerel and poetry around the house for us, tried to help us see the wonder in the world around us. I always remember Dad as being an emotional man. He and

Jack and Cathy, Laburnum, 1959.

Mum loved watching the sunsets from Laburnum,
and they would sometimes bring him to tears, as
much of nature often did.[7]

Reid's daily round through their childhoods always had a slow
start. Besides the neuropathy that left his feet especially tender,
a more debilitating result of the war was his digestive sensitivity.
Jock, one of three of Reid's six children who became doctors (Tony
and Mary the others), describes the pattern of his days and his
practice:

A typical day for him was to begin work at ten,
break for lunch at twelve (if the weather was nice
he would come home — a ten-minute drive — and
sit in the backyard with a sandwich and book), then
work like a fiend through the afternoon. In a day, he
would see thirty to forty patients, despite his shortened hours. Mrs. Cashman, Dad's long-time nurse
at The Clinic, told me that in her later years he had
to get a new nurse because she could no longer keep
up with him. He would get home at five-thirty or
six having done two or three house calls on the way.

Dad reportedly had one of the best save rates
for myocardial infarction and was regarded as a
top teacher by the residents at Vancouver General
Hospital. Apart from teaching, he had little contact
with the university. Dad was a superb doctor, but he
was not an academic.[8]

Away from work, Reid often crossed the road to Quilchena
Elementary School to bash a tennis ball off the wall, as he had
done at Runnymede Public School in his youth. Weekends were

family time — outings to Stanley Park, the University of British Columbia Endowment Lands, and especially the beach at English Bay where Reid continued his wartime habit of sawing wood — in this case, driftwood. If on their outings they encountered a point of interest — a lighthouse, a fire hall — Reid insisted that his children's curiosity be satisfied. Tavish recalled: "'Do Not Enter' meant 'Welcome' to Dad."[9]

A delight in nonsense and a blithe penchant for dispensing unexpected and sometimes questionable crumbs of erudition were Reid specialties. Coming home from Quilchena with her girl-friends, Mary might come upon her father reading in the main floor den. His greeting was never, "How was school?" Instead, it was his latest line of playful gibberish: "Did you ickle the bibble-back today?" or "How go the oofanoos? Were they confubling the dandereens again?"[10]

Mary may have been slightly discomfited, but her friends always chuckled.

The background to Reid's tongue-in-cheek devotion to the Aston Villa Football Club of Birmingham, England, remains a mystery of his childhood. He never played soccer, yet following the fortunes of the "Villans" was a pet passion, and the family was given to understand what a black day it was when the club was downgraded from the Premier League to the second division in 1967, and a day blacker still when it sank to the third division, a few years later. Despite illness, Reid's elation, mock or no, was fulsome when "his team" was restored to the Premier League in 1975.[11]

"Keep everyone guessing," says his son, Jock. "That was his style. He would come up with these seemingly outrageous statements of fact that were just close enough to reality to keep disbelievers off balance. Once stated, he was inscrutable and nothing would move him off the point — like the famous bird story":[12]

> One summer at Savary Island, Mum and [a friend]
> were birdwatching on the beach — they had books
> out and were using binoculars. Dad casually looked
> up from his book to remark that an overflying bird
> was a Parasitic Jaeger. Mum and [her friend] insisted
> that couldn't be. But after a frenetic thumbing-
> through of their bird books they admitted they
> weren't sure, and just maybe it *was* a Parasitic Jaeger
> — blown slightly off course.
>
> Of course, Dad went too far when he declared
> there was a Puffin sitting in the apple tree in the
> back yard at home. There may be Puffins on the
> west coast, but they aren't sitting in apple trees with
> their webbed feet! The puffin experience tainted his
> reputation as an ornithologist.[13]

With Reid's focus on family and work, outside social life was limited by choice. Cathy's sisters and several of her friends were close, and occasionally one or other of Reid's colleagues would be entertained, though not often.

While this comfortable reclusiveness was Reid's habitual social preference, he paid attention to people who interested him, uncon-cerned with their station in life: Charlie, the cook at the officers' mess, who provided the family with French fries for their weekend jaunts; Scotty, Reid's car mechanic; the hardware chap who sharp-ened the blades of his cast-iron lawn mower; Ed the butcher at McGee's Grocery, right behind the "49th house," who came for a drink at Christmas. Those who spent time with him speak of his "presence," his quiet politesse as a host, his casual elegance (even in scruffy khakis with an old sweater on backward — for extra chest warmth — he was impressive), the way he looked you in the eyes, the inevitable cigarette.

Jack and daughter, Mary, Savary Island, 1965.

Clearly a homebody — in part because of his physical sensitiv-
ities — Reid wasn't interested in travel. For many years, summer
holidays were spent at a cottage on Savary Island in the Strait of
Georgia, rented from one of Reid's colleagues. Here, family time,
swimming, beachcombing, reading, and the inevitable sawing and
chopping of wood were Reid's pastimes.

He loved dogs, most dearly Cinders, the family's beloved black
female cocker spaniel, who was his companion in another favourite
ritual: the sedate evening walk the two would methodically take
after dinner down Laburnum to 41st Street, up Cypress Street,
then around the block and home. When Cinders died at the age of
17, Reid was devastated.

Reid's last trip east for a Muskoka visit with Tony and Jon was in the summer of 1964. The next year, Tony was a full-time counsellor and Jon a counsellor-in-training at Hurontario, the camp in Georgian Bay they had been going to for a month each summer since 1959. The annual connection between father and sons was now broken.

But well before these teenage activities supplanted their childhood fortnights at Muskoka, the boys had been feeling a strain with their father. As they grew, so did their expectation of a changing relationship with him. They loved him in their way and admired him: as they grew up, Jean never spoke of Reid except in positive terms, explaining his adverse behaviour as a result of his wartime experience, which had been heroic. Yet their lives had been deeply affected by his personal decisions, and Tony to begin with, Jon soon after, yearned for Reid to talk about what had happened to him, to explain himself as best he could. But as summer followed summer into the 1960s, the Muskoka visits would unfold and carry on as if they were still eight and ten years old. Reid wouldn't open up — wouldn't or couldn't respond to the natural wish of his maturing sons to know him better, to understand the choices he had made in his life that had so radically affected theirs. In the last year of high school, Tony wrote a formal letter asking his father for some candid answers about the past and advice about his own future. He received no reply.

Ironically, Tony and Jon were unwittingly the cause of a different strain in Vancouver. In 1959, with three boisterous children to manage and a fourth on the way, Cathy finally consented to move to Laburnum, where there was more room inside and out. Given her long-standing resistance, her passion for painting and repainting Laburnum's rooms may have been a way of making it her own.

Once there, she was the perfect neighbour and friend of the street — a warm, welcoming woman whose door was always open for anyone wanting a cup of tea and a chat, ever ready to offer a sympathetic ear or sage advice to all and sundry, including her sons' ex-girlfriends who had become *her* friends. But according to Jock, alcohol was not her friend. On occasion, Reid's two Toronto sons became the targets of her Scottish temper:

> Mother could be very passionate, particularly if she had had a drink. The arguments always happened at night and never seemed to make any sense; I think it was the disinhibition caused by alcohol.
>
> One of the recurring subjects of Mother's nighttime rants was that Tony and Jon were receiving some form of privilege that was not available to us because of the money that had to be sent east. This was certainly not an argument that any of the four of us children bought because we were glad that we had Dad.
>
> We would hear Mother with raised voice, crashing around their bedroom. Father's voice, much lower register, always seemed to be trying to mollify, which paradoxically seemed to upset Mother even more. We children, just across the hall in our bedrooms, would hear Mother start to "tune up" with slightly raised voice, progressing to overt yelling at Dad. There was never any hitting, but Dad, in his attempts to calm Mother, would put his arms around her and she would struggle against him, resulting in some — what must have been — spectacular falls onto the bed, judging by the crashing and the scene of havoc that we sometimes found in the morning: them asleep together in a bed tilted at an odd angle, the slats holding the mattress having

given way. But they always found a way to let the night before dissolve in the morning and there was no rancor the next day....

They were a loving couple who really seemed content with one another in a way that I have rarely seen in others.[14]

Reid kept in touch with three friends from the pre-war years. Bill Bigelow, now a world-renowned heart surgeon, was one; Frank Woods and Doug Dadson from University of Toronto Schools and University College days, the others.[15]

Reid's visits to their homes were often unannounced, said Woods. If he was in Toronto on a summer visit or for a medical meeting, he would just turn up full of mischief. Long gone, thanks to the war, was the slightest concern for lightweight social conventions. On arrival, he might take off his shoes, lie down on the living room carpet, and carry on conversations from there, chain-smoking his Black Cats and using his pant cuff as an ashtray. He liked things a bit off balance. It amused him to bend the norms.

"Once, we met at the Royal York and he deliberately got me drunk," recalled Woods. "You could tell he had planned it, and you watched him take control. He could really hold his whiskey."

Dadson remembered a visit to Vancouver when he was dean of education at the University of Toronto. He and his wife, Patricia, dropped in to Laburnum for a drink before going on to an official function at the University of British Columbia. Reid was close to them both — he and Pat had a particularly sympathetic bond — and he must have been enjoying the visit, not wanting it to end, because in his easygoing way Reid did everything he could to keep them late.

"You could tell he enjoyed the game," said Dadson. "He kept saying, 'Don't worry so much about etiquette!'"

Aleck Dadson, Doug's son, remembers the first time he was aware of Reid visiting their home in North Toronto. Aleck was about 12 years old when this wide-smiling stranger in a smart blue suit and tie was welcomed into the house by his parents and introduced as Dr. Reid, the friend of his father he'd heard so many stories about. Reid was carrying an odd bundle, which Aleck soon learned was the doctor's dinner, wrapped up in his evening attire. Disappearing upstairs to change, Reid reappeared in old army clothes and a worn pair of running shoes, food supplies in hand. As though he were home, he headed for the kitchen, trailed by a wide-eyed Aleck, and proceeded to whip up his favourite postwar meal: three soft-boiled eggs mashed in a bowl with lots of melted butter and several thick slices of well-buttered bread on the side. Reid's enjoyment of the modest meal made it seem like a feast.

"He made a very strong impression on me," says Aleck, 55 years later. "And I was conscious of the very high regard that my own father had for him."[16]

With his Toronto sons, Reid kept in sporadic touch, usually with a letter and a present on birthdays. Books were his choice for many years — classics like *Wind in the Willows, Alice in Wonderland, Greenmantle, Pepys Diaries, Moby-Dick*, and of course, *Tristram Shandy.*

Later on, he began sending pieces of Japanese art, a liking formed in prison camp starting with the Hiroshige prints given by Dr. Iino — pastoral views made real in the sculpted landscapes he had seen while travelling by train from Hitachi to Sendai and back in August 1945.

For Jon's birthday in September 1971, he sent a framed Japanese watercolour painted on parchment. On the right of the picture is a dominating rock cliff, suggesting to some eyes a giant head sketched in profile. Rooted at the top of the cliff and over-hanging its rounded face leans an old, gnarled tree. As though drifting in space, a sampan floats midpicture, with a solitary figure on one knee at the stern, paddling obliquely away from the viewer. All is calm. Perhaps Reid chose it because it tells a story he saw as his own:

Dear J-Bug:

I'm late again as I couldn't get out for a few days with torn leg muscle. But here's hoping you had a great Birthday and enjoyed yourself.

A little picture is on the way. The pine tree is symbolic of strength, the rock of eternity, and the inscription in the corner signifies that the artist has been through many tribulations in life and has found through them patience and humility and has learned to think of himself as like a grain of sand in the vastness of the universe. Hope you like it....

My best love,
Dad[17]

In 1972, more than a quarter of a century after the war ended, Reid attended his first and only meeting of "Hong Kong" veter-ans, gatherings that had been taking place in one form or another in locations across the country for 25 years. It may have been out of curiosity to see some of his men, and the fact the meeting was just across the water in Victoria, that he went. According to his daughter, Mary, it was uneventful. "Characteristically, he didn't talk about it. Mum [Cathy] simply said it was appreciated that he attended. He gave me the memento they were all given — a tin about the size of a 5.5-ounce tomato paste can, but taller. It represented their daily ration of rice in prison camp. I kept it for many years in my room."[18]

Apart from his persistent physical reminders — the postprandial dumping syndrome that caused cramping and bowel dysfunction, his foot tenderness caused by neuropathy — it seems that Reid had suppressed his war experience. It is unlikely that he ever read the tribute to him, recorded in the *Official History of the Canadian Medical Services 1939–1945*, published in 1956. The two-volume history is written *sine nomine* — no one is identified by name:

> In January 1943 about 650 Canadians were sent to Japan to work in ship-building and mining industries. Three later drafts brought the total of Canadians transferred to Japan to one medical officer and 1183 other ranks. The medical officer, chosen by lot to accompany the first work party to Japan, served as commanding as well as medical officer for a group of 500 since he was the only one holding commissioned rank. The measure of his success in extracting every possible concession from the Japanese, in making fullest use of the most inadequate medical facilities, and in persuading his fellow prisoners to make the best of things, is that only 23 of this particular group died. This, the largest

group of Canadians in Japan, had the smallest number of deaths.[19]

Preserved in Jean Reid's wartime scrapbook is first-hand testimony to Reid's wartime conduct — a yellowed clipping from the *Regina Leader-Post*. The item is about 27-year-old Private Bernard Jesse, a Winnipeg Grenadier who was interviewed on his way home to Lampman, Saskatchewan, in October 1945. Private Jesse had been a prisoner of the Japanese at North Point Camp and Sham Shui Po in Hong Kong, and Camp 3D and Sendai Camp 1B in Japan.

"We were more fortunate than most and managed to get out of each camp before things got too tough," Jesse told the reporter. "We suffered no brutal punishment in any of the four camps we were at. This was due to the efforts of Capt[ain] J. Reid of Toronto. He fought hard for us and no matter where we were at was able to talk to the Japs and get enough supplies to pull us through. Most of us have Capt[ain] Reid to thank for being alive today. He was untiring in his efforts."[20]

Forty-five years later, ex-Signalman Lionel Speller put it this way: "[Reid] was the only Canadian officer that was sent to Japan. And if you can imagine with nothing to work with, and I mean nothing, and to look after 500 men and be the Camp Commandant, the liaison between the Japs and us, nobody, but nobody could have done better.... If there was ever a man that should have got their DSO or their DCM it was Dr. Reid because, I don't care, you'd have to be something out of this world to do the job he did after we went to Japan."[21]

– 18 –

Stricken: Past the Point of Marginal Reserve

In January 1974, without warning, Reid was felled by a severe infection of the brain. Feeling unwell the day of onset, he at first thought he had a gastrointestinal bleed and was driven to The Clinic for blood tests. By the time he got home, he was disoriented and clumsy, then suddenly overcome by a piercing headache. An ambulance was called, and he was rushed to the hospital. By night-time, he had developed a high fever. In his delirium, he was calling out for Jean — not seen in almost 20 years.

The diagnosis was acute encephalitis — inflammation of the brain caused by a viral infection, in Reid's case so severe that it left him stuporous, immobilized, and speech-impaired. He spent the winter and most of the spring in Shaughnessy Hospital before returning home, physically and mentally diminished, to the care of Cathy and his family.

Home proved therapeutic. He became more lucid, gaining limited mobility and improvement in speech. On July 27, 1974, seven months after the attack, he was able to attend the wedding of his

July 27, 1974: Wedding day of Jock Reid's first marriage, Laburnum, prior to the service. From left: Jack Reid, Jock Reid, Sandy Reid, Philip Tisdall (brother of the bride), and Tavish Reid. Seven months after his attack of encephalitis, Reid is seen shorn, due to his recent brain biopsy.

son, Jock, at St. Mary's Anglican Church in Kerrisdale. Although haggard from illness, his head shaven from the brain biopsy procedure he'd recently undergone, Reid was still his elegant self in blue suit and tie. Unable to walk on his own, he entered the church with his son, Sandy, on one arm, and Philip, the bride's brother, on the other. For Jock, two of the most poignant moments of the ceremony were when his father rose to his feet with the congregation — first, as the bride was escorted up the aisle, and later as the newlyweds proceeded out of the church: "The front row was left empty so that Dad could hold on to the back of its pew. When everyone stood, he struggled to get up, not permitting anyone to assist him, by gripping the back of the seat in front of him and pulling himself to standing. He was very unsteady on his feet, but remained upright, refusing to give way. I will never forget the look of determination on his face."[1]

The limited improvement that Reid made over the coming year led to his attempt to return to work. This was unsuccessful and short-lived, and his condition soon began to worsen again. But in the summer of 1975, the family was able to support his return to Savary Island for a short holiday. It was the last time he would see this place he loved. From now on, except when in hospital, Reid was almost entirely confined to home.

With no personal connections between the Reid families, it was almost a year before any news of Reid's illness reached Jean and her sons through Bill Bigelow, who learned of the encephalitis attack from medical colleagues in Vancouver.

Jon had last seen his father in June 1968. On that occasion, he was 19 years old, just back in Canada from a year abroad and on his way to find a summer job in northern British Columbia before university. His memories of that visit are bittersweet:

> When I arrived at the Vancouver bus station I phoned Dad at The Clinic, out of the blue. He was surprised and delighted. I went to his office and he took me home for the weekend. It was great to see him again and to meet his two youngest children, Sandy and Mary, for the first time. Given the history, I think both Cathy and I were uncomfortable when we were introduced, but she was warm and welcoming and kept quietly in the background while I was there.

Overall, it was a happy visit — catching up on the four years since I'd last seen Dad in Muskoka. He listened to my adventures, asked about my plans, showed me around. We took walks, played tennis at Quilchena, and I became instant pals with Sandy, who was ten, and Mary, who was eight, who seemed to enjoy having a new big brother.

The tough time was my last night there. Everyone else had gone to bed; Dad and I were in the den downstairs, the scotch flowing. Feeling grown up from my travels and wanting Dad to finally talk about himself — about the war, the chaos of my childhood years, his treatment of Jean — I poured out the questions. But no matter what I said, no revelations were forthcoming. He balked. He could not open up. Finally, well after midnight, I stood up in exasperation. Dad got out of his chair, tears running down his face, and took me in his arms: "Dear heart," he kept repeating, "dear heart...."

It was all he could say.[2]

In June 1976, Jon, by now working in Los Angeles, made arrangements to spend a day at Laburnum on his way back to Toronto after finishing a film. He found his father a much-changed man:

Sandy and Mary picked me up at the airport. At Laburnum, Dad must have seen the car come up the drive because he was waiting, Cathy by his side, at the front door. His welcome was joyous, effusive. But I could see from his movements how unstable and restricted he was. His speech was slightly slow, yet he seemed oblivious of his difficulties. I was exhausted and sleep-deprived and asked for a twenty-minute lie-down before we started catching up. I had less than a day to spend with him and wanted to make the most of it.

Twenty minutes later, on the dot, Dad knocked. Moving slowly, we went down the hall and turned into the master bedroom. He shut the door. There were two armchairs, one on each side of the bed, and we sat down, facing each other.

More than forty years since that conversation, much is now blurred. But my impressions of him that afternoon, and some of his words, remain. He was open in a way I'd never known him to be, eager to talk about himself.

He described his illness, what it had done to him. All through his life, he said, when faced with tough times, he had been able to keep going, to push through. But "this" — referring to his present state — he wasn't sure of. He was fighting on, he said, but towards an unknown outcome.

He asked what I was doing, what Tony was doing. Then he announced: "I want you to know that I've always loved your mother. Whatever happens to me, tell her that I have two insurance policies in her name. Twenty thousand dollars." He went on — for the first time admitting a sense of wrongdoing, and hoping, though only a gesture, that Jean would understand the policies represented a great deal of feeling.

In his reduced state, he was perhaps no longer sure what the truth was. The year after his death, I would learn that he had changed the beneficiary of

both insurance policies to his own estate in 1971,
and in January 1977, with finances tight, had surrendered both policies for cash. Not everything Dad
told me that day was true, but I think what he told
me was what he wanted to be true.

The next morning, he was helped to the curb to
give me a hug and wave me off. Leaning on Cathy,
one arm raised, smiling broadly — that was my last
sight of him.[3]

Over the following year, further deterioration in the form
of increasing dementia and gross incoordination signalled a new
problem: normal pressure hydrocephalus, requiring an operation
to insert a ventriculoperitoneal shunt to reduce the pressure on his
brain. In July 1977, Dr. Clyde Slade, director of family practice at
the University of British Columbia Department of Health Care
and Epidemiology, in summarizing Reid's history and present status shortly before the operation took place, is unequivocal about
the relationship between his illness and his war experiences:

Major Reid has had the misfortune of being a prisoner
of war in Hong Kong and thence in Japan until 1945.
On his return he was found to be suffering from
general malnutrition and concomitant disease of the
nervous system including peripheral sensation in the
feet and a post-prandial dumping syndrome which
has been permanent, so that anything but a minimal
amount of food in the stomach results in diarrhea.
This has been a very restricting disability throughout
the years following his brutal treatment in Japan.

He unfortunately developed a further onslaught
on his nervous system with an episode three years

ago characterized by an acute brain syndrome with stupor and later confusion that, following a variety of neurological investigations, was diagnosed as acute encephalitis.

Following this, a further neurological complication has arisen with increasing dementia, gross disturbance of coordination and gait and incontinence.

In my opinion, this present state of disability relates partially to his experience as a prisoner of war. If he did not have previous disease of the nervous system resulting from malnutrition, physical beatings and hypertension, he would probably be in better condition following his recent episode of acute encephalitis. Now the whole clinical state is much worse and the whole matter should be reassessed.[4]

The shunt relieved the pressure on Reid's cerebral system. But when he returned to Laburnum after the operation, he was temporarily unable to speak. His daughter, Mary, remembers being with him soon after his return home: "He had a way of intently looking at you with his eyes and flicking his fingers in anger and/or frustration while he pointed out the shunt, coursing along his neck, just below the surface of the skin.... He was diminished ... but still, to me, commanded a presence of dignity, love, and respect."[5]

Cathy wanted to care for Reid at home for as long as possible. With no significant recovery anticipated, Dr. Slade and several other Vancouver physicians drafted an appeal to the Department of Veterans Affairs to grant Reid a full disability pension.

Bill Bigelow visited Reid at Laburnum that fall. His letter to Dr. Slade in support of the pension initiative outlines both his medical and personal view of his old friend Jack:

December 15th, 1977

Dear Dr. Slade:

As you know, I spent an evening with Dr. Reid while in Vancouver the last week of September and was very disturbed to see the residual disability he has. I was very proud of the way he carried himself with such dignity and no complaints in spite of his severe disabilities of locomotion and speech. I would gather from what I saw that evening that he is really totally dependent upon his wife for all things. It would be quite impossible for him to venture outside the house without support and help. I am writing at this time to urge action in the matter of getting Dr. Reid a full pension, which I think he deserves.

I shall give you my reasons. I was a classmate and good friend of Dr. Reid's at university and he was quite the brightest student in the class. He was a top athlete with a brilliant academic and medical future. He was chosen by Professor Duncan Graham to be a senior resident in medicine and, when he returned from prison camp and had partially recovered from his long ordeal, he was offered a University staff appointment in medicine at the Wellesley Hospital. It was obvious to me, knowing him as well as I did, that he was suffering from some brain damage as evidenced by the difficulty he experienced in making up his mind whether to accept this appointment or not. After six months of vacillating, he decided to go to Vancouver to a private clinic. His reactions to his lovely wife were not typical, and the marriage unfortunately ended in divorce.

Considering his subsequent professional history in Vancouver, he never attained anything like the success in his profession, in the broad sense, that he was capable of.

I have discussed this case with Dr. Barney Barnett, Professor of Neurological Sciences at the University of Western Ontario. He feels there is very little doubt that the avitaminosis that the Canadian prisoners of war were exposed to in Japan and Singapore produced a very serious diffuse brain damage. A good many of these prisoners died in camp of brain damage ... and most of the returned veterans have developed neurological disorders of one kind or another, with many of them coming on in later life.

The general theory is that this diffuse brain damage has reduced the brain function to a point of marginal reserve. This makes the individual susceptible to neurological diseases, enhances the severity of the neurological illness when it does come, and it very often prevents adequate recovery from an illness that a normal person might be expected to recover from.

Applying this to Dr. Reid's situation it would explain his inability to recover from the encephalitis and, indeed, may have been the reason why he contracted it in the first place. As such, I think he should be on full pension.[6]

Dr. Barnett, Bigelow's neurologist colleague, added his voice of support after seeing Reid at Laburnum while in Vancouver for a Royal College meeting in January 1978:

Dr. Bill Bigelow, Cardiovascular Research Laboratory, Banting Institute, late 1950s.

> When [I] saw him ... he was slow in his think-
> ing, slurring his speech and hesitant in his move-
> ments. He had an impassive facies such as is seen in
> Parkinson's Disease.... He has no real grasp of the
> seriousness of his disability and decline. This might
> very well be a kindness but it is certainly not an ad-
> vantage.... I would judge that this patient is enti-
> tled to full pension benefit and if there is any allow-
> ance made for supervisory care that he requires ...
> I would think he should be given that as well.[7]

The initiative succeeded. Later in 1978, Reid was granted a full veterans disability pension.

Valerie Jerome, a Canadian Olympic sprinter and public school teacher, was a very close friend of the family after coaching Sandy and Mary at a local track club as well as teaching them at Quilchena Elementary School, across the street from Laburnum. Over the years, she was a regular guest at the Reids' Sunday dinners, always a lavish meal served buffet-style indoors or out. Cathy was Valerie's intimate friend, but "Dr. Reid" she greatly admired.

"Elegant, casual, handsome," Valerie remembers him. "He had an air of sophistication, but he wasn't a braggart. A gentleman with wonderful manners, not gabby but warm. His conversation was always meaningful. When he laughed he would get tears in his eyes. I often thought they were tears of sadness. He loved his family." Now, when Valerie came for Sunday meals, Reid remained in his room upstairs.[8]

In early 1979, Reid suffered a serious stroke and was rehospi-
talized at Shaughnessy, the veterans hospital where he had spent
many months since his illness began. This time, there would be no
return to Laburnum. On the night of July 7, 1979, like so many of
his "boys" at 3D in the terrible winter of 1943–44, Jack Reid died
of pneumonia, five and a half years after he was first stricken by
encephalitis. He was 65 years old — a far cry from the "good, ripe
ninety-six" he once prayed for.

In Search of Captain Reid: His Kind Testimony

On July 22, 1993, an article in Japan's *Asahi Evening News* caught the eye of Naoaki Kobayashi, managing director of the Tozai Engineering Company in Tokyo. As a very young man, Kobayashi had been a court interpreter at the war crime trials in Yokohama, and the article hearkened back to those days. Its headline read: "Former War Criminal Hopes to Thank Canadian POW."[1]

Spread over three columns, the article reported the story of Masao Uwamori, now retired from the securities business and living in Kamakura, south of Tokyo, who during the Second World War had been commandant of three Yokohama-area prison camps. It explained that after the war Uwamori had been prosecuted by the Allies at the Yokohama war crimes trials for charges of "abusing prisoners and causing many of them to die," and that Uwamori had been "prepared to be sentenced severely and was even resigned to being handed the death penalty." But these serious charges had been untrue, and because of the intervention of a Canadian officer, he had received a suspended sentence and been set free:

"Thanks to his kind testimony, my sentence was reduced," said Masao Uwamori. "I'm 89 years old. It's
been nearly 50 years since then, and I believe the
Canadian officer must be in his 70s by now. If I don't
contact him now, I may never be able to thank him."

According to Uwamori, a former lieutenant in
the Japanese Imperial Army, the name of the officer,
who belonged to the Royal Canadian Army Medical
Corps, is J.A.G Reid. Uwamori believes one of the
initials may stand for Anthony....

He is asking anyone who has information on
the Canadian medical officer to contact him at
0467-22-5321.[2]

Naoaki Kobayashi phoned Masao Uwamori, explained his personal history as a court interpreter at the Yokohama trials, and offered to help Uwamori in the search for Reid.

Kobayashi managed to get in touch with the Hong Kong
Veterans Commemorative Association in Canada, only to be told
that the association had lost contact with Major Reid. But the
association gave Kobayashi a lead. Dr. Charles Roland, a medi-
cal historian and Hannah Professor Emeritus for the History of
Medicine at McMaster University, was interviewing Hong Kong
veterans and their families for his book *Long Night's Journey into
Day: Prisoners of War in Hong Kong and Japan, 1941–1945*. When
Kobayashi contacted Roland in August 1993, Roland told him that
Dr. Reid had been dead for many years.

As soon as he learned of Reid's death, Kobayashi told Uwamori
by telephone. In failing health, Uwamori was hospitalized before
he could respond to this sad news. Suffering cardiac problems, kid-
ney and pancreas ailments, and difficulty in walking, Uwamori remained in hospital until January 1994, the month he turned 90.

Once back at home in the care of his daughter, he wrote to the man who had laid to rest the search for Reid:

February 14th, 1994

Dear Mr. Naoaki C. Kobayashi,

I was finally released from hospital at the end of last month....

Many thanks for your kindness. I can see you must have gone through a great deal of effort to find out about Captain Reid, who had become one of my closest friends when we were working together in a POW camp during the last war, despite we were both enemies, against each other.

I was dazed when I learned that he had died at the age of 65. Closing my eyes, I still see him as a nice and gentle man, and yet a man of high calibre, with confidence and sincerity, who as an officer of the Canadian Army devoted himself to the sake of several hundred men under him.

I vividly remember the time when we met each other for the first time in January 1943. It was in the courtyard of the POW detached camp in Tsurumi, where all the POWs were assembled.

Standing in the middle, in front of the lines of his Canadian men, he commanded — "Attention!" — strong and loud, and gave me his first salute.[3]

Forest Lawn Memorial Park, Burnaby, British Columbia, October 11, 2019.

If I should die, my journey hence will be
Tinged with our sorrow, borne so slow with me;
My mind is clear, the universal light streams through
Sheer-shimmery as a summery morning's blue.
My atom, guided, must to dust unwind
And coil again eternal forms to find,
Still aches my heart in spring time leaving you,
Your heart so young, our tender love so new.
Fading, one call is echoed over time –
Waste me, forever gone, no poignant glance,
I herd the clouds, bequeath a sunny clime,
Your gaze be forward, where the kobalds dance
Lo, see the rising sun blush on your face
Throw wide your arms, life's golden day embrace.

— John Reid, personal notebook, Tokyo Camp No.
5, Spring 1943, Reid Family Papers

Afterword

Except for three friends — Leney Gage, Reid's schoolmate, university pal, and fellow Foot's Bay "shack dweller" who was killed during the Second World War; and George Pollak and Adelbert Franken, fellow POWs who, like Reid, both died at the age of 65 (lives shortened, inarguably, by prison camp damage) — most of Reid's close contemporaries outlived him by many years. Here are nine "after stories."

LENEY GAGE (1913–1944)

Leney Gage enlisted in the Royal Regiment of Canada in 1942, received officer training at Gordon Head Military Camp in Victoria, and was posted overseas in May 1943, three months after he was married. After the Allied invasion of Normandy in June 1944, his regiment was involved in the fierce fighting at the Battles of Caen and Falaise Gap and by October was part of the Canadian advance attacking the Nazis along the River Scheldt to open the port of Antwerp. On October 14, Captain Gage and three other company commanders were dispersing from a meeting with their colonel when enemy shelling began. Frank Woods, posted nearby with the Argyll and Sutherland Highlanders, learned what happened:

"Gage and the other company commanders were returning to their stations. He and a Captain Beatty took cover in a shallow shell hole. When there was a lull in the shelling, Beatty stayed put, but Leney said he wanted to get back to his men — he was going to make a run for it. He did and was hit."[1] Gage died the next day. He was 31 years old. In a letter to his parents, written the day before he was wounded, he said: "The Canadian troops received a wonderful reception from the Dutch people and they certainly deserved it for they are a body of men of whom I am proud."[2]

DOUGLAS DADSON (1913–1995)

Several years after the death of his wife, Patricia, Doug Dadson left the family home in Toronto's Lawrence Park and moved to the Garden Court Apartments in Leaside where he and his young family lived in the early 1950s — a place of happy memories for him. Throughout his retirement, Dadson engaged in his customary activities — smoking his pipe, drinking black coffee, reading widely, napping, and composing letters. He occasionally got up to mischief with his old University of Toronto Schools friends, including Frank Woods. Although small of stature, he was very dapper man and had a manner that seemed to appeal to women. He certainly enjoyed their company, particularly if they were prepared to chauffeur him around town in a big automobile. After he suffered a mild stroke, Dadson spent his last year at the George Hees Wing of the Veterans Centre at Sunnybrook Hospital. The institutional environment was comforting for him, seeming to remind him of his days in England during the war. Frank Woods, who served on the board of Sunnybrook Hospital earlier in his life, remained a close friend and strong advocate for Dadson until the end. Douglas Dadson died of pneumonia in December 1995 and is interred in Mount Pleasant Cemetery beside his wife.[3]

DR. WILFRED BIGELOW (1913–2005)

Dr. Bill Bigelow's hypothermia research led to the first safe open-heart surgery in the early 1950s, and his pioneering of electrical stimulation of the heart led to the development of the pacemaker, two discoveries that revolutionized heart surgery and have improved and extended the lives of millions of people with heart disease worldwide. He was founder and head of the first Division of Cardiac Surgery in Toronto, trained 40 cardiac surgeons, and was the author of 120 publications, including two books: *Cold Hearts* and *Mysterious Heparin*. His honours were legion, and his bust is one of the 10 sculptures of Canadian medical greats that grace the south foyer of the Medical Sciences Building at the University of Toronto. When Bigelow died on Easter Sunday 2005 at the age of 91, five years after his wife, Ruth, he had long been recognized as "one of the most distinguished surgeons Canada has ever produced … and stands among the world's titans of medicine."[4]

FRANK WOODS (1912–2009)

For a man who was cautioned about a heart condition in his youth, Frank Woods lived a long, useful life. Never married, Woods was close to his five nephews and nieces, their children, and his wide circle of friends. A delight in company with his humour, general knowledge, and legendary memory, Woods was in constant demand as a dinner guest, cottage visitor, and travel companion, often employing his talent as an artist to draw an amusing cartoon of the occasion as a thank-you note to his hosts. He remained devoted to old schoolmates and was a long-standing and active member of Toronto's University Club. His interest in education was paramount. Over the years, Woods provided continuing financial support to the University of Toronto's University College, ultimately bequeathing an endowment — now administered by the Munk School of Global Affairs and Public Policy — that funds both the

Frank W. Woods Lecture in the field of political science, open to the public and given each fall at the Munk School's Trudeau Centre for Peace, Conflict and Justice (PCJ), as well as the Frank W. Woods Lunchtime Lecture, where the Woods guest lecturer meets privately with PCJ students, one of whom is annually awarded the Frank W. Woods Medal and scholarship for outstanding contributions to the PCJ program. In his last years, his extraordinary memory unimpaired, Frank Woods resided at Belmont House, Toronto, where he bore the afflictions of Parkinson's disease with grace while continuing to entertain family and friends right up until his peaceful death at the age of 97.

ADELBERT "AB" FRANKEN (1908–1973)

After liberation, Ab Franken returned to the Dutch East Indies to find his wife and three children safe, despite nearly four years of Japanese occupation. The Indonesian nationalist movement was on the rise, and as an officer in the Royal Netherlands East Indies Army, he was involved in trying to re-establish Dutch control following the departure of the Japanese. When that failed and Indonesian independence was declared in 1949, Franken and his family were forced to move to the Netherlands. Now in a foreign country, and as a professional soldier of an army that no longer existed (he refused to join the Royal Netherlands Army), Franken had a hard time establishing himself in Holland, working first as a magician to make ends meet, later as an insurance broker, and finally, after much study, as a mathematics teacher. For pleasure, he played guitar and trumpet in Amsterdam jazz bands. Upon retirement, Franken opened a travel business and personally conducted small tour groups from Holland to his beloved Indonesia. It was during such a tour that he died in his homeland of a sudden heart attack in 1973. After he signed over the rights to their songs to John Reid in 1945, Franken and Reid were never in touch again. Remarkably, their families were reconnected by Franken's granddaughter, Marjolein de Klerk, 70 years later.[5]

EDWARD GEORGE POLLAK (1919–1984)

Lieutenant Commander George Pollak saw active service on the USS *Bexar* for two years during the Korean War. In the late 1950s, now promoted to commander, Pollak was posted to London, England, as assistant naval attaché at the American embassy. In the early 1960s, he resigned from the navy and returned to the Massachusetts Institute of Technology, his alma mater, where he obtained a doctor of science in 1966. Settling in York Harbor, Maine, where he could sail to his heart's content, Pollak spent his subsequent professional career with Arthur D. Little Inc. as a consultant designing ships and port facilities around the world. Pollak's first marriage ended in divorce in 1970, and though he remarried in 1972, his closest and happiest relationship remained with his daughter, Antonia (she would become Boston's commissioner of parks and recreation), in whom he instilled the importance of education, hard work, kindness, loyalty, and a great love of dogs. The effects of the war never left him.

When he heard of Reid's death in 1979, he wrote: "Those years in Japan changed each and all of us.... One might think that after those years, one would come home and be happy as a pig in mud in all the things we had missed. On the contrary, I suspect we built up such a romanticized and idealized vision that when we came back to reality it left us with some sort of unsatisfied hunger. And we flailed about in all sorts of foolish ways and wreaked havoc, and didn't do ourselves or a lot of other people any good.... [But] one might as well look ahead as worry about the past. It seems a shame that it takes us so many years to see things more clearly and leaves us little time to salvage anything."[6]

Pollak's job took him to Cambridge, Massachusetts, for the work week, and he would sometimes stay with his daughter and her dachshunds at Antonia's Charlestown home in Boston, another refuge. Yet 14 years later, his personal outlook was little changed. In his 1983 Christmas letter to Jean Reid, he wrote: "Looking back over the year, I can't report much progress in any direction. Put it this way, I don't feel any closer to the life or way of life I would have liked to achieve by age 65 (next February). Don't know whether this dissatisfaction is congenital, circumstantial, or just ill humor. Anyway, it makes me want to climb in a hole and pull the lid down, every once in a while."[7]

George Pollak died of a heart attack three months later.

On stormy day at Kittery Point, Maine — a place on the ocean that Pollak loved — his daughter, Antonia, later committed his ashes to the seven seas from a bridge over Spruce Creek: "It was an outgoing tide, very windy and light rain. I released his ashes downwind and said goodbye with tears and laughter both. He was probably bound for Europe."[8]

CATHY REID (1922–1992)

After John Reid's death, Cathy stayed on at the Laburnum house until 1985. Her family and friendships sustained her, and with Valerie Jerome, she enjoyed season's tickets to the ballet, and one year, a trip to New York City. The move to a smaller house on Schaeffer Avenue in Richmond, British Columbia, was a change of location and milieu, but with her natural warmth, Cathy soon made the neighbourhood her own as she connected with neighbours and local shopkeepers. She now had four grandchildren to dote on, and the Schaeffer house became the new haven for family and friends to visit for tea and chats. In February 1991, Cathy fell ill and was rushed to Richmond Hospital where she underwent emergency surgery for a ruptured aneurysm. She recovered and was able to return to normal life. A year later, she developed heart symptoms, and after being transferred to St. Paul's Hospital for further treatment, she suffered a cardiac arrest and died on February 25, 1992. Her graduation photo still hangs in a hallway of St. Paul's, where she trained as a nurse in the 1940s. She and Jack Reid are buried side by side in Burnaby's Forest Lawn Memorial Park.

JEAN REID (1914–2006)

In 1954, 5 Scholfield Avenue, the home Jean grew up in, became her home once again and would remain so for another 15 years. Given her need to earn a living, her friend, Bill Bigelow, provided her with employment as part-time administrator of the Cardiovascular Research Laboratory, which he had set up at the Banting Institute to pursue further studies of hypothermia, including the secrets of animal hibernation. As the research expanded, this part-time job developed into a full-time position, which Jean held until her retirement in 1985 at the age of 71. As well as bringing up her sons, she cared for her father, Jack Hodge, for eight years after the death of her mother until his death in 1969. Five Scholfield was then sold, and after five years in a duplex nearby, Jean moved to an apartment in the Claridge Apartments on Avenue Road where she lived contentedly for a quarter century. Her sons married sisters — granddaughters of Dr. R.I. Harris, a prominent orthopedic surgeon under whom Reid had trained at Toronto General Hospital in the late 1930s — and she was warmly welcomed into the family of her in-laws, with whom she eventually shared six grandchildren. Diminishment from a neurological incident in 1999 necessitated a move to the O'Neill Centre on Christie Street, where Jean had a glorious view of the trees and grounds of Christie Pits Park during the last seven years of her life. Remarrying had never been a consideration. As Bill Bigelow once said, like the swan and the wolf, Jean married for life.

GEORGE MACDONELL

George MacDonell, the man who knew Reid in wartime, the man who has been a primary source of knowledge about the "C" Force experience, the man who precipitated the writing of this biography by requesting a chapter on "The Doctor" seven years ago, is not only a war hero but a hero of a different sort in his remarkable peacetime career. Returning to Canada a decorated 23-year-old veteran with a grade ten education, MacDonell completed Ontario's five-year high school program with honours in 13 months. He enrolled at the University of Toronto in 1947 and completed his three-year bachelor of arts in two years while class president, and married Margaret Telford, a lecturer in the Department of Sociology, in September 1949. By the spring of 1950, he was pressing on with his master of arts when the telephone rang in the MacDonells' tiny attic apartment on Spadina Avenue. The call was a summons from H.M. Turner, president of Canadian General Electric (CGE), whose friend — and MacDonell's professor of economics — had given Turner "A Content Analysis of Rival Employee Publications," one of MacDonell's A-plus term papers. Based on the insight and originality of that paper, Turner hired MacDonell after one interview. MacDonell rose to be a CGE vice-president before moving on to become president of General Steel Wares, a member of the National Design Council, vice-president of Maple Leaf Mills, president of the John Wood Manufacturing Company, and ultimately, deputy minister of industry and trade in the Ontario government of Premier Bill Davis. Today, at the age of 98, George MacDonell resides at the Dunfield Retirement Residence, Toronto, and about once a month produces a political and economic discussion paper on the state of Canada.

THE PRESENT

John Reid's six children — Tony, Jon, Jock, Tavish, Sandy, and Mary — became and remain close friends.

Acknowledgements

In 1983, I asked retired American naval officer and prison camp survivor George Pollak what he remembered of my father. A month later, he began his marvellously detailed, 11-page response with the comment, "I suppose it is part of a biography." At the time, I had no such pretensions: to encompass my father's story seemed far beyond my ken. But I did start collecting things. Thirty years later, "C" Force veteran George MacDonell finally got the ball rolling by asking me to write a chapter called "The Doctor" for his wartime story collection *They Never Surrendered*. In the end, I wrote this book.

I am indebted to the veterans who shared their memories: William Allister and Robert P. Warren (in letters), and in interviews: Dr. Martin Banfill, Robert "Flash" Clayton, Jessie Clayton, Dr. John Crawford, Roger Cyr, Angus McRitchie, George Pollak, and the indomitable George MacDonell, who not only has been a constant source of first-hand information over the years but a great friend to the author and the lion-hearted supporter of this endeavour.

Friends of my father were generous with their time, especially Douglas Dadson and Frank Woods, who spent a day with me in 1983, and Dr. Bill Bigelow, my honorary uncle, who spoke of my father many times over the years. Their children, Ann and Aleck Dadson and Pixie Bigelow Currie, have been most helpful with pictures and memories of their own.

For his expert contribution to this story, and for honouring it with his foreword, I wish to thank historian Tony Banham, the world's foremost authority on the Battle of Hong Kong and its POW aftermath. Dr. Hoyle Campbell and Dr. Charles G. Roland lent their own expertise in early interviews. Victoria Gibb-Carsley, granddaughter of Dr. John Crawford, opened her family archives to me. Taeko Sasamoto, secretary-general of the POW Research Network of Japan, has provided much valuable information and photographs. To Naoaki C. Kobayashi, I owe the remarkable resurrection of the Reid-Uwamori friendship. Filmmaker Viveka Melki, whose historical interests parallel mine, has been a thoughtful confederate.

Special mention goes to Antonia Pollak and Marjolein de Klerk. Antonia has been unstinting in supplying information about her father, including historical materials and photographs, and personal memories. Our many long-distance conversations have been a source of strong encouragement. Her friend, genealogist Craig Ashley, supplied much useful background on the Pollak family. Due to Marjolein de Klerk's curiosity about her grandfather, Captain "Ab" Franken, she found her way from Amsterdam to me, and I was able to fill in the period my father spent in Camp Sendai 1B and describe the surprising Reid-Franken musical collaboration. Marjolein found this book's extraordinary cover photograph of my father, taken in Sendai 1B in August 1945, in an old album in her mother's attic.

My special thanks to the wonderful team at Dundurn Press: publisher Scott Fraser, for his instantaneous enthusiasm for my work; acquisitions editor Rachel Spence, for her excellent editorial suggestions, which I followed to the letter; project editor

Jenny McWha, for keeping me on track through turbulent times and for her scrupulous proofreading; designer Sophie Paas-Lang, for the book's evocative cover and elegant layout; freelance editor Michael Carroll, for his meticulous treatment of the manuscript and creation of the index; managing editor Elena Radic, for shepherding the book through the final prepress stage; editorial assistant Melissa Kawaguchi, for her assiduous final proofreading; publicist Elham Ali, for guiding this story into the world; and associate publisher Kathryn Lane, for besting COVID-19 by "getting books moving forward again."

To editorial specialist Jane McWhinney, for her infallible literary sensibility, I owe more than I can say.

To my family: my mother, Jean, a loving and devoted parent who never spoke ill of my father; my brother, Tony, for leading the way through our unusual childhood; my "Vancouver" siblings Jock, Tavish, Sandy, Mary, without whose candour and openness about their family life this story could not have been told; my sons, Giles and Julian, because they never knew their grandfather; my father, for all he gave, for all he suffered.

To Janey, for sharing the journey, my love — first, last, and always.

Notes

PREFACE
1. In June 1983, the Bureau of Pensions Advocates ruled in favour of splitting the veterans pension between the women.
2. Robert P. Warren, letter to Tony Reid, April 17, 1990, Reid Family Papers, held by Jonathon Reid, Toronto.

CHAPTER 1: THERE WAS A KINDNESS IN HIM
1. Anonymous classmate of John Reid, *Twig*, 1927, 150.
2. John Reid, Reid Family Papers.
3. John Reid, *Twig*, 1930, 78.
4. Reid, *Twig*, 1929, 64.
5. Author conversation with Doug Dadson and Frank Woods, March 1983.
6. Ibid.
7. Ibid.
8. Ibid.
9. Ibid.
10. Ibid.
11. Ibid.

12. Olive Reid, letter to Grace Reid, December 29, 1932, Reid Family Papers.
13. Author conversation with Doug Dadson and Frank Woods, March 1983.
14. Ibid.

CHAPTER 2: THE GOLDEN COUPLE AND THE PHONEY WAR

1. Reid Family Papers.

CHAPTER 3: CANADA'S TURN TO HELP: THE "C" FORCE MISSION

1. *Star Weekly* (Toronto), September 27, 1941, 2, 4–6, 8, 9–11.
2. Quoted in Edmund Leolin Piesse, *Japan and the Defence of Australia* (Melbourne: Robertson & Mullens, 1935), 15.
3. Public Record Office (PRO), Great Britain, W0106/2364; quoted in Carl Vincent, *No Reason Why* (Stittsville, ON: Canada's Wings, 1981), 6.
4. PRO, W0106/2365; quoted in Vincent, *No Reason Why*, 7.
5. Oliver Lindsay, *The Lasting Honour* (London: Hamish Hamilton, 1978), 6; quoted in Vincent, *No Reason Why*, 7.
6. PRO, W0106/2409; quoted in Vincent, *No Reason Why*, 12.
7. Library and Archives Canada (LAC), RG25, v.1696; quoted in Vincent, *No Reason Why*, 11.
8. PRO, W0106/2409; quoted in Vincent, *No Reason Why*, 26–28.
9. Ibid.
10. Ibid.
11. LAC, Duff Royal Commission, RG33/120; quoted in Vincent, *No Reason Why*, 32.

12. Ibid.

13. Ibid., 33.

14. Ibid.

15. Ibid.

16. LAC, Duff Royal Commission, RG33/120; quoted in Vincent, *No Reason Why*, 46.

17. John Reid, "HK & After," Reid Family Papers.

18. John Reid, "The Hong Kong Episode," Reid Family Papers.

19. Ibid.

20. John Reid, letter to Jean Reid, November 2, 1941, Reid Family Papers.

21. Ibid.

22. Ibid.

23. Reid, "HK & After."

24. PRO, W0106/2409; quoted in Vincent, *No Reason Why*, 36.

25. Reid, "HK & After."

26. LAC, King Papers, MG26, v.394; quoted in Vincent, *No Reason Why*, 99–100.

27. Reid, letter to Jean Reid and family, November 15, 1941.

28. Reid, letter to Jean Reid, November 15, 1941.

29. Reid Family Papers.

30. Autographed menu card dated November 15, 1941, preserved in the Dr. John Crawford Family Papers, held by Victoria Gibb-Carsley, Ottawa.

31. Reid, "HK & After."

CHAPTER 4: THE "VIBRATION OF ASIA": THE BATTLE OF HONG KONG

1. Reid, "HK & After."

2. Ibid.

3. Department of National Defence, Directorate of History, 593 (D4); quoted in Vincent, *No Reason Why*, 121.

4. Sergeant Major George MacDonell, *George: The Life and Times of George S. MacDonell* (Toronto: ORBIT Design Services, 2010), 95–96.
5. Ibid., 97–98.
6. John Reid, postwar debriefing, Department of National Defence, Directorate of History, 593 (D17), 21–22.
7. MacDonell, *George*, 96.
8. Tony Banham, *Not the Slightest Chance: The Defence of Hong Kong, 1941* (Hong Kong: Hong Kong University Press, 2003), 15.
9. Lindsay, *The Lasting Honour*, 25.
10. LAC, RG25, v.2865; quoted in Vincent, *No Reason Why*, 100.
11. Ibid.
12. Reid, "HK & After." "Wong Nei Chong Gap" is now named "Wong Nai Chung Gap."
13. PRO, Great Britain, 106/2400; quoted in Lindsay, *The Lasting Honour*, 25; quoted in Vincent, *No Reason Why*, 125.
14. Ibid.
15. Vincent, *No Reason Why*, 128.
16. Reid, "HK & After."
17. Winston S. Churchill, *The Grand Alliance* (New York: RosettaBooks, 2010), 562.
18. Quoted in Lindsay, *The Lasting Honour*, 79.
19. Ted Ferguson, *Desperate Siege: The Battle for Hong Kong* (Toronto: Doubleday Canada, 1980), 164; quoted in Nathan M. Greenfield, *The Damned: The Canadians at the Battle of Hong Kong and the POW Experience, 1941–45* (Toronto: HarperCollins Canada, 2010), 111.
20. Banham, *Not the Slightest Chance*, 142.
21. Ibid., 192.
22. Ibid., 193.

23. John Reid, "The Captain," Reid Family Papers.

24. Reid, postwar debriefing, 6–7.

25. Quoted in Vincent, *No Reason Why*, 178.

26. Reid, postwar debriefing, 8.

27. Wellcome Institute for the History of Medicine, Contemporary Medical Archives Collection (CMAC), Medical Women's Federation Collection, SA/MWF, Box 21, C/195, Work of British Medical Women in POW Camps, TLS Report by Dr. Annie Sydenham, Nethersole Hospital, Hong Kong, April 9, 1950, 1; quoted in Charles G. Roland, *Long Night's Journey into Day: Prisoners of War in Hong Kong and Japan, 1941–1945* (Waterloo, ON: Wilfrid Laurier University Press, 2001), 28–29.

28. Reid, "HK & After."

29. *South China Morning Post*, December 8–26 (minus Saturday, December 20); quoted in Banham, *Not the Slightest Chance*, 248.

30. Banham, *Not the Slightest Chance*, 248.

31. Lindsay, *The Lasting Honour*, 150.

32. Reid, "HK & After."

CHAPTER 5: PRISONERS OF WAR: FALSE HOPES AS CONTAGIOUS AS DYSENTERY

1. Tim Carew, *Hostages to Fortune* (London: Hamish Hamilton, 1971); quoted in Banham, *Not the Slightest Chance*, 286.

2. Reid, "HK & After."

3. Ibid.

4. Lindsay, *The Lasting Honour*, 163; Charles G. Roland, *Long Night's Journey into Day: Prisoners of War in Hong Kong and Japan, 1941–1945* (Waterloo, ON: Wilfrid Laurier University Press, 2001), 48; Nathan M. Greenfield, *The Damned: The Canadians at the Battle of Hong Kong and the*

POW Experience, 1941–45 (Toronto: HarperCollins Canada, 2010), 238.

5. Reid, "HK & After." "Chungking" is now named "Chongqing."

6. William Allister, *Where Life and Death Hold Hands* (Toronto: Stoddart, 1989), 50–51.

7. Les Fisher, *I Will Remember: Recollections and Reflections on Hong Kong 1941 to 1945 — Internment and Freedom* (Totton, Hampshire, UK: A.L. Fisher, 1996), 33; quoted in Tony Banham, *We Shall Suffer There: Hong Kong's Defenders Imprisoned, 1942–45* (Hong Kong: Hong Kong University Press, 2009), 36.

8. Kenneth Cambon, *Guest of Hirohito* (Vancouver: PW Press, 1990), 35; quoted in Banham, *We Shall Suffer There*, 36.

9. J.E.C. Robinson, "Work and Problems of a Medical Officer Prisoner of War in the Far East," *Journal of the Royal Army Medical Corps* 91 (1948): 52; quoted in Banham, *We Shall Suffer There*, 36.

10. Canadian War Museum, White Diary, entry for December 30, 1941, 1; quoted in Roland, *Long Night's Journey into Day*, 65.

11. Allister, *Where Life and Death Hold Hands*, 55; quoted in Banham, *We Shall Suffer There*, 37.

12. Karl Hack and Kevin Blackburn, eds., *Forgotten Captives in Japanese-Occupied Asia* (New York: Routledge, 2008), 135–36.

13. Author conversation with Sergeant Major George S. MacDonell, confirmed by email, December 15, 2019.

14. Reid, "HK & After."

15. Ralph Goodwin, *Hong Kong Escape* (London: Arthur Barker, 1953), 36; quoted in Banham, *We Shall Suffer There*, 24.

16. Cambon, *Guest of Hirohito*, 36.

CHAPTER 6: BELIEVED TO BE ALIVE —
JOY OVERSHADOWED: THE HOME FRONT I

1. *Globe and Mail*, November 16, 1941, 1; *Toronto Evening Telegram*, November 17, 1941.
2. *Toronto Evening Telegram*, November 17, 1941.
3. *Globe and Mail*, December 8, 1941.
4. *Toronto Evening Telegram*, December 15, 1941, 17, 20, 22; *Globe and Mail*, December 23, 1941, 1.
5. *Globe and Mail*, December 26, 1941, 1.
6. *Globe and Mail*, December 22, 1941, 1.
7. LAC, J King Papers, MG26, v. 394; quoted in Vincent, *No Reason Why*, 217.
8. Vincent, *No Reason Why*, 217.
9. King Papers, MG26, v.394; quoted in Vincent, *No Reason Why*, 217.
10. King Papers, MG26, v.369; quoted in Vincent, *No Reason Why*, 217.
11. Greenfield, *The Damned*, 253.
12. Ibid., 253–54.
13. Press clipping, unidentified Toronto newspaper, May 1942.

CHAPTER 7: THE SECRET MEDICAL DIARY:
THE BITTERNESS OF PLAYING GOD

1. Reid, postwar debriefing, 12.
2. Allister, *Where Life and Death Hold Hands*, 65–66.
3. Reid, "The Hong Kong Episode."
4. Reid, postwar debriefing, 16.
5. Geoffrey Marston, "The Scourge of Dysentery," 1993, facsimile found on mansell.com, mansell.com/pow_resources/camplists/tokyo/tok-15b-niigata/Memoirs_of_POW_1941-1945_Geoffrey_Marston_TOK-15-s.pdf; quoted in MacDonell, *George*, 127–29.

6. Reid, "HK & After."
7. Vince Calder, "A Guest of the Emperor"; Ken Ewing, "Surviving Against All Odds"; Tom Forsyth, "Hong Kong Diary and Memories of Japan"; Sergeant Tom Marsh, "Memoirs of Tom Marsh": all found under Personal Accounts, Hong Kong Veterans Commemorative Association, hkvca.ca/historical/index.php (HKVCA); Roland, *Long Night's Journey into Day*, 70; Greenfield, *The Damned*, 273–74.
8. Reid, postwar debriefing, 13.
9. Reid, "The Hong Kong Episode."
10. Sergeant Lance Ross, "Lance Ross's Diary," HKVCA; quoted in Roland, *Long Night's Journey into Day*, 165; quoted in Greenfield, *The Damned*, 273.
11. Private Frank Harding, interview, in Gustave Gingras and Carol Chapman, *The Sequelae of Inhuman Conditions and Slave Labour* ... (Toronto: War Amputations of Canada, 1987), 7; quoted in Roland, *Long Night's Journey into Day*, 160.
12. Reid, postwar debriefing, 14.
13. J.N. Crawford and J.A.G. Reid, "Nutritional Disease Affecting Canadian Troops Held Prisoner of War by the Japanese," *Canadian Journal of Research* 25, no. 2 (April 1947): 61.
14. Dave McIntosh, *Hell on Earth: Aging Faster, Dying Sooner — Canadian Prisoners of War of the Japanese During World War II* (Whitby, ON: McGraw-Hill Ryerson, 1997), 25.
15. Reid, "The Hong Kong Episode."
16. Allister, *Where Life and Death Hold Hands*, 89.
17. Reid, "HK & After."
18. Author conversation with Dr. Martin Banfill, March 13, 1994. In March 1943, two months after Reid's departure for Japan, Banfill would learn that his wife, Anna, devastated on

learning in early 1942 that he was reported dead, had taken her own life.

19. Reid, postwar debriefing, 18.
20. Reid, "The Hong Kong Episode."
21. Reid, "HK & After."

CHAPTER 8: TOKYO CAMP NO. 5: "YOU CANNOT WIN THIS WAR!"

1. Ross, "Lance Ross's Diary," HKVCA.
2. Marsh, "Memoirs," HKVCA.
3. Reid, postwar debriefing, 18.
4. Allister, *Where Life and Death Hold Hands*, 92–93.
5. Ibid., 93–94.
6. Ibid., 94.
7. Marsh, "Memoirs," HKVCA.
8. MacDonell, *George*, 140.
9. Reid, postwar debriefing, 27–28.
10. Ibid., 35.
11. Author conversation with Roger Cyr, May 5, 1996.
12. Allister, *Where Life and Death Hold Hands*, 98.
13. Ibid., 147; quoted in Brereton Greenhous, *"C" Force to Hong Kong: A Canadian Catastrophe* (Toronto: Dundurn Press, 1997), 137.
14. In conversation with the author on December 10, 1996, Royal Rifle Roger Cyr, who became a human resources specialist after the war, and ultimately, director of personnel at Canada Post Corporation, apparently spoke for many when he pronounced Keenan "an asshole of the first magnitude." Keenan's excessive co-operation with the Japanese was seen as currying special favour for himself — breaking an unspoken code of honour among the prisoners by kowtowing to their captors for personal benefit. In conversation with the author

on January 28, 2020, Sergeant Major George MacDonell confirmed unequivocally Cyr's assessment and said that Keenan, to his knowledge, was the only one to break the code. MacDonell added that, right after the war, there was discussion among his fellow POWs of reporting Keenan to the military authorities for fraternizing with the enemy. "You forget a lot of things," said 97-year-old MacDonell, "but not the ones who let you down."

15. Reid, postwar debriefing, 25–26.

16. Allister, *Where Life and Death Hold Hands*, 169.

17. John Reid, "Medical Diary, by JAG Reid, Capt. RCAMC, Camp No. 5, Tokio Prisoners' Camp," March 8, 1943, 10, Reid Family Papers.

18. Reid, postwar debriefing, 21.

19. Ibid., 93–94.

20. Ibid., 125.

21. Ibid., 136.

22. Ibid., 53.

23. Marsh, "Memoirs," HKVCA.

24. Reid, postwar debriefing, 115.

25. Sergeant Major George MacDonell, *They Never Surrendered: Allied POWs Who Defied Their Captors in World War II in Hong Kong & Japan 1941–1945* (Toronto: ORBIT Design Services, 2014), 90–92.

26. Author conversation with Sergeant Major George MacDonell and Sergeant Robert "Flash" Clayton, October 19, 2002.

27. Ibid.

28. Ibid.

29. Reid, "The Hong Kong Incident."

30. Reid, postwar debriefing, 94–95.

31. Ibid., 95.

32. Ibid., 46.

33. Ibid., 46–47.
34. Ibid., 49; Reid, "The Hong Kong Incident."
35. Reid, postwar debriefing, 96.
36. Ibid., 63.
37. Ibid., 80–81.
38. Ibid., 82
39. Reid, "Medical Diary," February 19, 1944, 57; Reid, postwar debriefing, 122.
40. Reid, postwar debriefing, 83.
41. Ibid., 125.
42. Ibid., 83.
43. Ibid., 89.
44. Ibid., 128.
45. Ibid., 91.
46. Ross, "Lance Ross's Diary," HKVCA.
47. Allister, *Where Life and Death Hold Hands*, 149–50.

CHAPTER 9: 1944: COPING, COMMUNICATING, AND THE CANDLE CONSPIRACY

1. Reid, postwar debriefing, 129–30.
2. Sergeant Léo Paul Bérard, *17 Days Until Christmas* (Barrie, ON: Léo P. Bérard), 142.
3. Lance Corporal Georges "Blacky" Verreault, *Diary of a Prisoner of War in Japan 1941–1945* (Rimouski, QC: VERO, 1996), 250.
4. Reid, postwar debriefing, 131.
5. Ibid., 135.
6. Author conversation with Sergeant Major George MacDonell and Sergeant Robert "Flash" Clayton, October 19, 2002.
7. Allister, *Where Life and Death Hold Hands*, 157–58.
8. Reid, postwar debriefing, 48–49.
9. Ibid., 20–21.

10. Ibid., 19–20.

11. Ibid., 134.

12. MacDonell, *George*, 137–38.

13. Reid, postwar debriefing, 40.

14. Roland, *Long Night's Journey into Day*, 256.

15. Reid, postwar debriefing, 74.

16. Ibid., 60–61.

17. Ibid., 75–76.

18. Henry C. Strohm, postcard to Jean Reid, July 6, 1943, Reid Family Papers.

19. Canadian Department of National Defence, Army, letter (Quote No H.Q.C.9050–26–2 [SAAG]) to Mrs. Jean Louise Reid, July 13, 1943, Reid Family Papers.

20. Reid, "Medical Diary," December 28, 1943, 51.

21. Ibid., March 19, 1943, 11.

22. Ibid., March 17, 1944, 63.

23. John Reid, letter to Jean Reid, January 15, 1944, Reid Family Papers.

24. Reid, "Medical Diary," January 9, 1944, 52.

25. George Pollak, "War Memoir," 10, Pollak Family Papers, held by Antonia M. Pollak, Portsmouth, New Hampshire.

26. Ibid., 11, 13.

27. Ibid., 13.

28. Ibid., 11–12.

29. MacDonell, *George*, 147.

30. Lieutenant Commander George Pollak, U.S. Navy, 86792, Navy Department deposition, Washington, D.C., March 25, 1947, 1, Pollak Family Papers.

31. Reid, postwar debriefing, 112–13.

32. Pollak, Navy Department deposition, 1–2.

33. Ibid., 3.

34. Reid was promoted to major in 1946. Pollak's U.S. Navy

Department deposition, from which this quotation is taken, was given in March 1947.

35. Pollak, Navy Department deposition, 2.

36. MacDonell, *George*, 147.

37. Ibid., 148.

38. George Pollak, letter to the author.

39. Pollak, letter to Jean Reid, December 7, 1979, Reid Family Papers.

40. Pollak, letter to the author.

41. John Reid, letter to Jean Reid, April 20, 1944, Reid Family Papers.

42. Reid, postwar debriefing, 142–45.

43. Author conversation with Angus McRitchie, March 13, 1994.

44. Reid, postwar debriefing, 142–45.

45. Ibid., 147.

46. Ibid., 97–98.

47. Ibid., 98.

48. John Reid, "The Green Buddha," Reid Family Papers.

49. Ibid.

CHAPTER 10: THE ASSOCIATION OF RELATIVES OF MEN AT HONG KONG: THE HOME FRONT II

1. John Reid, postcard to Jean Reid, June 3, 1943, Reid Family Papers.

2. Dr. Lyall Hodgins, letter to Ernest Maag, Delegate in Canada for the International Red Cross Committee; quoted in Ernest Maag, letter to Lieutenant-Colonel F.W. Clarke, Canadian Department of National Defence (Army), February 4, 1943, Reid Family Papers.

3. Dr. Lyall Hodgins, report, June 1, 1942, BCSC Papers, RG 36/27, vol. 3, PAC; quoted in Ann Gomer Sunahara, *The Politics of Racism: The Uprooting of Japanese Canadians*

During the Second World War (Ottawa: Ann Gomer Sunahara, 2000), 63.

4. Ernest Maag, letter to Dr. Lyall Hodgins, February 4, 1943, Reid Family Papers.
5. Ernest Maag, letter to the Comité International de la Croix-Rouge, Palais Général, Genève (Suisse), Ref: Canada M/1068, February 4, 1943, Reid Family Papers.
6. Dr. Lyall Hodgins, letter to Jean Reid, February 24, 1943, Reid Family Papers.
7. Lance Corporal William Bell, Winnipeg Grenadiers, "Adsum" ("We Are Present"), Personal Accounts, HKVCA.
8. *Sydney Morning Herald*, June 15, 1943, 6.
9. Allister, *Where Life and Death Hold Hands*, 82.
10. Kanao Inouye, alias the "Kamloops Kid," was a Nisei (second-generation Japanese Canadian) who returned to Japan in 1938 to study and later served as a prison camp guard and interpreter for the Imperial Japanese Army and Kenpeitai Political Police during the Second World War. He was known for his extreme brutality to Canadian prisoners. Former POWs testified that he was responsible for the torture and deaths of at least eight Canadian POWs. Inouye was executed for war crimes and high treason in Hong Kong's Stanley Prison in 1947.
11. Allister, *Where Life and Death Hold Hands*, 83. John Norris, the brave Grenadier captain who defied the Japanese and shouted out "Fake!" to the Red Cross observers, survived the war but returned home to Winnipeg permanently disabled. After spending months in hospital, Norris, with the help of his wife, Cleo, took over his father's Garry Street tailor shop, where he had worked before the war. In 1947, he rejoined the local militia (he had first joined up in 1923), helped form the Hong Kong Veterans Association, and was elected its first

president. In 1949, age 44, Norris died of his wartime injuries, leaving behind Cleo and his young son, John Jr. Said fellow POW Tom Forsyth, who witnessed his beating by Kanao Inouye: "Norris lived to come back, but he'd been struck so often in the head that he was never right, he was never right ... he never got back to being normal." (Thomas Forsyth, "Remembering the Kamloops Kid," Heroes Remember Interviews, Veterans Affairs Canada, veterans.gc.ca/eng/video-gallery/video/6524.).

12. Prime Minister Winston Churchill, November 10, 1942, *Guardian*, November 11, 1942.

13. Maude Crawford, letter to Jean Reid, September 16, 1942, Reid Family Papers.

14. Maude Crawford, letter to Jean Reid, July 9, 1943, Reid Family Papers.

15. Clipping from unidentified Toronto newspaper, Jean Reid's wartime scrapbook, Reid Family Papers.

16. Marianne Pollak assumed Lieutenant Finn, an American, was brought to Japan with her son and Lieutenant Commander Dockweiler in the fall of 1942. In fact, Finn was brought to Japan for interrogation in January 1943 and immediately put in Tokyo Camp No. 5 with Reid and the Canadians.

17. Marianne S. Pollak, letter to Jean Reid, August 31, 1944, Reid Family Papers.

18. George Pollak, transcription of message from Radio Tokyo broadcast recorded at 3D in July 1944, forwarded to M.S. Pollak by Provost Marshal General Lerch, WM56 WMUC GOVT NL- WUX WMU WASHINGTON, D.C., August 31, 1944, Reid Family Papers.

CHAPTER 11: ALLIED BOMBING BEGINS: THE END OF POW CAMP TOKYO 3D

1. Marsh, "Memoirs of Tom Marsh," HKVCA.
2. Verreault, *Diary of a Prisoner of War*, 147.
3. Standing order of Japanese War Ministry; this copy from the journal of the Taiwan POW Camp HQ, Taihoku, August 1, 1944, Doc 2701, Exhibit "O": National Archive and Research Administration, War Crimes, Japan, RG24, Box 2015. There is scholarly dispute concerning the official status of the "kill-all order." See the online discussion posted by historians Linda Goetz Holmes, R. John Pritchard, and others at fepow-community.org.uk/monthly_revue/html/atrocities.htm.
4. Reid, postwar debriefing, 147.
5. Pollak, letter to the author.
6. Reid, postwar debriefing, 153–54.
7. Author conversation with Sergeant Major George MacDonell, November 24, 2016.
8. Pollak, letter to the author.
9. Reid, postwar debriefing, 153.
10. Marsh, "Memoirs," HKVCA.
11. D. Burke Penny, *Beyond the Call: Royal Canadian Corps of Signals Brigade Headquarters, "C" Force, Hong Kong and Japan 1941–1945* (Nepean, ON: Hong Kong Veterans Commemorative Association, 2009), 281–82.
12. Reid, postwar debriefing, 155.
13. Ibid, 156.
14. Reid, "The Hong Kong Episode."

CHAPTER 12: SENDAI CAMP 1B: DIGNITY AND DISARMAMENT

1. Marsh, "Memoirs of Tom Marsh," HKVCA.

2. Ibid.
3. Ibid.
4. Ibid.
5. Ibid.
6. Reid, postwar debriefing, 161.
7. Ibid., 158–65.
8. Ibid., 162.
9. Ibid.
10. Ibid., 166.
11. Ibid., 165.
12. Warren, letter to Tony Reid.
13. Marsh, "Memoirs," HKVCA.
14. Warren, letter to Tony Reid, April 17, 1990.
15. Pollak, letter to the author.
16. Marsh, "Memoirs," HKVCA.
17. "Mr. Breeze," lyrics and music by John Reid, Reid Family Papers.
18. Richard B. Frank, *Downfall: The End of the Imperial Japanese Empire* (New York: Penguin Books, 2001), 102.
19. Harry J. Wray and Seishiro Sugihara, *Bridging the Atomic Divide: Debating Japan-US Attitudes on Hiroshima and Nagasaki* (Washington, DC: Lexington Books, 2018), 102.
20. Frank, *Downfall*, 229.
21. Ibid., 230.
22. George R. Goethals, Georgia Sorenson, and McGregor Burns, *Encyclopedia of Leadership, Volume I* (Thousand Oaks, CA: Sage Publications, 2004), 661.
23. Thomas McKelvey Cleaver, *Tidal Wave: From Leyte Gulf to Tokyo Bay* (London: Osprey, 2018), 298.
24. Frank, *Downfall*, 269.
25. Ibid., 295–96.
26. Ibid., 296.

27. Ibid., 302.

28. Ibid., 299.

29. Ibid., 311.

30. Ibid., 315.

31. Kazuo Yagami, *The US-Japan Relation in Culture and Diplomacy: Japanese Perspective* (Bloomington, IN: Balboa Press, 2018), Appendix D.

32. Jim Smith and Malcolm McConnell, *The Last Mission: The Secret History of World War II's Final Battle* (New York: Broadway Books, 2003), 176.

33. Frank, *Downfall*, 102.

34. Reid, postwar debriefing, 169–70.

35. Ibid., 170–71.

36. Ibid., 171.

37. Ibid., 172.

38. Adelbert Franken, "Declaration of Musical Rights," Reid Family Papers, De Klerk Family Papers, held by Marjolein de Klerk, Amsterdam.

39. Marsh, "Memoirs," HKVCA.

40. Reid, postwar debriefing, 172–73.

41. John Reid, "Report on Sendai Conference," Reid Family Papers.

42. Reid, postwar debriefing, 175.

43. Ibid., 174.

44. Ibid., 175.

45. Marsh, "Memoirs," HKVCA.

46. Reid, "The Hong Kong Episode."

47. Headquarters 498th Bombardment Group, USAF, "Confidential 14900," Subject: Transmittal of Missing Air Crew Reports, Declassified by NARA 1973, mansell .com/pow_resources/camplists/sendai/Sendai_1_yumoto/ MACR_42-65345.pdf.

48. Author conversation with Sergeant Major George MacDonell and Sergeant Robert "Flash" Clayton, October 19, 2002.

49. Ibid.

50. Bérard, *17 Days Until Christmas*, 169–70.

51. Reid, postwar debriefing, 175–76.

52. John Reid and Charles Finn, letter to Masao Uwamori from Sendai IB, August 27, 1945, Reid Family Papers. Uwamori's handwritten copy of the letter was provided by N.C. Kobayashi in his letter to the author of February 18, 1994. Uwamori stated to Kobayashi that the original letter was submitted as evidence for the defence at his war crime trial and never returned.

CHAPTER 13: SAFE IN ALLIED HANDS — A TIME OUTSIDE OF TIME: THE HOME FRONT III

1. Reid, postwar debriefing, 177.

2. Ibid.

3. Author conversation with Doug Dadson and Frank Woods, March 1983.

4. Author conversations with Jean Reid.

5. U.S. War and Navy Departments V-Mail Service, June 5, 1945.

6. John Reid, Radio Tokyo broadcast message to Jean Reid, May 27, 1945, recorded March 1945.

7. Reid, postwar debriefing, 178–79.

CHAPTER 14: PICKING UP THE PIECES: A BUNCH OF CANES

1. Jean Reid, interview with Dr. Charles G. Roland for *Long Night's Journey into Day*, November 2, 1993.

2. Author conversation with Dr. Hoyle Campbell, March 14, 1994.

3. Pollak, letter to the author.

4. Jean Reid, letter to George Pollak, January 20, 1980, Reid Family Papers.

5. Pollak, letter to the author.

6. Ibid.

7. LAC RG24 Vol. 2898 File HQS 8959-9-4/17; quoted in McIntosh, *Hell on Earth*, 177–78.

8. Ira Kaye, "Defense Motion for Modification of Sentence in the case of United States of America vs Masao Uwamori," Case Docket no. 133, Headquarters Eighth Army Judge/advocate Division APO 343, 26–27, Reid family papers; NARA, Review of the Yokohama Class B and Class C War Crimes Trials by the U.S. Eighth Army Judge Advocate, 1946–49 (M1112).

9. Masao Uwamori, letter to John Reid, December 1, 1948, Reid Family Papers.

10. Pollak, letter to the author.

11. Author conversation with Doug Dadson and Frank Woods, March 1983.

12. Major P.F.L. Sore, "for Lt.-Colonel N.S. Cuthbert AOD, A/Officer IC Administration, Central Command," CC 60/HON PRES/8 (H&A), Ortona Barracks, Oakville, Ontario, covering letter and citation to Major J.A.G. Reid, MBE, November 3, 1948, Reid Family Papers.

CHAPTER 15: VANCOUVER AND THE DOUBLE LIFE: A CONFUSING CORRESPONDENCE

1. Mary Reid Ramsey, email to the author, February 21, 2015.

2. Author conversation with Diane Poole, November 28, 2018, Reid Family Papers.

3. William Shakespeare, *Henry V*, 3.2, *The Histories and Poems of William Shakespeare* (London: Oxford University Press, 1912), 44.

4. John Reid, letter to Cathy Gillies, undated (spring 1949), Reid Family Papers.
5. Ibid.
6. Ibid.
7. John Reid, letter to Cathy Gillies, October 6, 1949, Reid Family Papers.

CHAPTER 16: THE DOMESTIC TIGHTROPE OF A MENTALLY DISTURBED MAN

1. While on shift duty, Cathy stayed at the hospital Nurses Residence. Otherwise, she continued to live at the family home on Angus Drive, where her extended family helped take care of baby Jock.
2. Pollak, letter to the author.
3. John Reid, letters to Jean Reid, August 10 and 25, 1950, Reid Family Papers.
4. John Reid, letter to Jean Reid, July 1952, Reid Family Papers.
5. Ibid.
6. John Reid, letter to Jean Reid, early August 1952, Reid Family Papers.
7. John Reid, letter to Jean Reid, mid-August 1952, Reid Family Papers.
8. John Reid, letter to Jean Reid, August 20, 1952, Reid Family Papers.
9. John Reid, letter to Cathy Reid, July 8, 1953.
10. Dr. Bill Bigelow, letter to J.W. Stark, Bureau of Pensions Advocates, Toronto, December 17, 1981, Reid Family Papers. At this time, the author was preparing a submission to the bureau on his mother's behalf in favour of Jean Reid receiving half of the full spousal veterans pension awarded to Cathy Reid on Reid's death, in 1979. Bigelow's letter was in support of this submission. The Bureau of Pensions Advocates ruled

in favour of splitting the pension between the two women in June 1983.

CHAPTER 17: A SIMPLER DAILY ROUND: PEACE AT LAST

1. In June 1954, Jack and Eva Hodge were both about to turn 75. Suddenly, the third floor of their quiet house became living quarters for their downcast daughter and her two little boys. Their welcome was unreserved. Jean and her sons would live at 5 Scholfield until Jack Hodge's death in 1969.
2. Author conversations with Pixie Bigelow Currie, December 12, 2019, and January 12, 2020.
3. The other cottages were "Seven Persons," "The Black Cat," and "The Lurch." Bill Dadson was a talented musician who played in a military band during the First World War and in the 1920s formed a musical group with his daughters called Bill Dadson & the Doo-Dads. After vaudeville's demise during the Great Depression, Professor Dadson gave his brother make-work projects building guest cabins on his Foot's Bay property. "The Lurch" was Bill's cabin because, he said, that's where the Depression left him.
4. Neither set of John Reid's children was aware of the other's Muskoka visits until the summer in the early 1960s when Eva kept calling Tony "Jock": the Vancouver contingent had just vacated the cottage the day before Tony and Jon arrived and Eva was having trouble adjusting. Tony and Jon had been told from a young age that their father had another family. In Vancouver, revealing the existence of two half-brothers in Toronto was on a need-to-know basis. Jock was told by Cathy when he was 10 or 11 because he asked why their father spent time in Ontario every year without them. Mary was seven when Tony came to Savary Island to see his father after

finishing a summer job on the Prairies in 1967. The day Tony was to arrive by ferry, Cathy sat Mary down on a beach log and told her who this mysterious visitor was. Rather than be shocked, Mary thought it was great: "I was thrilled I had two more brothers!"

5. John Reid, letter to Cathy Reid, August 1958, Reid Family Papers.

6. John Reid, letter to Jean Reid, January 9, 1958, Reid Family Papers.

7. Mary Reid Ramsey, email to the author, February 21, 2015, Reid Family Papers.

8. Jock Reid, emails to the author, March 10, 2014, and March 7, 2015, Reid Family Papers.

9. Tavish Reid, email to the author, February 21, 2015, Reid Family Papers.

10. Mary Reid Ramsey, emails to the author, January 31, 2020, and February 2, 2020, Reid Family Papers.

11. Jock Reid, emails to the author, January 30, 2020, and February 1, 2020, Reid Family Papers.

12. Jock Reid, email to the author, April 10, 2016, Reid Family Papers.

13. Jock Reid, emails to the author, April 10, 2016, and November 9, 2018, Reid Family Papers.

14. Jock Reid, email to the author, June 10, 2015, Reid Family Papers.

15. Author conversation with Doug Dadson and Frank Woods, March 1983; author conversation with Frank Woods, May 6, 2006; author conversations with Dr. Bill Bigelow. Bill Bigelow and his wife, Ruth, were Jean Reid's closest friends and supports after her return to Toronto in 1954. Bigelow arranged her job as office administrator of the Cardiovascular Research Laboratory that he set up at the Banting Institute in

the 1950s. Jean remained in the position until her retirement in 1981. The Bigelows were "honorary" aunt and uncle to the author and his brother, Tony.

16. Author conversation with Aleck Dadson, October 18, 2019.

17. John Reid, letter to the author, September 24, 1971, Reid Family Papers.

18. Mary Reid Ramsey, email to the author, January 7, 2020, Reid Family Papers.

19. W.R. Feasby, ed., *Official History of the Canadian Medical Services 1939–1945, Volume One: Organization and Campaigns* (Ottawa: Queen's Printer, 1956), 307. The death rate in Reid's group was 4.6 percent — for the rest of the Canadians in Japan, well over 16 percent. Without Reid, loss of life at Camp 3D would have been nearly four times higher.

20. Bernie Jesse made good use of the time left to him. Married in 1946, he became a civil servant, successful businessman, and pillar of the community in Estevan, Saskatchewan, where he died at the age of 90 in 2008, leaving behind four children, eleven grandchildren, and eight great-grandchildren to remember him. He was a member of the Royal Canadian Legion for 60 years and spent countless hours sharing his war experiences with schoolchildren across Saskatchewan.

21. Lionel Speller, interview with Dr. Charles G. Roland, May 27, 1990; quoted in Banham, *We Shall Suffer There*, 116.

CHAPTER 18: STRICKEN: PAST THE POINT OF MARGINAL RESERVE

1. Jock Reid, emails to the author, December 17, 2013, and January 13, 2020, Reid Family Papers.

2. The author, personal recollection.

3. Jonathon Reid, "Submission on Behalf of Jean Reid" to J.W. Stark, Bureau of Pensions Advocates, Willowdale, Ontario,

January 7, 1982, Reid Family Papers; the author, personal recollection.

4. Dr. Clyde Slade, director, Division of Family Practice, University of British Columbia Department of Health Care and Epidemiology, letter to Cliff Lowe, provincial service officer, Pacific Command, Royal Canadian Legion, July 13, 1977, Reid Family Papers.

5. Mary Reid Ramsey, email to the author, January 7, 2020, Reid Family Papers.

6. Dr. Bill Bigelow, letter to Dr. Clyde Slade, December 15, 1977, Reid Family Papers.

7. Dr. H.J.M. Barnett, letter to Dr. Michael Jones, February 7, 1978, Reid Family Papers.

8. Author conversation with Valerie Jerome, March 31, 2016.

CHAPTER 19: IN SEARCH OF CAPTAIN REID: HIS KIND TESTIMONY

1. *Asahi Evening News*, July 22, 1993.

2. Ibid.

3. Masao Uwamori, letter to Naoaki C. Kobayashi, February 14, 1994, Reid Family Papers.

AFTERWORD

1. Author conversation with Frank Woods, May 10, 2006, Reid Family Papers.

2. "Capt. Leney Gage Dies in Holland," *Toronto Daily Star*, October 26, 1944, 8.

3. Aleck Dadson, email to the author, February 16, 2020, Reid Family Papers.

4. Canadian Medical Hall of Fame, cdnmedhall.org.

5. In March 2015, Marjolein de Klerk of Amsterdam, Franken's granddaughter, used a genealogy website and Google Maps

to track down Jock Reid in Vancouver. She was researching her grandfather's past and among his effects had found items from prison camp days belonging to John Anthony Gibson Reid. The author met Marjolein in Toronto in November 2015, and before and since that meeting, she has provided information about her grandfather, Sendai Camp 1B, as well as this book's cover photograph of John Reid, likely taken by Franken in Sendai 1B shortly after the Japanese surrender in August 1945. The photo was pasted into an old album of her grandfather's, which Marjolein found in her mother's attic.

6. George Pollak, letter to Jean Reid, December 7, 1979.

7. George Pollak, letter to Jean Reid, December 18, 1983, Reid Family Papers.

8. Antonia Pollak, email to the author, March 5, 2020, Reid Family Papers.

Bibliography

PRIMARY SOURCES

Archival

Library and Archives Canada (LAC): RG24 Vol. 2898 File HQS
     8959-9-4/17; RG25, Vol. 1696; Vol. 2865; RG33/120; King
     Papers, MG26, v.394.
National Archives and Research Administration (NARA) (U.S.).
Public Record Office (PRO) (United Kingdom), 106/2400.

Personal Papers and First-Hand Written Accounts

De Klerk Family Papers, held by Marjolein de Klerk, Amsterdam.
Dr. John Crawford Family Papers, held by Victoria Gibb-Carsley,
     Ottawa.
Hong Kong Veterans Commemorative Association, Personal
     Accounts, hkvca.ca/historical/index.php.
Pollak Family Papers, held by Antonia M. Pollak, Portsmouth,
     New Hampshire.
Reid Family Papers, held by Jonathon Reid, Toronto.
Royal Rifles of Canada, Hong Kong War Diary, December 1–
     December 25, 1941.

Wellcome Institute for the History of Medicine, Contemporary
Medical Archives Collection (CMAC), Medical Women's
Federation Collection, SA/MWF, Box 21, C/195, Work of
British Medical Women in POW Camps.

Author Conversations and Correspondence

Dr. Martin Banfill; Dr. Bill Bigelow; Dr. Hoyle Campbell; Robert
"Flash" Clayton; Dr. John Crawford; Pixie Bigelow Currie;
Roger Cyr; Aleck Dadson; Ann Dadson; Douglas Dadson;
Valerie Jerome; Marjolein de Klerk; Naoaki Kobayashi;
George MacDonell; Angus McRitchie; Sandy Pitcher;
Antonia M. Pollak; Diane Poole; Mary Reid Ramsey; Jean
Reid; Jock Reid; Sandy Reid; Tavish Reid; Tony Reid; Frank
Woods.

SECONDARY SOURCES

Books

Allister, William. *Where Life and Death Hold Hands.* Toronto:
Stoddart, 1989.

Banham, Tony. *Not the Slightest Chance: The Defence of Hong
Kong, 1941.* Hong Kong: Hong Kong University Press, 2003.
———. *We Shall Suffer There: Hong Kong's Defenders Imprisoned,
1942–45.* Hong Kong: Hong Kong University Press, 2009.

Bérard, Léo Paul. *17 Days Until Christmas.* Barrie, ON: Leo P.
Bérard, 1997.

Cambon, Kenneth. *Guest of Hirohito.* Vancouver: PW Press,
1990.

Carew, Tim. *Hostages to Fortune.* London: Hamish Hamilton,
1971.

Churchill, Winston S. *The Grand Alliance.* New York:
RosettaBooks, 2010.

Cleaver, Thomas McKelvey. *Tidal Wave: From Leyte Gulf to Tokyo Bay*. London: Osprey, 2018.

Feasby, W.R., ed. *Official History of the Canadian Medical Services 1939–1945, Volume One: Organization and Campaigns*. Ottawa: Queen's Printer, 1956.

Ferguson, Ted. *Desperate Siege: The Battle for Hong Kong*. Toronto: Doubleday Canada, 1980.

Fisher, Les. *I Will Remember: Recollections and Reflections on Hong Kong 1941 to 1945 — Internment and Freedom*. Totton, Hampshire, UK: A.L. Fisher, 1996.

Frank, Richard B. *Downfall: The End of the Imperial Japanese Empire*. New York: Penguin Books, 2001.

Goethals, George R., Georgia Sorenson, and McGregor Burns. *Encyclopedia of Leadership, Volume I*. Thousand Oaks, CA: Sage Publications, 2004.

Goodwin, Ralph. *Hong Kong Escape*. London: Arthur Barker, 1953.

Greenfield, Nathan M. *The Damned: The Canadians at the Battle of Hong Kong and the POW Experience, 1941–45*. Toronto: HarperCollins Canada, 2010.

Greenhous, Brereton. *"C" Force to Hong Kong: A Canadian Catastrophe 1941–1945*. Toronto: Dundurn Press, 1997.

Hack, Karl, and Kevin Blackburn, eds. *Forgotten Captives in Japanese-Occupied Asia*. New York: Routledge, 2008.

Lindsay, Oliver. *The Lasting Honour: The Fall of Hong Kong 1941*. London: Hamish Hamilton, 1981.

MacDonell, George S. *George: The Life and Times of George S. MacDonell*. Toronto: ORBIT Design Services, 2010.

———. *One Soldier's Story 1939–1945: From the Fall of Hong Kong to the Defeat of Japan*. Toronto: Dundurn Press, 2002.

———. *They Never Surrendered: Allied POWs Who Defied Their Captors in World War II in Hong Kong & Japan 1941–1945*. Toronto: ORBIT Design Services, 2014.

MacDonell, George S., and Sue Beard. *A Dog Named Gander.* Toronto: ORBIT Design Services, 2017.

McIntosh, Dave. *Hell on Earth: Aging Faster, Dying Sooner — Canadian Prisoners of the Japanese During World War II.* Whitby, ON: McGraw-Hill Ryerson, 1997.

Penny, D. Burke. *Beyond the Call: Royal Canadian Corps of Signals Brigade Headquarters, "C" Force, Hong Kong and Japan, 1941–1945.* Nepean, ON: Hong Kong Veterans Commemorative Association, 2009.

Piesse, Edmund Leolin. *Japan and the Defence of Australia.* Melbourne: Robertson & Mullens, 1935.

Roland, Charles G. *Long Night's Journey into Day: Prisoners of War in Hong Kong and Japan, 1941–45.* Waterloo, ON: Wilfrid Laurier University Press, 2001.

Stacey, C.P. *Official History of the Canadian Army in the Second World War Volume I, Six Years of War.* Ottawa: Queen's Printer, 1955.

Sunahara, Ann Gomer. *The Politics of Racism: The Uprooting of Japanese Canadians During the Second World War.* Ottawa: Ann Gomer Sunahara, 2000.

Verreault, Georges "Blacky." *Diary of a Prisoner of War in Japan 1941–1945.* Rimouski, QC: VERO, 1996.

Vincent, Carl. *No Reason Why: The Canadian Hong Kong Tragedy, an Examination.* Stittsville, ON: Canada's Wings, 1981.

Wray, Harry J., and Seishiro Sugihara. *Bridging the Atomic Divide: Debating Japan-U.S. Attitudes on Hiroshima and Nagasaki.* Washington, DC: Lexington Books, 2018.

Yagami, Kazuo. *The U.S.-Japan Relation in Culture and Diplomacy: Japanese Perspective.* Bloomington, IN: Balboa Press, 2018.

Newspapers and Magazines

Asahi Evening News (Tokyo)

Globe and Mail (Toronto)

Guardian (United Kingdom)

South China Morning Post (Hong Kong)

Star Weekly (Toronto)

Sydney Morning Herald

Toronto Evening Telegram

Twig, school magazine of University of Toronto Schools

Websites

Center for Research on Allied POWS Under the Japanese. mansell.com.

Hong Kong Veterans Commemorative Association, "C" Force Reports and Stats. hkvca.ca/cforcedata/index.php.

Video

McKenna, Brian, dir. *The Valour and the Horror*. Documentary film series, episode 1, "Savage Christmas: Hong Kong 1941." Aired January 12, 1992, on CBC.

Image Credits

Ann and Aleck Dadson: 12, 21

Antonia M. Pollak: 302

C.C.J. Bond/Historical Section, General Staff, Canadian
 Army: 72, 456–57

George MacDonell: 143

Jonathon Reid: 24, 322

Library and Archives Canada: 60

Marjolein de Klerk: 240, 253

Naoaki Kobayashi, Taeko Sasamoto, POW Research Network
 Japan: 131

Pixie Bigelow Currie: 380

Reid Family: 3, 4, 6, 19, 26, 28, 32, 47, 299, 301, 304, 320,
 337, 357, 359, 363, 372

Shutterstock: 128

Tavish Reid: 386

Twig/University of Toronto Schools: 8

Index

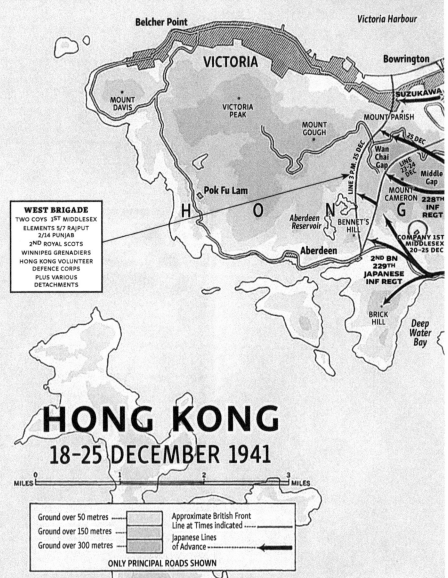

KOWLOON

Victoria Harbour

Belcher Point

VICTORIA

Bowrington

MOUNT
DAVIS

VICTORIA
PEAK

SUZUKAWA

MOUNT PARISH

MOUNT
GOUGH

LINE 3 P.M. 25 DEC

25 DEC

Wan
Chai
Gap

LINE
23-24
DEC

Middle
Gap

Pok Fu Lam

H   O   N

Aberdeen
Reservoir

BENNET'S
HILL

MOUNT
CAMERON

228TH
INF
REGT

G

WEST BRIGADE
TWO COYS 1ST MIDDLESEX
ELEMENTS 5/7 RAJPUT
2/14 PUNJAB
2ND ROYAL SCOTS
WINNIPEG GRENADIERS
HONG KONG VOLUNTEER
DEFENCE CORPS
PLUS VARIOUS
DETACHMENTS

Aberdeen

COMPANY 1ST
MIDDLESEX
20-25 DEC

2ND BN
229TH
JAPANESE
INF REGT

BRICK
HILL

Deep
Water
Bay

HONG KONG
18-25 DECEMBER 1941

MILES 0   1   2   3 MILES

Ground over 50 metres ----
Ground over 150 metres ----
Ground over 300 metres ----

Approximate British Front
Line at Times indicated ----
Japanese Lines
of Advance ----

ONLY PRINCIPAL ROADS SHOWN

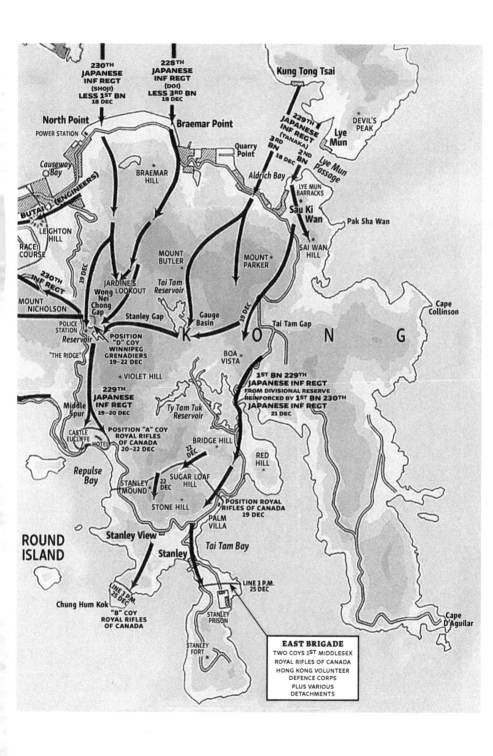